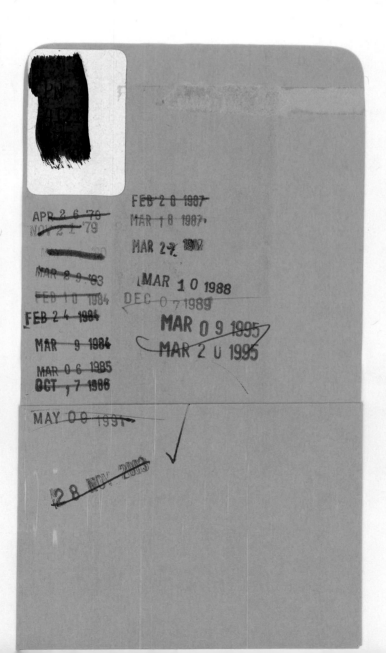

SPEAKING

SPEAKING

Back to Fundamentals

Cal M. Logue

Dwight L. Freshley

Charles R. Gruner

Richard C. Huseman

The University of Georgia

ALLYN AND BACON, INC.

Boston • London • Sydney • Toronto

Library of Congress Cataloging in Publication Data
Main entry under title:

Speaking : back to fundamentals.

   Includes bibliographical references and index.
   1. Public speaking. I. Logue, Calvin McLeod.
PN4121.S73   808.5'1   75-23102

ISBN 0-205-04864-1

Fourth printing ... September, 1977

CONTENTS

PREFACE

This book will help you improve your speaking, and the requirements necessary for becoming a better speaker are discussed in the chapters that follow. We have tried to write about speaking in such a way as to make the book both understandable and helpful.

A unique feature is the emphasis on the importance of *problem solving* to the speaker. Before you speak on a topic you will want to understand the many aspects of your subject. Prior to taking a strong stand on an issue you should be confident that *you* have first made the best choice of the alternatives. For example, before advocating that more money should be spent on public relations to stop the decline of sales in your company, you would be wise to investigate the problem very carefully to determine what is actually *causing* the decline of sales. Otherwise, even if you give an effective, persuasive speech and convince your company to invest more funds in public relations, you will not solve the problem if you are talking about the wrong cause. And you will also waste a considerable amount of the company's profits. So the attention given in this book to deciding what to say *before* you write your speech is an important area of study.

You will also learn more about the value of training in speaking and how such experience can help you personally. You will read two diaries actually written by student speakers while they went through the basic steps of preparing to speak. You will see where they did well and what they discovered on their own which they needed to improve. This will help you as you take the same type of steps in preparing your own speeches.

This book will also suggest how you can relate more meaningfully to your listeners, how and where to find supporting materials for your speeches, kinds of supporting materials to use, the best ways to organize your ideas, the available kinds of supporting materials, how to use visual aids effectively, and how you can improve your use of words and your overall speaking delivery.

Special emphasis is given also to three kinds of speaking. First is the informative speech. Teachers, executives, students, government officials, religious leaders, and citizens generally do a great deal of informative speaking. The other two kinds of speaking are persuasive speeches and speeches for special occasions. At different times all of us feel so strongly about an issue that we want to tell other people what we believe should be done, so we stand before a small or large group and attempt to persuade our listeners. This book will help you understand the nature of persuasion in society and how you can be a more effective persuader.

The chapter on speeches for special occasions will be particularly useful for you. A unique aspect of this chapter is its emphasis on the speech to entertain and how humor works generally. Knowledge of humor is also important because you may want to use this means of communication, to a limited degree, not only in speeches for special occasions but also in informative and persuasive speeches. This chapter also tells you briefly how to give talks of introduction, welcome, presentation, tribute, acceptance, farewell, eulogy, and nomination.

Whereas our book *Speech Communication in Society* was written for the basic course which includes both public speaking and interpersonal communication, this work, *Speaking: Back to Fundamentals,* is written for the public-speaking-oriented course. While some material was taken from *Speech Communication in Society,* in general this is a new work.

Appreciation is expressed to Mrs. Marsha W. Gruner and Mrs. Virginia K. Tubbs for typing the manuscript and to Mr. Frank Ruggirello, editor, College Division, Allyn and Bacon, Inc., for his helpful assistance.

CML
DLF
CRG
RCH

CHAPTER 1

THE VALUE OF
TRAINING
IN SPEAKING

After you leave school for other pursuits, what courses have you had, do you think, which will prove to be the most valuable? This was the question in which Professor James Costigan was interested. He found a partial answer in a survey conducted by the Dean of Faculties at his college, Fort Hayes (Kansas) State College. The survey asked the 1964, 1967, and 1970 graduates of Fort Hayes State to indicate which of the fourteen required courses in general education they considered "the best." The course which ranked Number One for all three classes was their course in Public Speaking.[1] These college graduates had found that after college the training they'd received in speaker-audience communication was of great value.

The evaluation of instructors and courses at the University of Georgia reveals similar findings. On anonymous questionnaires, students who have been required to take the basic speech communication course are asked at the end of the term whether they feel that the course should continue to be required. Between 85 and 90 percent reply that it should.[2]

IMPORTANCE OF COMMUNICATION TO MAN

Obviously, the bulk of people who have had training in speaker-audience communication consider it valuable, and it is not difficult to understand why.

Man is the only animal alive with a communication system as complex and as flexible as speech. Lower animals "communicate" with each other, it is true, but the maximum number of displays or "messages" available to the rhesus monkey, closest in social organization to

1. James Costigan, "College Graduates Evaluations of the Value of Training in Speaker-Audience Communication," *Speech Teacher* 21 (September 1972), p. 226.
2. Charles R. Gruner, "Student Evaluation of Speech Courses and Teachers," *Speech Teacher* 21 (March 1972), pp. 145–46.

that of man, is thirty-seven;[3] on the other hand, humans can use speech and language to make up an infinite number of messages. And it is this speaking and language using that clearly distinguishes man from other animals and gives him such mastery over his world.

If speech and language using is man's most distinguishing characteristic, it would stand to reason that those people who speak and use language the best should be better able to develop their potential. And this is generally true, whether considering success in school, at work, or in the community in general.

In school you use speech and language a great deal. How well you express your thoughts and knowledge in class participation, student-teacher interviews, or in group work projects will undoubtedly affect your instructor's opinion of you and, perhaps, your grade. How well you listen to lectures and other presentations may well determine how much you will learn from your courses. And how well you communicate with your peers in "rap sessions" and other social contacts will determine to a large extent how you will get along socially.

It is difficult to conceive of gaining success in business or the professions without a modicum of communicative skill. In fact, several years ago one of the authors observed a high school class discussing the question, "What kinds of work could one engage in that would not require speaking and in which success might not depend upon the degree of speaking skill?" After many minutes of discarding lines of work in which speaking skill would, in part at least, contribute to success on the job, they finally came up with just one: teaching sign language to deaf-mutes. And, even at that, the admission was made that one would probably have to use speech to communicate with fellow workers, supervisors, secretaries in the office, and so on.

LEARNING TO BE CONFIDENT

Young people today do not have to be told that this is a highly competitive world. Securing and keeping a good job usually involves "beating out the competition." Once your job is relatively secure, you will usually be in competition with others for promotions and increases in salary. Being able to speak communicatively, with knowledge and authority, will help to insure a competitive edge.

3. Edward O. Wilson, "Animal Communication," in *Communication* (San Francisco: *Scientific American*, 1972), p. 32.

The competition between opposing ideas is equally strong in our society. Not only will rival politicians, newspapers, and advertisers vie with each other for your vote, your readership, and your consumer dollars, but you yourself, as an educated citizen, may be called upon to champion a point of view in a public speaking situation.

Quite often we recognize conditions in politics, business, education, and religion which should be improved but decide not to become involved because we are reluctant to speak. Failure to speak may be caused by a number of factors. You may not participate in a student government campaign because you become too nervous when you speak before people. Confronting an audience can be a frightening experience. While there is no simple prescription which will guarantee self-confidence, study and practice can help. This book and this course will provide you with the opportunity to study and practice to improve your speaking performance. Training in speaking can give you more faith in your own ability. In his study of the effect of the Basic Speech course on students' attitudes, Professor James C. McCroskey found that "we may conclude that one of the benefits derived by a student in a basic course in speech is increased confidence in his speaking ability."[4]

ORGANIZING YOUR THOUGHTS

Training in speaking can help you improve other skills. Perhaps you are willing to speak but you have difficulty communicating what you are thinking to other people. You may have a good idea for improving the relationship between students and administration on your campus, for example, but you have difficulty organizing your thoughts orally. Maybe you have had the experience of talking for awhile on a topic about which you were greatly concerned, but when you finished your listeners looked at each other with the expression, "What did he say?" Or you and the rest of a class may have conscientiously listened to a professor lecturing and suddenly he said, "Now for my sixth point . . .," and everybody seems to be wondering, "What were the first five points?" Thus, how you organize your thoughts is extremely important in determining whether your audience will be able to understand your message. In this book you will be given specific suggestions for improving the organization of your ideas.

4. James C. McCroskey, "Effect of the Basic Speech Course on Students' Attitudes," *Speech Teacher* 16 (March 1967), p. 117.

DEVELOPING SPEECH CONTENT

A chief reason many persons give for not speaking in public is that they do not have anything to say. You will often hear students ask, "What can I talk about?" In this book you will be shown how to find materials on almost any topic. The key to success is to know what research tools to use. For example, if you were looking for a plumber in the phone book, you would probably look in the "Yellow Pages." The "Yellow Pages" is an index to the phone book. If you want to find articles in journals on drugs, abortions, education, business, politics, art, or history you will use the appropriate index. In this book there are detailed discussions on the kinds of supporting materials you can use to develop your message, such as examples, analogies, statistics, kinds of reasoning, as well as visual aids. These are the raw materials you will use in presenting your thoughts.

What if in your Political Science class you are asked to prepare a ten-minute oral report in which you define the basic philosophies of the Republican and Democratic Parties in the United States. You first must know where to go to find related information by competent authorities. For this topic you would probably use the *Social Sciences and Humanities Index*. Then you have to select specific examples, statistics, and concepts which will help define the two parties. After, you must organize your materials so you can achieve your assigned purpose within the ten-minute time limit. A person with the necessary communication training could actually enjoy such an assignment. A person lacking communication skills may well perceive the task as baffling and even frightening.

STUDYING SPEAKING PRINCIPLES

Many people speak in public ineffectively. The person untrained in speaking skills may present a report to the class totally unaware that the audience failed to follow his line of reasoning, that he rambled on and on well over the time limit, and that in the end the listeners had no better understanding or appreciation of the subject than before they heard the speaker. Increasing your awareness of what is required to be an effective speaker, then, is an important step in improving your own communication behavior. You must know that simply because you say something to other persons on a particular subject does not mean they will perceive what you intended to say.

ADAPTING TO AN AUDIENCE

Analyzing and adapting to your audience is a basic requirement for successful speaking. For example, you might be called upon in a history class to characterize the region of the United States called "The South." Let us say you are a student who has grown up in California. You stand and say, "The South is composed largely of slow-talking farmers and is ruled socially and politically by white Protestants." After developing this theme for a few minutes you proudly take your seat, innocent of the fact that several of the persons in the class have recently migrated to California from the Deep South—a Catholic from Atlanta, a person from Nashville, and a farmer from Alabama. Imagine the possible reactions to your comments. The native Southerners may be offended by what they perceive as character assassination of their region, their races, and their religions. You might be surprised by their aggressive reaction to what you feel was a fairly mild and accurate assessment. No matter, the words you used one way were perceived by your listeners—because of their different attitudes, beliefs, experiences, and self-interests—in an entirely different manner. Other persons in the class may criticize you because they believe you were too kind to the South. Others may ask, "Have you ever been there?"

The point to be learned from this example is how much better it is for you to realize *before* you speak the kinds of different reactions your message may provoke. Then you will be better able to anticipate audience attitudes and by adjusting what you say have a better chance to produce a more predictable reaction. Training in the principles of speaking can make you more sensitive to the many possible effects which your speaking can have on the speaker and the audience.

Whether you participate effectively, then, in a public discussion will be determined to a large extent on whether you know the basic principles of good communication. In this first chapter we have cited as examples of important speaking skills self-confidence, organization, knowledge of your subject, and audience analysis. Other communication principles you will study in this book are analysis of the causes of a problem, effective use of words, improving your listening habits, delivering your message, informative speaking, and speaking on special occasions. Read the assignments carefully. Work on the speaking assignments diligently. Search for ways you can use the principles discussed in this book to improve your own speaking. Become a better observer of the speaking you see and hear on television, radio, and in person. Then apply those insights to the improvement of your own performance.

PREPARING TO PARTICIPATE

So far the stress on the value of learning to speak has concerned the value of learning *public speaking*. You may be wondering, "Why learn *public speaking* if I am apt to do little of it in later life?" First, the authors of this text believe that, if you really improve your skill at public speaking, you are far more apt to *use* your new-found skill. They think you will be much more likely to speak out at the PTA meeting or the public hearing on the proposed new zoning ordinance at the County Zoning Commission meeting if you are only minimally bothered with stage fright and feel confident that you can say something worthwhile in a clear and forceful manner. They think you will be much more inclined to engage political candidates in dialogues at rallies and be more willing to accept chairmanships of committees in church, social, and civic organizations if you have had training in public speaking. They also believe that you will be more willing to speak before groups when asked by program chairmen to speak on your vocational or avocational specialty if you feel comfortable giving public speeches. But they believe that training in public speaking is also valuable in another way.

SPEAKING CONVERSATIONALLY

Although admitting that it would be difficult to prove, scientifically, your authors feel that skills gained in becoming a better *public* speaker will make you a better speaker—period; that you will improve in your interpersonal communication with your family, your friends, your fellow workers, and your chance acquaintances. They believe this because much of what is *good* in public speaking is also good in conversation; and much of what is *bad* in public speaking is also bad in conversation. Let us look at some comparisons.

We expect anyone with whom we converse to have something worthwhile to say. We expect him to speak of things of interest and worth to us; if he does otherwise, we will "turn him off" and drift away either mentally or physically. We do the same thing to the public speaker who speaks of matters we neither care about nor understand. Good speaking means good content.

We prefer our conversational partner to speak in a manner as pleasing as possible. We want him to speak loudly so we can hear easily but not so loudly as to sound overbearing. We will be pleased if he speaks fast enough to keep from boring us but slow enough so that we can follow easily. We will be delighted if his voice shows change and variety in pitch and melody instead of dragging along in a monotone. In other words, we wish for good delivery in our conversational partner no less than in the public speaker.

We wish both the public speaker and our conversational partner to speak in organized sequences that are easy to follow. Everyone, perhaps, has known at least one joker who asks, "Have you heard the one about ... " followed by the punch line of the joke to the accompaniment of his own hilarious laughter. Then he gives the body of the joke so that you can see why the "punch line" was funny. This kind of bore is mostly the victim of poor organization, which also plagues so much public speaking today.

When conversing with someone, our interst is held and heightened (or lessened and lost) by physical delivery. Both the good conversationalist and the good public speaker will look at his auditor(s), maintaining direct eye contact rather than conducting a monologue with himself while staring at his fingernails, the ceiling, or out the window. This is true whether speaking from the pulpit, the lectern, or the other side of the desk or coffee table. The posture and gestures of the interested and interesting speaker or conversationalist will suggest poise, and an alert, dynamic quality; the disinterested or frightened speaker or conversationalist may suggest with his posture and movements those feelings.

The good conversationalist is one who constantly analyzes his audience as he talks, continually showing concern for the way his words are being understood and reacted to. The good public speaker is also a good audience analyzer, and he has a heightened concern over how his words are being received.

Therefore, the authors feel that through mastery of the principles of this book and their practice in actual public speaking situations, the student will learn the valuable lessons of using good content, organization, and delivery in both his public and private speaking and will practice both with more concern and empathy for his auditor(s).

OPPORTUNITY TO SPEAK

Your authors have one final reason why Americans should study the theory and practice of public speaking: the historical link between such study and the flourishing of the kind of social and political freedom that is found in a relatively open and free country. The careful scrutiny of problems, the weighing of alternatives, and then the choosing of particular rhetorical strategies with which to advocate solutions to those problems is not a course always taught. However, in a relatively free society there is greater opportunity for the study and practice of public speaking. The emergence, for example, of public speaking as a practical art that could be taught and learned coincided with the birth of freedom in ancient Greece. For this reason, a brief sketch of the historical development of the public speaking tradition is given next.

STUDY OF SPEAKING IN HISTORY

The study of speaking was one of the original liberal arts and was included in the Trivium of grammar, logic, and rhetoric (theory and practice of speaking). As early as the fifth century B.C., the Greeks valued highly one's ability to communicate well orally. After the collapse of tyranny in the sixth century B.C., an intensely active political life developed in Athens and other Greek Cities.[5] Greek communication consisted of activities such as "the sermon, the political pamphlet, the educational treatise, the funeral encomium, and the imaginative exercise, as well as the more expected judicial and deliberative orations."[6] With these activities came a need for training in politics and persuasion. Eduard Zeller found that "whoever wished to play a role in public life required not only a more extensive knowledge than had been hitherto usual, but above all a thorough formal training in thinking and speaking . . . ."[7]

When you live in a free society, you must learn how to work effectively in that situation. Much is left to individual choice and personal initiative; one must fend for himself. To survive the competition of an open society, one has to discover ways of adapting, confronting such questions as: What are the available means of informing and persuading? How can I best organize my ideas? What words should I choose to accurately and interestingly convey my feelings and thoughts to individuals and groups? What are the ideas inherent in this topic which require analyzing and explaining? How can I know my examples or statistics are correct and appropriate?

5. H.I. Marrou, *A History of Education in Antiquity* (New York: New American Library, 1956), p. 77.

6. George Kennedy, *Art of Persuasion in Greece* (New Jersey: Princeton University Press, 1963), p. 7.

7. Eduard Zeller, *Outline of the History of Greek Philosophy*, 13th ed. (New York: Meridian Books, 1955), pp. 93–94.

Both before and after the time of Aristotle (384–322 B.C.), persons have struggled with such questions. To provide some answers Aristotle wrote an important work on persuasive speaking called *Rhetoric*. Viewing rhetoric as "the faculty of discovering in the particular case what are the available means of persuasion," Aristotle discussed the importance of a speaker's credibility, emotion while speaking, and use of supporting materials.

Aristotle divided persuasive speaking into three kinds: *deliberative* speaking, such as takes place in a legislative assembly, in which you exhort or advise in behalf of the most expedient policy; *forensic* speaking, often in the courtroom, in which you accuse or defend in behalf of justice; *epideictic* or ceremonial speaking, such as a dedication service, in which you praise a person or institution on the basis of honorable service.

Romans, such as Cicero and Quintilian, further systematized the five canons of classical speaking theory: *invention* (discovery and analysis of ideas for a speech), *style* (use of words), *organization, delivery,* and *memory.*

In 1776 George Campbell wrote his *Philosophy of Rhetoric,* one of the books which strongly influenced the teaching of speaking in American colleges from 1776 to 1870. In his work Campbell broadened the study of rhetoric to include wit, evidence, logic, style, human nature, the doctrine of the association of ideas, and the "infusing of vivacity into ideas." He believed that "there is no art whatever that hath so close a connection with all the faculties and power of the mind as eloquence, or the art of speaking, in the extensive sense in which I employ the term." Campbell thought that "all the ends of speaking are reducible to four; every speech being intended to enlighten the understanding, to please the imagination, to move the passions, or to influence the will."[8]

In the United States, theorists and speakers have continued to systematize and add to our understanding of speech communication theory. Experiences in the classroom have been as varied as the interests and abilities of the teachers and students. In 1859, just months before the Civil War, students at The University of Georgia were giving orations on topics such as "Insufficiency of Human Happiness," "The Reformers," "Patrick Henry," "The Battle of Marathon," "Southern Chivalry," "Mohammedanism," "Death of the Girondists," "Heroes," "The Destiny of America Is beyond the Reach of Human Investigation," "Motives for Marrying," "The Italian War," and "African Slave Trade."[9]

8. George Campbell, *The Philosophy of Rhetoric,* ed. by Lloyd F. Bitzer (Carbondale: Southern Illinois University Press, 1963), p. 1.
9. *Southern Watchman* (August 4, 1859), Athens, Georgia.

The need for a better understanding of both the theory and practice of speaking in society increases. With the shift from a rural-agrarian population to an urban-industrialized society, with the conflict between the generations, races, and societies, and with the influence of the mass media has come a critical need for meaningful communication. Donald C. Bryant, in his important article on the functions and scope of rhetoric, suggested that "the rhetorical function is the function of adjusting ideas to people and of people to ideas."[10] Study of speaking, based simply on that one definition, includes such important areas as thought, language, human behavior, decision making, and personal adjustment. One can readily see, then, the interdisciplinary nature of speech and how it closely relates to disciplines such as psychology, sociology, philosophy, history, political science, and other social studies.

Just because a country historically has experienced a free society does not mean it will automatically continue. Whether the relatively open society serves man's needs will depend in large measure on the ability and willingness of citizens to speak. Informed individuals sharing ideas freely have a good opportunity to make wise choices. Whether it be an interested student discussing the quality of life, a woman debating equal rights for women, or a home owner speaking about a proposed zoning law, the decisions made on any matter will be determined by those concerned enough to become involved. We urge you to develop your abilities as a citizen-speaker so you will be able to contribute effectively to man's ongoing search for a better life for all.

EXERCISES/ASSIGNMENTS

1. Evaluate one of the following kinds of speaking. How important is the speaking in this area to the progress of mankind: political, educational, religious, business, radio-television.

2. Prepare a three- or four-minute (written/oral) statement defining the means a student should use to influence decisions in society.

3. List methods of influence you believe to be acceptable in a democratic society; list ways you believe to be unacceptable. Be prepared to explain your conclusions.

4. If you categorized the kinds of speaking you have heard, what divisions would you use? Give examples of each kind of speaking.

10. Donald C. Bryant, "Rhetoric: Its Functions and Its Scope," *Quarterly Journal of Speech* 39 (December 1953), p. 413.

5. What are the limits of speaking as a means of making decisions?
6. Observe a speaker and evaluate his or her performance. What were the strengths? What needed improving?

CHAPTER 2

BASIC PRINCIPLES
OF SPEAKING
AND LISTENING

In Chapter 1 you were apprised of the value of speaking skills to each individual. Free, responsible, and successful speech communication is one of the bases of our society. Having an interest in politics, business, or religion, you may be wondering where you begin to improve speaking skills that are so vitally needed. In a large sense you have already begun. You learned to talk at an early age and have been practicing in one way or another ever since. "But," you may protest, "that has been on an informal, conversational level most of the time. Giving speeches is not my line. I wouldn't know what to talk about, or how to organize what I wanted to say, or anything." That is an understandable reaction. The purpose of this chapter is to help you get started in your development as a skilled and responsible communicator.

Mastery of all of the principles and techniques of speaking and listening is an exacting process and takes considerable time. But you need to be acquainted with at least the basic principles for your very first efforts, so we present them here with an outlined overview of the steps to be taken in preparing to speak, the diaries of two students' preparation, a section on how to approach speaking with confidence, and finally a brief explanation of how understanding listening behavior can help improve the communication process. We hope these guides will help point the direction for your improvement as a communicator.

SEVEN BASIC PRINCIPLES

Free, responsible, and successful speaking must be based on acceptable and, when possible, proven principles. Seven principles are stated briefly here and followed by the basic steps to carry them out. Elsewhere in the book these precepts will be amplified and their importance demonstrated for the individual who wants to improve as a communicator.

The responsible and skillful speaker will:

1. Choose a fitting subject to achieve a specific purpose.
2. Adapt to the audience and occasion seeking the highest good for that audience.
3. Use the most reliable supporting materials available.
4. Organize materials into understandable, retainable patterns.
5. Choose clear and appropriate language.
6. Utilize the most communicative vocal and bodily manner of speaking.
7. Be a person of confidence, competence, and integrity.

These are the general principles one must develop. Speaking, however, involves specific skills. To improve as a speaker one must translate these general goals into practical performance. Let us now look more closely at the specific practices which one must perfect if he is to be an effective communicator.

Selecting the Subject and Purpose

You will probably get to choose most of your speech class topics, so start with your own experience and interests at the outset so that you feel more confident in handling the material and are more highly motivated to speak to the group. Relating an aspect of your summer job working in a federal park, for example, may be more interesting to you and the audience than trying to explain, say, the federal court system.

Limit the topic to something manageable within the time allotted. It is said that the amateur speaker worries about material to put into his speech and the expert worries about what he will have to leave out. Suppose your hobby is amateur photography. You would be quite qualified to speak on the topic of "photography." However, you could hardly cover the history of photography, the various photographic processes, the different kinds of equipment, and how to shop for a camera in a single short speech. You would be wise to limit your speech to a much narrower aspect of photography, such as the basic difference between the rangefinder and single lens reflex types of cameras.

The three general purposes of speaking are to inform, to persuade, and to entertain. Determining the general purpose will very likely be done for you in class—but not necessarily after you graduate. The above purposes will be considered in greater detail later in the chapter. Here it is important to remember that the chief end of communication is to elicit a response or achieve a specific purpose. It is not enough just to talk "about Rh incompatibility"; your purpose would be "to clarify existing misconceptions about the subject of Rh incompatibility and present some of the basic principles, problems, and solutions of this undesirable affliction." Better than a "talk about doctors," your specific purpose might be "to convince the audience we need to assign a high priority to medical education, especially increasing the capacity of our medical schools."

Analyzing the Audience and Occasion

If the purpose of speaking is to elicit a favorable response, you have to know your audience well enough to predict their interest in your topic, their level of understanding, and their attitude toward the subject. Then if your favorite subject, such as the history of railroads, is not important to your audience, you must try to find ways to make the topic more meaningful to them. For instance, if your audience is the local chapter of the Civil Air Patrol, you might compare and contrast the history of railroads with that of commercial airlines.

For most assignments you will have a time limit to which you must adapt. Because other classmates are waiting their turn to speak, you should time your talk carefully. This is good training in how to adapt to the occasion. Many civic clubs meet during the noon hour, for example, and members have to be back to their places of business promptly. A speaker who is insensitive to this situation may see his audience slowly disappear before his eyes. Analysis of the audience and occasion is presented in more detail in Chapter 3.

Gathering and Using Materials

Once you have a topic and purpose and have some idea of the audience and occasion, you are ready to search for materials. If your subject comes from your experience, it is natural for you to exhaust your personal storehouse of knowledge first. You should supplement your experience, however, with findings from the library. The card catalogue and *Readers Guide* will be good places to begin; then go immediately to more specialized indexes which cover the particular subject you are to speak on. If a student grows up on a tobacco farm, his knowledge is considerable, but his father's authority on this subject would be welcome. The doctor's daughter who reports on the latest cancer therapy will find a ready source at home. Discussion of the open classroom in public schools would be enhanced by views of a local education professor, high school principal, or open classroom teacher.

Put your researched materials on 3 x 5 or 4 x 6 cards, preferably one item to a card on one side only so that when you begin to organize your information you can simply put your cards in orderly categories.

Use broad topic headings at the tops of your cards and be sure to get the full reference. It is always a good idea to know your exact source in case you need to return to it for additional information.

We have been discussing sources and handling of speech materials. Now we preview what these materials are. They will be taken up in detail in Chapters 6 and 7. Your content may be classified as personal assertion, supporting materials, reasoning patterns, and visual aids. You cannot report the status of the welfare program without statistics. To explain the effects of additives to food, you need facts. To know how a laser beam works, an audience needs explanation and examples. Convincing an audience that violence on TV programs is harmful to children requires testimony. The most successful speeches never lack substance.

Organizing Your Material

When you first decide on your topic and purpose you should do some preliminary thinking as to what major points you want to get across. This will help direct your search for materials. If you were interested in the struggle for freedom in Africa, for example, you would need to limit your treatment to representative countries. Perhaps early in your reading you discover that Rhodesia, South Africa, and Mozambique provide an overall picture. You then have a ready-made geographical or spatial type organization and have three main points to cover.

Once you have decided on your points, you can assure yourself a more systematic analysis and presentation if you will outline the main ideas. Taking a different topic, note how, in the brief outline below, we have eliminated everything about photography except what will achieve our specific purpose: to explain the basic difference between the rangefinder and single lens reflex cameras.

I. The rangefinder camera uses separate lenses for composing and taking the picture.
   A. The area to be covered by the picture is seen through two small windows in the top front of the camera.
   B. The picture is taken through the main lens below the rangefinder lenses.
   C. Since the two lens systems "see the picture" from different angles, there may be what is called a "parallax" problem wherein what one sees in the viewfinder may not be quite what the main lens will cover.

II. With the single lens reflex camera the lens that takes the picture is the one through which you view the subject.

    A. Light enters the camera lens and is directed straight upward by a mirror slanted 45 degrees from the light.

    B. The light travels through a pentaprism and onto a ground glass screen as an upright image of the subject.

    C. At the moment the shutter is tripped the mirror snaps up, allowing the light to pass onto the film behind it, and then it snaps back down.

    D. Since the picture is composed and taken through the same lens, there is no parallax problem.

Add a conclusion and then an introduction to this and you will have a skeleton speech outline. See Chapter 5 for suggestions on organizing, the rules for outlining, and several ways to introduce and conclude your speech.

Wording the Speech

With the preparation above you are ready to "talk out" your speech on photography. It will not flow as easily as it might if you were recounting a personal experience where first one event happened and then another. But if you will establish the overall pattern in your mind and let your note cards remind you of the main points and subpoints you want to discuss, after several attempts it will become almost as familiar as a personal experience. The speech will *become* your experience. Each time you practice you should polish the wording for maximum clarity. Further help with choice of language is found in Chapter 9 where clarity is broken down into elements of concreteness, simplicity, precision, and appropriateness. The nature of words and characteristics of oral style are also set forth and should help increase your communication effectiveness.

Rehearsing the Delivery: Voice and Body

When you began to flesh out your outline in words, you of course began to rehearse. Adding the dimensions of voice and body, the speech now comes alive. Simulate the real situation as closely as possible. Stand while practicing. Strive for a conversational, communicative manner. Chapter 8 discusses principles of presentation, kinds of delivery, and the use of voice and body in communication in more detail.

Being a Confident, Credible Communicator

The final principle says more about what you the speaker are than what you do. Following the first six principles should help you become confident, competent, and be perceived as a person with integrity. Gaining confidence is discussed later in this chapter. The need for credible communicators in contemporary society has been painfully obvious. This text is dedicated to the proposition that "ends" in speaking must be considered with "means," that achieving a right response for a wrong reason may be indefensible. Hopefully the text will provide enough communication strategies for your arsenal that you will lose few battles for just causes.

Now that we have considered several basic principles of effective speaking, we will study the diaries which two student speakers kept while preparing their speeches for class. Note also the comments which accompany the diaries.

Diaries of Two Student Speakers

Diary of Speaker 1	Comments
Sunday afternoon: Began to rack my brain for a topic that would be interesting to me, the class, and meet the ten minute deadline.	Good to consider audience and self-interest when selecting topic. Good to adapt to time limits. Needs to consider specific purpose carefully.
Since I had strong feelings in favor of the police department, I knew this would do the trick.	But did it meet interests of audience? (Of course on occasion the purpose of speaking is to create an interest.)
Monday: Went to the library and found many good books.	Did he use an index to find recent articles? What method did he use to find books on police? See Chapter 4.
That night I realized that I wanted to present my views on the police department in an unusual way.	What would be attitude of audience? What kinds of materials would be required to make the topic appealing? What kind of delivery? What visual aids would help clarify?
Began to doodle with an outline and rough paragraphs.	Good to give careful thought to organizing your ideas. Did Speaker 1 consider the methods one can use when outlining? See Chapter 5.
Tuesday: Put it all together and realized it wasn't long enough and seemed to lack cohesiveness.	A critical stage in speech writing is when one takes materials found in books, articles, interviews, and personal experience and organizes them in an original

way so as to be clear and interesting. Often the first draft of a speech will "lack cohesiveness" and one must continue to struggle with organization, use of clear and interesting language, and delivery.

Went and talked to my instructor.

Reactions by other people will help you communicate your ideas clearly and with interest.

That night I finished writing the speech and began to practice giving it out loud.

Facts don't always speak for themselves. They must be presented in such a way that people will listen and comprehend. Chapter 8 will demonstrate different kinds of delivery and how to present your thoughts in an attractive manner.

Wednesday: *Day before the speech! I didn't touch the speech until 2:00 this afternoon. I presented it to several different people. They seemed to like it; this gave me confidence.*

Some listeners are more candid than others; it is wise to get the reaction of several people. Good to practice *orally*, to become familiar with language and to time the speech. Self-confidence is very important. Persons who have not often talked in public are very nervous. Informed practice will give you more confidence.

By late that night I had given it out loud so many times I was starting to not like the speech so went to bed.

There is no one formula for practicing a speech. During this process, however, look for specific ways to improve the organization, word choice, and audience adaptation. How many times one should give the speech will differ with the individual.

Thursday: *The day has arrived. I didn't touch the speech until the chairman in the class introduced me to the class. I was nervous but confident. I gave it.*

Be certain you have all your materials together (outline, bibliography, note cards, visual aids). Be certain you have anticipated any special problems: electric plug if needed, place to hang visual aid. See Chapter 7.

Afterthought: *I don't think I began preparing for this speech soon enough. I was not satisfied with my end product. I was too rushed the last couple of days.*

Writing a speech takes time. Research often is long and involved. Then one must invent an original speech from raw data gathered from numerous sources. Be sure you give considerable thought to audience attitudes and interests and what you must add or delete from the speech to make your topic interesting to this particular group.

Diary of Speaker 2

My last speech was thought of before my first speech. I gave my first speech to give the class a background in phosphate pollution so that they would understand the urgency that I felt in my final speech.

All of the information in my final speech, with the exception of the introduction and conclusion, was taken from a Chemistry II term paper I did at the U.S. Coast Guard Academy.

The main task I faced was modifying and condensing the information so that it could be understood by just about anybody. I began work on my final speech six days prior to its performance.

Sunday evening: I organized the information that I wanted to present. I had originally planned to explain the whole tertiary plant, but I decided that evening that it would take too long. I narrowed it down to just the phosphate removal portion and that appeared to be enough.

Monday evening: I made the visual aids that I knew would be necessary to explain the phosphate removal system. I originally made three large posters, but my wife showed me where it might be more effective if I used a "tack-over" technique which I did end up using.

Comments

When one knows his or her schedule of speaking activities well in advance, he or she can coordinate two or more speeches.

While individual instructors may differ on this, usually one is expected to write an *original* speech, not a warmed-over term paper. The Coast Guard research would have been *one* important source from which to draw, but the student should supplement with data from current books, articles, and interviews. All data should then have been put together for an *oral* communication. See Chapter 9 for a discussion of the use of language in oral communication. Also the original speech should incorporate many materials of particular interest to this particular audience which a Coast Guard term paper would not have at all. See Chapter 3 for help with audience analysis.

Speaker 2 was wise in looking for ways to make the speech fit within the time limit and to be certain all members of this audience could understand. As stated above, he should have considered other tasks: adapting both to audience comprehension and audience interests and audience attitudes.

Look in Chapter 5 for ways to organize speech material. Speaker 2 was very wise in limiting his topic. Too many speakers try to explain in seven minutes such topics as "pollution," "psychology," or "education." This speaker took a broad subject and divided it to something he could handle in ten minutes.

Speaker 2 here demonstrates a genuine interest in communicating with his audience. He asked himself, "What must I do to explain to this audience a process that many probably know nothing about?" One answer was to use visual aids. Visual aids are not easy to use, but they add both interest and understanding to almost any topic. See Chapter 7.

Tuesday evening: I typed out the body of the speech as I wanted to present it. I ended up typing it twice, because I decided it would be best to put the results of the Lake Tahoe plant at the end of the speech rather than prior to the explanation of the system.

Wednesday evening: I gave a live performance for my wife. I then made up note cards on the points I was hazy on. My speaking was all extemporaneous. I knew the material backward and forward; the problem was a matter of stating it in the simplest terms. When I made a statement that was too difficult for my wife to comprehend, she would stop me and I would modify the statement until she could understand it.

Thursday evening: I went through the speech six times with my wife. Each time she would tell me what method of presentation she liked best. I would make a note of it and attempt to incorporate it in the speech the next time. After the sixth time I figured I was ready.

Friday: I gave the speech. (Instructor's Note: The student used no notes and forgot very early in his speech. He glanced at the outline which the instructor had and went on with no further trouble or use of notes.)

Different instructors will suggest a variety of ways to prepare the final speech. This speaker found writing out the entire speech to be of help. Certainly such a process permits one to check carefully such communication principles as organization, use of language, reasoning, and supporting material. You would do well to follow the procedure used by this speaker of continuing to revise the speech in search of the best way to communicate the message.

Again the speaker shows his real concern for communicating his ideas clearly. He practiced orally; he revised his word choice when some words were vague, unknown, or too complex for his listener. While there are several ways to deliver a speech (see Chapter 8), the extemporaneous method does permit conversational speech, audience adaptation during the speech, and a friendly contact with the audience. But to achieve an extemporaneous delivery one must do as the speaker did — one must practice extemporaneously!

Enlightened practice is important. Just as is true in playing the piano or in developing a surgical skill, one must apply substantive theory to practical use. In communication you must study the principles discussed in this book carefully and then *look* for ways to apply them when speaking to other people. Speaker 2 was wise to practice orally; he may have profited even more had he varied his practice audience. Certainly he would want to ask all through this process what he would have to add or delete to make his topic of interest to this particular audience, with its interests, attitudes, apathy, and concern.

Even though the speaker knew the topic backward and forward, he became overconfident. A note card or two with key words to remind him of what he wanted to say could have saved a bad moment. He recovered beautifully, however, and the total impact was favorable.

SPEAKING CONFIDENTLY

Your attitude toward your speech and the speaking situation will influence your performance. Indeed your attitude toward the speech becomes part of the speaking process. If you approach the event with confidence, chances are you will be perceived by the audience as a confident communicator. If you have followed steps that assure adequate preparation, you will be more likely to develop confidence. Remember that speaking is a skill which must be learned, an art to be mastered.

But for some of us anxiety remains. A 1973 survey by the R. H. Bruskin Associates involving 2,543 male and female adults indicated that speaking before a group was feared by 40.6 percent of the respondents.[1] They were asked to pick the items from a list representing situations in which they had some degree of fear. The first ten items chosen are as follows:

Speaking before a group	40.6%
Height	32.0
Insects	22.1
Financial problems	22.0
Deep water	21.5
Sickness	18.8
Death	18.7
Flying	18.3
Loneliness	13.6
Dogs	11.2

The report elaborates on speaking before a group:

About 46% of women have this fear, while 36% of men indicate some concern. There is little difference by age, but people in the $15,000 plus income group seem somewhat less concerned about public speaking. The more education a person has, the less likely he is to fear addressing a group. People living in the southern part of the United States seem to have the greatest fear while those in the northeast seem concerned.[2]

Earlier research showed that *some* degree of stage fright, as psychological or physiological arousal, is common among both experienced and inexperienced speakers. So, you know now it is common.

You should know also that research indicates that (1) the symptoms of stage fright seem to be less apparent to the observers than to

1. Survey by R. H. Bruskin Associates, reported in *Spectra* 9 (December 1973), p. 4.
2. Ibid.

the speaker; (2) men are more likely to have their stage fright observed while women are more likely to be aware of it themselves; and (3) there is no apparent correlation between stage fright and intelligence, reasoning ability, or major phases of personality as reflected in standard tests.[3] The more you know about the phenomenon of stage fright, the less you will shrink from it, for knowledge dissipates fear.

Though probably no one simple cause exists for all people who experience anxious feelings, the speaking situation contains both attractive and distasteful features and, thus, an approach-avoidance conflict results. Precipitating this conflict may be faulty evaluations of the situation, in which the speaker expects too much of himself and the audience, or one may imagine dreadful consequences for not measuring up to his own expectations.

Where do you go for help? First of all, knowing the results of the research on stage fright tells us that you are not alone and that talk of intelligence and personality differences will not suffice. On the other hand, you should understand that natural tensions may heighten your alertness and prevent your performance from being dull and routine.

Secondly, sound preparation cannot be stressed enough. This is this book's reason for being — to help you learn how to prepare. Choose a topic that interests you, do thorough research, and rehearse to coordinate the mental and physical components of your message.

Thirdly, at the time of the speech, talk *with* not *at* your audience, and endeavor to move around if you still need to relax.

Finally, consider your role as a speaker positively. When you change posture from being seated among your peers to standing before them as the focus of attention, when twenty or so people take five minutes or more out of their lives to listen to you, be a responsible communicator who has faithfully followed the steps of preparation and has earned the right to speak. Welcome the challenge.

GENERAL PURPOSES OF SPEECH

Speaking should be purposeful. We live in a time and a society in which many social and political problems exist. Our talk should be meaningful. The three general purposes of speaking are to inform, to persuade, and to entertain.

3. Jon Eisenson, J. Jeffery Auer, and John V. Irwin, *The Psychology of Communication* (New York: Appleton-Century-Crofts, 1963), p. 322.

To Inform

Probably the most common purpose is to share information. A log of any day's events will confirm this: the early morning announcer with the news, the weatherman forecasting, a campus policeman explaining where Zone D parking lot is, an instructor lecturing on European history. The goal is understanding so that the knowledge may be useful. In the age of the information explosion it is especially important to speak with clarity on important topics. But listeners have so many competing incoming stimuli the speaker will also have to create a desire in his audience to listen. How people learn information and the kinds of informative speeches are included in Chapter 10.

To Persuade

In our society with incessant advertising for goods and services, the second general purpose—to persuade—permeates our lives. Persuasion attempts to change beliefs, reinforce feelings, or modify behavior. A speaker may try to convince you that there should be stricter gun control laws, that you should appreciate the USA even more after hearing about a trip abroad, that you should try transcendental meditation. These specific persuasive purposes are amplified in Chapter 12 along with the nature of persuasion and the contribution of classical rhetoric and modern empirical research to the theory of persuasion.

To Entertain

In a society with increased leisure time, the final general purpose—to entertain—is also significant. Whereas informing and persuading carry listeners through several organizational steps to achieve their serious purposes, the speech to entertain can be counted as successful if it captures the attention of an audience successfully for an appointed time. Chapter 6 treats humor and other supporting materials appropriate for a speech to entertain, and Chapter 13 develops further the entertaining speech.

LISTENING

A study of listening is important both to one who is striving to get the attention of an audience and to one who is in the audience. In this section we define listening and suggest ways to improve that behavior.

What is listening? Listening is the reception, recognition, understanding, interpretation, and evaluation of aural stimuli. *Reception*
means you can hear. You could nod your head that you hear a piano
sound of twenty decibels. This is reception. If you can repeat a message, even though you don't know what it means, you show *recognition*. For example, if your instructor asked you to pronounce nonsense
syllables for laboratory articulation practice and you repeated and
wrote those nonsense syllables, you would have reached the second
level, *recognition*. When you demonstrate that you can get to a restau-
rant after being given directions, you have achieved *understanding*.
Interpretation is exemplified by deciding that, when a speaker talks of a
"general education," he means a two-year core of courses in college
and not an education common to all. Finally, *evaluation* occurs in daily
assessment of alternative messages or in critically analyzing evidence
presented in a given case. Let us consider a few ways you can improve
your listening habits.

Attitude Control

Why are you "turned on" by one speaker and "turned off" by another?
Though a number of reasons come to mind, one of the most common
is your attitude toward *what* the speaker says and *how* he says it. You
usually bring to a speech occasion some information about the subject
and an attitude toward it. The less information you have the more neu-
tral you are likely to be. If you have never heard of the I.L.O. (International Labor Organization) you will tend to be open-minded. But the
subject of student housing is one on which you probably have an opinion and may find yourself debating with the speaker after the first sentence. Resist this temptation. Hear the speaker out. Wait until you are
certain you understand his position. Otherwise you may sit there spin-
ning your emotional wheels and miss an opportunity to learn more
about housing on campus.

Environmental Control

Poor listening sometimes results when the speaking occasion is pol-
luted with too much noise, bad acoustics, a faulty public address system, a stuffy room, or hard seats. To be sure, once there, it may be too
late to change some of these conditions, but the efficient listener will do
what he can. It is not uncommon for lawn mowers or construction
equipment to be operating near an open classroom window. When this
happens some listeners might welcome the distraction and continue to

daydream. The good listener will close the window so the speech or lecture will not be further disrupted. Show initiative in your listening habits.

Physical Fitness

Listening is an active, not a passive, process. When you work at it the heart beats faster, there is quicker circulation of the blood, and there is even a slight increase in body temperature. This process takes more energy than just sitting relaxed. Research reports tell us that college students tend to come to class tired and begin listening too late, thus missing much which would aid comprehension of the entire lecture. The health clues are clear: be well-rested, assume a comfortably erect posture, and begin listening early.

Rate of Speech vs. Rate of Thought

If you are physically and mentally ready to listen, you may be so alert that the speaker who speaks at the average rate of 140 words per minute will leave your rapid-thinking brain with time to spare. These are the times daydreams intervene and mental meandering begins to take over. It has been found that many listeners can comprehend up to 275 words per minute without appreciable loss. Because this is true, you can, as a listener, (1) anticipate the organizational pattern of the communication; (2) decide what information category you are going to "plug" this new information into; (3) review your own experience with the topic and relate wherever possible; and (4) evaluate the speaker's points objectively, trying first to make sure you understand them from his point of view and then assessing their strength according to evidence and reasoning.

Seeking Ideas, Not Just Facts

Well-intentioned listeners continually deceive themselves by trying to "get all the facts." It seems the natural and logical approach in a culture with an established tradition of twelve years of schooling. In both school and nonschool studies, however, it is not unusual to find a mere 25 percent efficiency in understanding what message was intended. But we persist in trying to absorb facts when what the communicator is trying to do is present a central idea with two or three main points. Francis Drake reported an Air Force study in which a speaker in a brilliantly organized speech was developing the concept that we need to see the other fellow's point of view in world affairs, that we must understand countries in Asia in terms of their history. As an example, he mentioned that parts of China had been carpetbagged for years. In developing further the failure of Americans to recognize the Asian's attitude toward us, he noted that nationalistic pride dislikes charity. A few students, when asked, came up with the main idea, but far too many put down the miscellaneous points such as: "China has been carpetbagged," and "Asiatics are proud."[4]

Of course, concentration on specific facts will sometimes take priority over trying to discern generalizations, but even then facts will be remembered longer, if the main points are isolated. Seek first the central ideas, and some facts will more likely be noted.

Use of Notes

The most time-honored method of remembering what a speaker has said is some method of note-taking. Here again there is no one magic method. The major finding to come out of studies on the subject is the usefulness of a review and reflection period some time after hearing the speaker. If the listener has followed the above suggestions on recognizing a pattern of organization and seeking the central idea, note-taking follows easily.

Listen for Total Meaning

In public communication and interpersonal communication, the receiver should always try to listen for total meaning. The words of the message taken in a straightforward manner may not be what the speaker intends. We need to discover early if the speaker is fond of irony, for instance. The nonverbal communication also plays an important role here. Some speakers deliver the funniest lines with a straight face and their most cutting remarks with laughter. It is to underlying feelings as well as words that we must respond if we are to be successful listeners.

EXERCISES/ASSIGNMENTS

1. Interview a local person who speaks regularly and discover what procedure that person follows when preparing a speech. Be prepared to report your findings to the class.

4. Francis E. Drake, "How Do You Teach Listening?" *Southern Speech Journal* 16 (May 1951), pp. 268–71. See also Ralph Nichols and Leonard Stevens, *Are You Listening?* (New York: McGraw-Hill, 1957).

2. Prepare a three- to five-minute informative speech based on a personal experience you have had. Try to follow the steps outlined in the chapter.

3. Keep a diary on how you prepared a speech. How close did you stay to the suggested procedure? Share with the class your experience with the difference between theory and practice.

4. Study the seven principles for free, responsible, and successful communication. Some relate to the content of the speech and some to delivery. Which factor do you think is most important for successful communication? Be prepared to defend your position in class discussion.

5. Poll five or ten people as to their attitude on giving a speech to a group they don't know.

6. Go to listen to a speaker on campus or in town. Could you easily summarize his or her main ideas? Did supporting materials or main points stand out the most? How attentive was the audience? What were the chief listening problems *you* encountered?

CHAPTER 3

ADAPTING TO THE OCCASION AND AUDIENCE

THE SPEAKING SITUATION

The total environment in which a speech takes place may be called the speaking situation and will have direct influence on the different ways you develop and present your ideas. The speaking situation has both historical and immediate characteristics, and both make demands on the communicator. Historical factors are those which provide a wider context and require of the speaker a broad perspective. Immediate characteristics of the speaking situation are those which relate to the present needs, interests, and views of people actively involved.

To better understand the effects of the total speaking situation on the speaker, ask yourself, for example, "What factors during World War II were different from those during the Vietnam struggle, and how would these differences affect the *speaking* of persons who lived through these wars?" How would one handle "patriotic-type arguments" when discussing events and issues inherent to those two wars? What problems were different? Were there similarities growing out of those two conflicts which would affect speaking? What attitudes and beliefs would one confront during the two periods?

What kinds of communication requirements, then, does the speaking situation make upon you as speaker? The speaking situation may help determine which issues and arguments are most appropriate. The speaking environment will influence the type language and delivery you can use successfully, whether direct or indirect, formal or informal. The key point to remember here is that as speaker you will be confronted with numerous communication choices as to what kind of speaking will work. Very important also is your own personal choice. For example, after studying the speaking situation carefully you may determine that a particular argument or position is popular with most people; however, you believe that view to be dishonest. Thus one can only go so far when adapting to the demands of a speaking situation; you must also maintain your own personal moral principles.

To better understand the requirements placed upon you by the situation in which you will speak, we will now discuss two important aspects of the speaking environment: the occasion and the audience.

THE SPEAKING OCCASION

You should carefully study the occasion on which you will speak. A primary concern will be to identify the purpose of the meeting and the role you are expected to perform. Why are the people meeting? What topics are appropriate for the occasion? What physical arrangements will influence your speech? What is the size of the room, the quality of the acoustics, and the amount of lighting? Will you have a reliable public address system? Will the audience be comfortable? How will the seating arrangements affect what you do? Will there be child care facilities or an audience filled with children? Here are a few examples of general type occasions you could confront.

Ceremonial Speaking

Historically, persons writing on communication have discussed epideictic or ceremonial speaking. This would include Fourth of July orations, a Labor Day rally, or an annual teacher-of-the-year awards dinner on campus. Your job is to discover what your speaking role should be on such occasions. What kind of talk are you to make—informative, persuasive, or inspirational?

Deliberative Speaking

Purposeful speaking occurs when individuals or groups feel a need exists which deserves attention. Deliberative speaking takes place when persons discuss publicly what should be done concerning a need or problem in the community. Students at a school or university may discuss in a forum the need for an improved curriculum. Persons in a community might become concerned about water and air pollution, and gather to explore or advocate what can be done. Deliberative speaking often results in new policy. Problem-solving communication will be discussed at length in Chapters 11 and 12.

Forensic Speaking

When you speak on some occasions you will find that you must share the podium with other speakers. Forensic speaking is a give-and-take between two or more speakers or debaters. Court room communication is a good example, where we have the prosecutor and defender. Some of you have observed high school and college debaters presenting an "affirmative case" for some change in society and a "negative case" which is constructed to defend a situation the way it is. There are many occasions on which one finds himself involved in both deliberative and forensic speaking. You may stand, for example, before a group of farmers and speak in behalf of government support for commodities and, before you are finished, find you are engaged in a forensic exchange with persons who disagree with your point of view. The speaking will often deal with whether there is a problem and what should be done about it.

Other Occasions

While some speaking is directed at serious social problems, much of our communication is devoted to the fulfillment of personal desires. For example, you may develop a need for fun or variety of relationships with other people, an occasion where you can share interests or time with other people. From felt needs have developed such communicating groups as the Liar's Club, the Mystic Valley Railway Association, little theater, and an organization of antique collectors.

Finally, a group of persons could meet on a particular occasion because of the creative thought of an individual. One need not wait until a situation or problem emerges or becomes critical before taking action. A person who is widely read and experienced can inquire into better ways of doing things before that state is reached. This kind of preventative speaking is badly needed in the United States. Too often individuals and governments at every level allow a situation to become a crisis before meaningful analysis and interaction occur. In practical terms preventative speaking means a daily dialogue on affairs of society rather than crisis rhetoric designed to treat problems in a palliative fashion.

Adapting to the Occasion

The occasion of a speech is an important part of the total speaking situation and one you should study carefully. When analyzing the occasion, investigate what requirements and choices it places upon you in your role as speaker. There will be some characteristics of a unique occasion which you can only discover when studying that particular event. On the other hand there are stock questions you can ask which will help prepare you for the demands of this aspect of the total situation: What led to this situation? Who were involved in bringing it about? What are the key issues? What self-interests are involved? What groups are concerned? To what extent are religious, economic, political, and social forces at work? What expectations are inherent to this occasion? Must I be formal or informal in dress, use of words, and delivery? Are there physical factors which should be considered? How will the time of day and amount of time allotted for the speech affect my speech? What is the purpose of the meeting? What role am I expected to play? What do my personal convictions require that I do?

THE AUDIENCE

Of vital importance to successful speaking is knowing the audience. Communication is a process of interaction between two or more persons. At any one moment in the speaking process one can be either speaker or listener. Whether you talk to a small or large group, in order to determine how they may feel and think about you and your subject and how you can reach them with your message, you should study that audience carefully. Audience analysis is the study of all characteristics of your listeners, including their age, sex, education, knowledge of subject, personal experience, values, cohesiveness, responsiveness, and their beliefs. Each audience will be different, and you will have to consider many factors. First we will discuss these audience characteristics which will influence how they react to your speech.

Age

The age of persons in your audience may indicate something of their interests or experience with a particular topic. Persons twelve years old can be as excited in proposed improvement in playground equipment as their parents, but for different reasons. Persons over eighteen will be more concerned about marriage or choosing a career than those much younger. Age can be a good indication of one's knowledge, level of formal education, and experience.

Sex

Audience reaction is also influenced by the sex of the audience members. Attitudes toward sex roles are changing, and the speaker should be cautious in generalizing about males and females. Historically in the United States more men than women have been interested in auto mechanics, but you would be wise not to make a blanket assumption. A wise speaker doesn't generalize too quickly about audiences on the basis of sex. Study the particular audience you will address before jumping to conclusions. You may discover, for example, that many men are not interested in investments and many women are.

Level of Education

The general level of education is an important characteristic of a group of listeners. Education provides more resources for making comparisons, drawing conclusions, and possibly making informed decisions. Education equips persons to handle new situations, and a well-educated person can probably understand new materials and ideas more easily than an audience with little background knowledge to draw on. At the same time educated people often form firm beliefs. For example, a scientist may hold to a principle his educational experience has taught him, yet others with similar training will reject it. Members of the American Medical Association may be convinced that private medicine is the best means of providing adequate health services to the public. Such conclusions would certainly influence their reaction when confronted by a speaker who disagreed.

Knowledge of the Subject

The listeners' knowledge of the subject you are to discuss is a key factor in communication. You want to adapt your treatment of a topic to the level of understanding of your audience. The audience's knowledge of the subject, for example, will determine where you begin your discussion. If they are unfamiliar with an issue, you will have to devote the introduction to an orientation. Do not move too quickly into the main body of your speech until you are certain the audience understands the meaning of technical terms and knows clearly what you plan to do. These are critical choices which only an alert speaker can make when analyzing the knowledge of an audience.

Personal Experience

One's knowledge of a field may not depend solely on one's formal education. Personal experiences are also important. To experience something is to have an excellent opportunity to understand it. To speak before persons who have had wide experience with the subject is a real challenge. They will soon perceive whether you have a practical understanding of the subject you are explaining. In such a circumstance you would do well to be willing to learn from your audience.

Values

The values held in high esteem by your auditors should also be considered when you think of ways of adapting your speech. These may grow out of religious beliefs, social mores, tradition, study, or from personal conviction. A speaker would be naive who, without consideration of the fact, advocated a position which offended an audience's values. Of course the speaker might also hold strong values which require that he speak, even if they conflict with those held by the audience. On such occasions conflict probably is unavoidable. However, the speaker can anticipate such a condition and emphasize areas of agreement and encourage an exchange of ideas.

Cohesiveness

The relative unity of members of a group is an important characteristic to consider when analyzing an audience. Is the audience composed of persons bound together by a common purpose? Is it a heterogeneous group? For example, members of a church might be so committed to a particular belief that they are able to overcome differences which may exist among them. On the other hand a second congregation may be so divided that eventually the church splits into separate denominations. When analyzing an audience, then, explore the degree of cohesiveness among the members. Determine why a particular group is so united. These findings will provide valuable information concerning their attitudes and beliefs.

Responsiveness

When preparing your speech, anticipate whether your audience will respond in some way before, during, or after your presentation. In the 1950's in the United States, one could often assume he would enter an auditorium, sit on the stage, be introduced, and then lecture to a silent audience. The 1960's taught us that speaking situations can be more varied than that. Political campaigners visiting campuses were often met with hostile signs, comments, and questions. On some occasions audiences may not be willing to wait until the conclusion of the speech to ask questions; they want a response at the time a statement is made. In many of these kinds of speaking situations the speaker, at some point, becomes a listener and the listeners become speakers.

Such conditions have important implications for one who hopes to communicate meaningfully in those situations. You, for example, could not plan a prepared text with the assumption that you will not be interrupted. Your word choice, organization, and delivery must be flexible so if a member of the audience jumps up and asks a question or yells, "You are wrong!" you can stop and deal with that situation. The audience may not allow you to slip by with broad generalities and weak arguments. You will understand your topic, or under the pressure of questions and comments from the audience, be revealed as one who does not know what he is talking about.

Beliefs

In our search for security, status, safety, happiness, material wealth, comfort, and other goals, we have built up beliefs concerning how to go about achieving them. Beliefs may be acquired from education, religion, society, personal experiences, individual decisions, and so forth. When you confront an individual or group, you have come face to face with persons who have strong feelings and thoughts and who often believe they too are "right," whatever their education, level of competence, experience, vocation, or religion.

An example will help picture the situation a persuader faces when one confronts someone with an opposing belief. When your listeners disagree with you on an issue, it may well be because they sincerely "see" the situation differently. For example, you may honestly believe from your study and experience that "anyone who wants to work can find a job and that welfare programs should be abolished." On the other hand, the person you are addressing—an individual who has experienced job discrimination, lives in poverty, has had little education, and has had no contact with prosperity—also "knows" that many people who want to work can't find a job. How can this situation be resolved? Both persons sincerely believe they are right. For there to be a better understanding between the two persons, there has to be a sharing of the different perceptions which are as real to each as are the environments in which they spend most of their time. The speaker should attempt to anticipate these differences and *discover some common reality* which will establish communication and possibly resolve the conflict.

Professor Gary Cronkhite, after surveying the research literature on attitudes and beliefs, concluded that "one of the best-established findings of social psychology is that individuals who have well-established attitudes and beliefs act so as to maintain them; the more extreme the attitudes, the more difficult they are to change." He also warns that "individuals will reject communications which urge too much attitude change."[1] Communicating with persons who have different beliefs from your own will not be easy. You will do well to develop a sense of patience, respect, and understanding for the other person *as he is* before you seek ways of changing his actions and beliefs.

DEDUCTIVE REASONING

When analyzing your audience, then, you should investigate numerous listener traits which may provide insight into their role in the speaking situation. But how do these audience characteristics operate in a speaker-audience situation?

One way these factors influence audience perception and response is through deductive reasoning which takes place *between the speaker and listener*. Reasoning deductively involves going from a general belief or premise about a group or category to the application of that general belief to a specific member of that group. We can illustrate that deductive process by putting it in the form of a syllogism:

Listener responds: All Americans love wealth.
Speaker states first: John is an American.
Listener concludes: John loves wealth.

Most people have formed opinions about the Republican party, Boy Scouts, Frenchmen, laborers, abortion, or sex education, for instance. When such subjects are discussed ("John is an American") most persons automatically supply their preconceived general beliefs ("All Americans love wealth") and draw conclusions ("John loves wealth") based on these beliefs. When members of an audience supply the same basic beliefs, they are in agreement. When they supply opposing premises, there is conflict. Members of a group who hear a statement may supply different basic beliefs and thus react differently. For example, what if you say in a meeting, "House Bill 1–A is a sales tax"? Two of your listeners might respond as follows:

Listener 1

Listener responds: All taxes are bad.
You say first: House Bill 1–A is a sales tax.

Listener 2

Listener responds: Taxes are necessary for better public services.
You say first: House Bill 1–A is a sales tax.

1. Gary Cronkhite, *Persuasion: Speech and Behavioral Change* (New York: The Bobbs-Merrill Co., 1969), pp. 139–40.

Listener concludes: House Bill 1-A is bad.	*Listener concludes:* House Bill 1-A is necessary if we are to have better public services.

This is how deduction works in our daily lives, and understanding this process teaches us to anticipate all kinds of reactions to our words and our ideas. All of us carry with us basic beliefs about many subjects, and when the subject is discussed we often, depending upon how strong the belief, supply conclusions that cover the topic and thus *answer for ourselves* what we believe about the issue. A communicator faces a difficult challenge to try to crack these beliefs enough to just get a fair hearing. One can see too how critical it is to analyze one's listeners to anticipate what conclusion they are likely to supply when confronted with any particular topic. While you talk they are "talking to themselves." After you identify what *probable premise they will impose upon your subject,* you will know better how to direct your discussion and your supporting materials. In the case of Listener 1 above, you would have to consider ways of getting that person to re-think the belief that "all taxes are bad," if you hope to change his conclusion that "House Bill 1-A is therefore bad." To persuade Listener 1 you might argue, "None of us likes taxes; we all wish they would just go away. But you would not like to think of a fire gutting your home and realize that there were no firemen to help. It takes money to pay for a fire department and the money must come from a tax such as Bill 1-A." Anticipate the fundamental reaction of your audience to your message and search for honest ways of convincing your listeners to reconsider their initial judgment.[2]

KINDS OF AUDIENCES

As a speaker you will try to anticipate the beliefs, deductions, and responses of your listeners. Let us look more closely at audiences we can classify as uninformed, apathetic, favorable, and hostile.

The Uninformed Audience

When people are unfamiliar with a topic, unless they associate it with something they do know about, they will probably have no preconceived attitude toward that subject. In this situation your goal is to

2. Cal M. Logue, "Persuasion in a Competitive Society," in *Readings in Interpersonal and Organizational Communication,* ed. by Cal M. Logue, Richard C. Huseman, and Dwight L. Freshley, 2nd ed., 1973.

inform your audience so they will have an understanding of this new information. This process of learning can also be persuasive. For example, your college-age audience may not know how widespread venereal disease is among college students nor that it is a serious disease. A concrete and vivid explanation concerning this topic could well influence the sexual behavior of your listeners. There are unlimited opportunities and need for information sharing in a society which is influenced by complex economic forces, multiple levels of government, big business, and personal frustration.

The Apathetic Audience

In a society which is too often depersonalized, both young and old alike find it easy to be apathetic. Decisions seem to be made far off in Washington or by management or the Establishment. The authors of this book, however, believe that individuals do matter. It is in the interests of each citizen to become informed and to participate in affairs of society. One task of the speaker is to influence persons who are indifferent or who don't care to become involved. This is no easy task. Using principles discussed in this text, however, you will be able to demonstrate forcefully and vividly to an apathetic audience how drunk drivers, tax inequality, and poverty do affect their lives, no matter whether they live in urban or suburban areas. Appeals can be made on the basis of humanitarian concern and personal welfare. First, however, you will want to study your audience carefully to determine the nature of their indifference.

The Favorable Audience

On some occasions you will talk to persons who support either you personally or your attitude and beliefs. Senator Edward Kennedy would generally be better received by liberal Democrats than would many conservative speakers. Of course, once he began speaking, audience reaction would depend also on what Kennedy had to say. One cannot take a supportive audience for granted. Senator George McGovern, for example, after the Democratic nominating convention in 1972, had to work very hard to retain the support of the young people who opposed the Vietnam war. His audiences listened carefully to his speeches and, when he seemed to compromise on the war, they responded vocally against him.

With a friendly audience, however, the speaker can assume areas of agreement. Earlier in this chapter we explained how listeners supply stored beliefs when they hear a speaker. When speaking to a favorable audience, the speaker and audience often agree on at least broad principles or beliefs; thus, they would react to social and political issues in much the same way. In this speaking situation, the speaker must look for ways to reenforce existing attitudes and to mobilize participants.

The Hostile Audience

Although conflict and disagreement may not always be as visible in the United States as during the 1960's, division does exist. Many times when you speak to an audience they will be hostile, either to you, your position on a topic, or both. What if, for example, you attempted to convince a committee of physicians that we should have socialized medicine? You would first search for areas of agreement, i.e., for beliefs you and the physicians might share. Although speaker and listeners in this case disagree strongly about the solution (socialized medicine), all of you probably want to provide the best health care possible for the people.

You might begin, then, with that friendly position, that you all want the best health care possible. If you introduce your subject with a view you and your audience share, perhaps the physicians will give you a fair hearing when you reach areas of disagreement. Along with this strategy you must answer the audience's objections to your proposal with valid reasons and reliable information. If the physicians believe socialized medicine means giving up individual control of their own medical practice, you must answer this objection candidly and informatively. Here you use materials discussed in Chapter 6—illustrations, comparisons, examples, statistics, testimony, and others. While we do not guarantee you will convince your hostile listeners, we do know you will have presented an informed position in a competent manner. You have done all you can in a speech to share enlightened ideas on an important subject.

RESEARCHING AN AUDIENCE

Early in this chapter we discussed some general information about the speaking occasion that you as speaker should consider before developing your speech. In this section we offer some research activities you might use to discover more about the audience you will address.

Opportunity to investigate a potential audience will vary with the occasion. A candidate for governor in Georgia might hire people to travel in the rural and urban areas to investigate what the people are

concerned about and what their attitudes are toward taxes, government controls on farm products, busing of school children, or crime.
Polls are used by persons who can afford them to measure attitudes
toward specific issues and personalities.

Most of us, however, aren't so well-organized or financed. We have
to work with limited money and help. But there are some things you
can do. If invited to talk to a local group, ask specific questions about
their organization: When do they meet? Who comes? How many persons usually attend? What kinds of topics are usually discussed? Will
there be time for questions? What subjects will and will not interest this
particular group?

There are other sources you can use. Look in official publications
published or supported by groups to find out what their general philosophy is. Look through local newspapers for information relating to the
group's community involvement. Determine what attitudes and beliefs
are reflected in their activities and statements. On some occasions you
might even be able to use questionnaires or other type instruments to
measure audience attitude and information level.

SUMMARY

Remember that the words and supporting materials you use in your
communication may mean one thing to you and something different to
members of your audience. Listeners may be uninformed, friendly,
indifferent, or hostile to the position you are defending. Study the characteristics of your audience and the nature of the speaking occasion so
you will be able to adapt your speech effectively. Adapting to the occasion and the audience in each speaking situation requires wise choices.
The principles in this chapter will aid you in these decisions.

EXERCISES/ASSIGNMENTS

1. Observe a speech first hand and determine how the occasion and audience
   influenced what the speaker did and said (or should have done and said).
2. Select a timely topic and discuss it individually with five different persons.
   After each conversation record the positions taken by each and the probable premise (basic belief) which was supplied to cover those positions.
3. Prepare a three- to five-minute (written/oral) report on the characteristics
   and probable attitudes of your class which one should consider when
   speaking to that group.

SUMMARY **43**

4. Prepare a three- or four-minute (written/oral) analysis of information about yourself which any speaker would do well to consider if he were talking to you.

CHAPTER 4

FINDING SUPPORTING MATERIALS

$\mathbb{L}$earning can be fun and informative if you know how to find the necessary information. Before speaking on a topic, you should research that subject carefully. When preparing your speech, you will need such supporting materials as statistics, examples, testimony by authorities, definitions, explanations, comparisons, and visual aids. These materials will help explain your subject and, when appropriate, persuade your audience. Some supporting materials may come from your own personal experience. This might include your travel, reading for pleasure, and education.

You should supplement your knowledge with information and insight from journal articles and books. If you know how to find appropriate articles and books you can become informed on an endless number of subjects.

Suppose your instructor asks you and one other student to prepare a five-minute informative speech on "The Permissive Parent." The other student knows how to use research tools; you don't. Look at the advantage he has. Not only can he find materials, but more than likely he can enjoy doing it. Where are you? You are left with butterflies in your stomach and no idea of where to begin! Within a very brief period of time, the student who knows how to use the library can compile an impressive list of sources relating to parents and begin to read these materials while you will be lucky to find one book (which may well be out of date). Thus, the key difference between you and your classmate is not necessarily interest or intelligence but, in this case, is simply that he knows how to find sources and you don't.

The purpose of this chapter is to help you find materials on almost any topic you may want to study. The tools you learn to use will be helpful in any course and in any profession you may choose. It is not implied here that your task will always be easy or successful; research can be hard and frustrating work even when things go well. But we can say that with the knowledge discussed in this chapter you will usually be able to study subjects successfully.

DEVELOPING A RESEARCH ATTITUDE

One of the most difficult things for all of us to do is to be open-minded about a subject. Because of our past experiences—the influence of family, friends, and society—we form attitudes and beliefs even when we know relatively little about a matter. We tend to hold to what we have always thought. Of course, there is nothing inherently wrong with a belief or attitude simply because it is "old." However, we must be willing to approach any topic carefully, and with an open mind. If an old belief is "right," then it will certainly stand the test of careful study and reflection.

We are often told to "be objective" when studying or discussing an issue. Objectivity, however, is not an end in itself. It is only a means to an end, i.e., truth. Probably a better description than "objectivity" would be for one to be fair and open-minded. Surely you may express your *informed* judgment. You have every right, after investigating a subject carefully and fairly, to offer advice or defend a position on an issue.

You should try to know the "truth," then, of what you are discussing. You should have read widely and studied carefully so as to be well informed. At the same time, there will come a day, particularly if your goal is to persuade others of your point of view, when you must weigh all of the facts and judgments you have studied and decide for yourself. In doing this, you will want to treat your findings in a fair and interesting fashion.

Your search for answers to problems of society will seldom end. You have to develop a continuous state of mental inquiry. An ideal researcher-speaker is a seeker. You do reach certain informed conclusions but, at the same time, you realize there usually are more articles, books, opinions, and judgments to be studied which may later alter your understanding of a subject.

Most of us have a tendency to state strong opinions on all topics before we have taken the time to find "the facts." For example, if the discussion is on crime, we tend to conclude, "we need stricter law enforcement," or "we need fewer policemen and more social workers." The important question is: Have you earned the right to make those statements? Only when you have studied a matter carefully and fairly can you know enough to offer knowledgeable advice. The only way to be relatively certain of your information is to verify your findings through reliable sources. In this chapter, you will learn how to find those sources.

Assuming you have a speech topic, where do you locate information about that topic? Depending upon the subject, you may use interviews, personal observations, newspapers, pictures, taped recording, letters, diaries, books. The personal interview, for example, is an excellent way to gather information from a well-qualified source. You can actually go and talk with a salesman, a clothing store owner, a prostitute, or a preacher. You can ask the person what you want to know. Often the place to begin your research will be in your library. There you will find certain *research tools* which will aid you in finding available books, periodicals, newspapers.

FINDING BOOKS

The card catalog is the key to the library, of course. Learn how to use it. You can find a book by looking up the author, title, or general subject.

By Author.   If you know the author of a book, look in the author-title catalog under the author's last name. All books that the library possesses by that author will be listed alphabetically by title under his name. The "author" for some books may be the name of an institution, society, a government agency, or other organization.

By Title.   If you know the title of a book but not the author, look in the author-title catalog under the first word of the title disregarding *a, an,* or *the.*

By Subject.   Books may be located in the subject catalog by looking under the specific subject desired. All cards for one subject are arranged alphabetically by author.

FINDING PERIODICALS

Another important source of material covering a wide variety of subjects is the library's periodical collection. The term "periodical" is used to include the magazines, journals, and other publications which appear in continuing series. Popular titles, such as *Reader's Digest, Time,* and *Newsweek,* as well as hundreds of specialized journals in many subject fields, are included in the large group of periodicals which a library receives. As the current issues accumulate, they are usually bound into permanent volumes.

Suppose you wanted to find numerous articles in a wide variety of journals on the general topic of "public opinion." One method would be to look through every issue of every journal which might include articles on public opinion. This method, however, would take months and possibly years. Anyway, someone has already done this for you. There are books which include the title of article, author, magazine title, volume, page, and date of most articles which have been written on "public opinion" and almost any other topic you may want to study. These books are called *indexes*.

Periodical indexes provide the kind of shortcut and systematic method of finding current and past articles in magazines that the card catalog offers for books. Articles are listed by subject and, in some instances, by author. Usually you will find a bound volume of the index for each year (on occasions volumes are consolidated, and two or more years may be covered in one bound volume).

INDEXES, ABSTRACTS, AND BIBLIOGRAPHIES

Below are indexes in which you will find articles on many different topics. For example, one of the indexes is *Business Periodical Index*. Thus, if you wanted to locate what articles were published on "communication" in business in 1960, you would go to the 1960 edition of *Business Periodical Index* and you would find a list of articles with author, date, journal, article title, volume, and page of each. Then you would look up the call number, locate the journal, and read the articles you considered important.

Ulrich's International Periodical Directory. Approximately 55,000 periodicals are classified by subject. Indicates where the periodicals are indexed.

Winchell, Constance M. *Guide to Reference Books*. 8th ed. Three supplements published in 1968, 1970, and 1972. Lists reference books basic to research. For example, if you were researching the topic, "Guidance," you would find that to be a subheading in Table of Contents under, "Education." Turn to "guidance" and you find specific bibliographies and directories in area of guidance.

ERIC (See next item.)

Research in Education. Prepared monthly by ERIC (Educational Resources Information Center), a nationwide network for acquiring, abstracting, indexing, storing, and disseminating educational research reports. See "How to Order ERIC publications," in *Research in Education*, vol. 8, no. 11, 1973, p. 321.

Readers' Guide to Periodical Literature, 1900 to date. Indexes articles appearing in more than 160 well-known periodicals in general fields. Notes which of the journals are available in braille or on tape.

Biological and Agricultural Index, 1916 to date. Indexes articles dealing with agriculture and related fields.

Cumulative Subject Index to Psychological Abstracts.

Sociological Abstracts. Abstracts of lectures, papers, articles, and books.

Abstracts for Social Workers. Abstracts from numerous journals as varied as *Harvard Business Review, Race,* and *Exceptional Children.*

Art Index, 1929 to date. An index to a selected list of art periodicals and museum publications, covering both the fine and applied arts, including archaeology, architecture, ceramics, graphic arts, painting, sculpture, and landscape architecture.

Business Periodicals Index, 1958 to date. Indexes periodicals in the fields of business and industry.

A Guide to the Study of the U.S. of America. Representative books reflecting the development of American life and thought. Mugridge, Donald H., and Blanche P. McCrum.

Writings on American History, 1902–   . List of books and important articles on all phases of American history. There is a gap for the World War II years.

Index to the Writings on American History, 1902–1940. Index to work listed immediately above up to 1940.

The Encyclopedia of American Facts and Dates. Carruth, G. et al. 4th ed., 1966.

Education Index, 1929 to date. Covers educational periodicals, books, and pamphlets.

Applied-Science and Technology Index, 1913 to date. (Formerly *Industrial Arts Index*). Indexes journals, books, and pamphlets in the fields of technology and physical sciences.

Social Sciences and Humanities Index (formerly *The International Index to Periodicals*), 1907 to date. Covers scholarly journals in the humanities and social sciences.

The New York Times Index, 1913 to date. A subject guide (and author, if any) covering all articles that have appeared in *The New York Times.*

Public Affairs Information Service, 1915 to date. Commonly known as *PAIS.* Indexes periodicals, books, pamphlets, and government documents in the fields of economics and public affairs.

The Vertical File Index, issued monthly and helpful in locating pamphlet material published by a variety of organizations.

Cumulative Book Index (successor to the *United States Catalog*). Includes a record of nearly every book published in the U.S.

Catalog of the Theatre and Drama Collections, New York Public Library. More than 120,000 plays written in western languages appear in this catalog. By author and subject.

Music Collection, New York Public Library. Thirty-three volumes plus supplementary materials.

A Check List of Cumulative Indexes to Individual Periodicals in the New York Public Library. A cumulative index is to be understood as one which indexes at least three volumes of a file, and makes at least a slight attempt at the classification of the periodical's contents.

British Humanities Index, 1962 to date. Superseded the *Subject Index to Periodicals* which had been published since 1915 (with exception of the years 1923–25). More than 250 periodicals covered by author and subject.

The Metropolitan Museum of Art, New York. This catalog represents in book form the 147,000 volumes in this library.

Avery Index to Architectural Periodicals (Columbia University). "To comprehend architecture in its widest sense," including archaeology, decorative arts, interior decoration, furniture, landscaping, architecture, planning-and-housing.

Cumulated Magazine Subject Index, 1907–1949. A cumulation of the forty-three volumes of the *Annual Magazine Subject Index* which is now largely out of print. Designed to complement *Readers' Guide, Poole's Index,* and *Annual Library Index.* As early as 1907 covered seventy-nine American and English periodicals, with some emphasis on local and state history.

MLA International Bibliography of Books and Articles on the Modern Languages and Literatures.

Engineering Index

Biography Index

Index to Latin America Periodical Literature

Catholic Periodical Index

The Art Institute of Chicago

Index to Legal Periodicals

Industrial Arts Index

London Times Index

Occupational Index

Poole's Index to Periodical Literature, specially useful for articles published before *Reader's Guide* was begun in 1900.

Book Review Index

Essay and General Literature Index

Granger's Index to Poetry

Ottemiller's Index to Plays in Collections

Bibliographic Indexes. Each cumulative yearly edition includes more than four thousand bibliographies on numerous topics.

Stevenson's *Home Book of Quotations*

John Bartlett's *Familiar Quotations*

Mencken's *A New Dictionary of Quotations on Historical Principles from Ancient and Modern Sources*

Oxford Dictionary of Quotations

Hoyt's *Cyclopedia of Practical Quotations*

YEARBOOKS AND STATISTICAL INFORMATION

Yearbooks are publications, usually issued annually, that contain concise up-to-date facts and statistical information. Some of the many in your library are:

Ayers' Directory of Newspapers and Periodicals

Statesman's Yearbook: Statistical and Historical Annual of the States of the World, 1864 to date.

Statistical Abstract of the United States, 1878 to date. Published annually by the U.S. Bureau of Foreign and Domestic Commerce, is a "summary of authoritative statistics showing trends in trade and industry, as well as social progress."

World Almanac and Book of Facts, 1868 to date.

Facts on File

Information Please Almanac, 1947 to date.

Monthly Labor Review, data concerning payrolls, employment, cost of living, retail prices, industrial disputes.

Survey of Current Business, data on domestic and foreign trade, exports, imports, etc.

The Commerce Yearbook, provides information about business conditions in the U.S.

Representative American Speeches, 1937 to date, published annually, contains selected speeches made each year.

The Americana Annual, covers current events and biographical items for each year.

Britannica Book of the Year

New International Yearbook

World Book Encyclopedia Annual

SPECIAL DICTIONARIES AND ENCYCLOPEDIAS

Encyclopedia of the Social Sciences
Oxford Classical Dictionary
Cassell's Encyclopaedia of Literature
Thorpe's Dictionary of Applied Chemistry
Hastings' Encyclopedia of Religion and Ethics
Webster's Geographical Dictionary
Oxford English Dictionary
Good's Dictionary of Education
Dictionary of Speech Pathology (1970, Moore Publishing Co., Durham, N.C.)
Encyclopedia of Educational Research
Jewish Encyclopedia
Catholic Encyclopedia

BIOGRAPHICAL INFORMATION

Who's Who (British)
Who's Who in America
Who Was Who in America
International Who's Who
Current Biography
Webster's Biographical Dictionary, famous persons of all time plus
    pronunciation
Twentieth Century Authors
Directory of American Scholars
American Men of Science
Dictionary of American Biography (noteworthy dead)
Dictionary of National Biography (United Kingdom, dead)
Who's Who in American Education
Leaders in American Education
Who's Who in Engineering
National Cyclopedia of American Biography

NEWSPAPERS

For close-up pictures of the past and present, you will want to consult local and national newspapers in your library, many of which will be on microfilm. The book, *Newspapers on Microfilm,* lists approximately 21,700 entries, representing 4,640 foreign newspapers and nearly 17,100 domestic.

Atlanta Constitution
Chicago Daily Tribune
The Christian Science Monitor
The (London) *Times*
Manchester Guardian
New York Herald Tribune
  (now out of print)
The New York Times
Portland Oregonian
St. Louis Post-Dispatch
The Wall Street Journal

The Boston Globe
The New Orleans Times-Picayune
Washington (D.C.) *Star*
Louisville Courier-Journal
Des Moines Register
Los Angeles Times
Minneapolis Star
Omaha Bee
Denver Post
San Francisco Chronicle

MAGAZINES

The American Scholar
The Atlantic
Fortune
Harper's Magazine
The Nation
Newsweek
The Reporter
Saturday Review
Time
United Nations Review
U.S. News and World Report
Vital Speeches of the Day
New Republic

Monthly Labor Review
Financial World
Current Events
Annals of the American Academy of
  Political and Social Sciences
Current History
National Geographic Magazine
Yale Review
North American Review
United States News
American Economic Review
Barron's Weekly
Foreign Affairs

ATLASES

Atlases contain carefully indexed maps and statistical information.

Rand McNally Commercial Atlas
Encyclopaedia Britannica World Atlas
Adams' Atlas of American History
Westminster Historical Atlas to the Bible

GOVERNMENT PUBLICATIONS

The United States government publishes numerous documents on agriculture, education, labor, and many other topics you may be interested in. Your library, particularly if it is a "government depository," will have many of these materials. Publications of the bureaus and departments of the federal government are indexed in *Monthly Catalog of United States Government Publications*. Many of the government's publications can be ordered from Superintendent of Documents, Government Printing Office, Washington, D.C.

OTHER SOURCES

There is, of course, no end to sources available for study. Above, we have cited works which will aid you in finding materials. By spending some time in your library, you will probably find speeches and music on tape, possibly the newspaper edition which announced your birth to the world, and many other interesting and important findings. After you have explored the library holdings, you may want to continue your research through personal interviews, first-hand observation, letters, questionnaires, radio, television, and through scientific experimentation. Research seldom ends. Use every available source in trying to better comprehend your subject.

TESTING YOUR SOURCE

After you have found available materials, you will have to decide which will be the most reliable. All written words are not dependable. Ask the following questions concerning your source, whether that source be a taped recording, article, or personal interview.

1. Is the source (author, magazine, etc.) qualified to comment knowledgeably on the topic he is discussing? Has he had wide experience in this area? Has he demonstrated competency in this field?
2. Has the source been in a position to observe? Was he there? Could he see? Was he prepared to observe?
3. Can you trust this source? Is he fair and open-minded? Is he primarily concerned with his own self-interests? Has he been honest in finding, handling, and reporting judgments and data?
4. Is this source corroborated by other sources? Are there significant differences among other competent observers?
5. Are sufficient supporting materials (examples, statistics, analogies, testimony, for instance) provided to warrant the conclusion? Are the data typical? Have they been carefully compiled and classified? Are they based on reliable methods of reporting and experimentation? Are the data relevant to the topic and conclusions? Are there significant exceptions to the materials reported?

TAKING NOTES

After you have finally found a comment or statistic you want to use for your speech, you will need to copy it carefully and systematically. If you leave out something, you will have to go back later, so record accurately everything you need the first time.

You must work out a systematic method of taking notes. There is no one way, but a few guidelines will help. Use only one side of a 4 x 6 index card. If you write or type on both sides, you will find it most difficult to order and classify topic areas once you are ready to compose your speech. An index card can be easily filed and handled.

It is best to place only one item (one idea, one comment) on each card. For example, if you find in the *Harvard Business Review* that businessmen are able to write letters well you would record *only* that information on a single card. Then if you find similar information from three other sources, when you get ready to write your speech, you could place all four cards concerning the same topic together, even though they were compiled from four different sources.

Be certain on the note card you have:

1. Bibliographical data (author, title of article, book or journal, volume, date, pages).
2. Subject area under which the quotation or paraphrased materials fall.

3. An accurate record of the selected passage—one must report not only the correct wording but also the intent of the passage. For instance, without the last sentence in the quotation below, one might believe that the authors are simply quoting the opinions of others rather than implying that their own empirical study has provided "hard data" for the support of those opinions:

"Archie Bunker's Bigotry: A Study in Selective Perception and Exposure," by Neil Vidmar and Milton Rokeach. *The Journal of Communication,* vol. 24 (Winter 1974), pp. 36–47.

Topic: Results of a questionnaire study of Canadian and American viewers' reactions to TV's "All in the Family" characters suggests that selective perception involved reinforces rather than diminishes racial and ethnic prejudices.

"Both Hobson and Slawson have asserted that by making Archie a 'lovable bigot' the program encourages bigots to excuse and rationalize their own prejudices. Sanders has charged that 'already there is evidence that impressionable white children have picked up, and are using, many of the old racial slurs which Archie has resurrected, popularized and made acceptable all over again.' Our empirical research suggests that at the very least those charges have a valid psychological base." (p. 47)

EXERCISES / ASSIGNMENTS

1. Go to the library and, using microfilm, try to locate your birth announcement.

2. Go to the library and, using microfilm, look through (a) *The New York Times,* and (b) a local newspaper, and take notes concerning what happened in those newspapers on the day you were born. Look at the prices, fashions, news items, sports, and other aspects.

3. Find the index (or indexes) which covers the journals in your major field of study. For example, if your major is some aspect of education, find the index which covers all the education journals.

4. Locate, in addition to number 3 above, four indexes which cover journals of interest to you.

5. Find the main national and regional organization in your major field of study. What are the journals sponsored by those major organizations? Where are those journals indexed?

CHAPTER 5

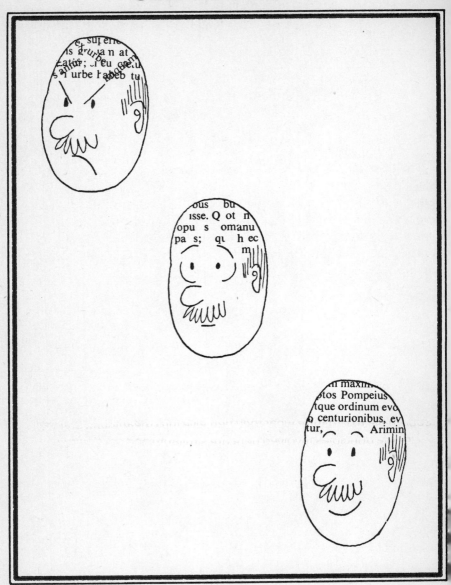

ORGANIZING SPEECHES

The speech and its supporting materials have to be put into an understandable order if you are to successfully communicate a message to an audience. Toward that end this chapter considers psychological and logical needs for order, patterns of organization, planning the introduction, planning the conclusion, outlining, additional organizational aids, and a sample outline. Organizational devices for speeches to inform and persuade are provided in Chapters 10 and 12 respectively.

PSYCHOLOGICAL NEEDS

Most minds dislike chaos. Listeners are especially particular about some semblance of order in material presented. Psychologically, people have to organize what they perceive into meaningful patterns. Two of the principles involved here are similarity and contiguity.[1]

Similarity

The first principle is: So much of our symbolic behavior is determined by past experience that similar items in our environment are preferred to dissimilar items. Thus we will more readily focus our attention on the group below which contains the similar items.

    A. Apollo, Montezuma, stalactite, paranoid, allegro
    B. registration, dormitory, co-ed, examination, degree

It would be unusual if you did not choose the items in B. Your audiences too will welcome and retain ideas that are similar and organized systematically. Ideas should be selected which cluster meaningfully around the central idea of your speech.

1. Donald C. Bryant and Karl R. Wallace, *Fundamentals of Public Speaking,* 4th ed. (New York: Appleton-Century-Crofts, 1969), pp. 28–30.

Contiguity

The second principle is: Items in a person's experience must be near enough in space and time to be taken as a whole.[2] The audience must be able to see a connection between ideas, issues, or causal relationships. Would a person touch a hot stove if he knew it were hot? You may smile at such a question. But would a person smoke a cigarette if he knew it would cause cancer? We do know that smoking does cause cancer but more and more people smoke. If the connection between smoking and developing cancer were as immediately obvious as pain is when touching a hot stove, it is unlikely that as many people would smoke. But there is considerable time lag between smoking and the recognized presence of cancer, between air pollution and what it does to our environment, between educational discrimination and what it does to individuals and their society.

The speaker, then, must vividly demonstrate a link between ideas, events, and attitudes if he hopes to convince his audience to become concerned. One must look for ways to vividly picture for the audience what will happen if action is not taken. The challenge is not easy. Many people don't worry about fastening their seat belts because in their experience it has never made any difference. Those kinds of worries are for television announcements and for others! The well-planned speech can stimulate an audience out of their indifference but it is not easy. The task will be easier if you understand that we tend to be most attentive to those relationships that are adjoining in space and time.

LOGICAL NEED

A corollary to the above psychological needs is the requisite for order which we label a logical need. Most of us have grown up with a parental admonition that "There's a place for everything and everything should be in its place." We have discovered the truth of this many times when we waste minutes looking for an item which "was right here the last time I looked." This is especially true when doing library research, if one is not careful to categorize and arrange his raw materials. Our experience is replete with the classification of things in our environment. We come to learn the genus and species of plants and animals. For example, *Quercus alba* is the white oak tree with *Quercus* being the

2. See Wayne C. Minnick, *The Art of Persuasion*, 2nd ed. (Boston: Houghton Mifflin Co., 1968), p. 102.

genus oak and *alba* designating the species.

We ourselves constantly classify in everyday life. Your class in school is determined by number of hours accrued, history courses are classified according to time period covered, boxing tournament participants according to weight, and so on.

Also, in speeches, we can follow many of these same kinds of patterns. The time sequence might suggest steps in a process such as how to plant a garden or how personality develops according to Freudian theory. Effects suggest causes to the orderly mind, so the devastation from a tornado creates the question "why," and a speech pattern emerges.

Let us look at some speech patterns in more detail.

PATTERNS OF ORGANIZATION

Subject matter and purpose influence patterns of organization for speaking as it does in other activities. In deliberating post-secondary education, for example, you consciously or subconsciously chose from an array of alternatives which may have been organized like this:

Vocational-Technical School
    Auto Mechanics
    Business Education
    Data Processing
    Radio–TV Technician
    Practical Nursing
    Restaurant Management
    Radio Electronics
    Dental Assistant
    Medical Lab Technician
Community College or Junior College (two-year)
Liberal Arts College (four-year)
Service Academy
University
Professional Schools
    Agriculture
    Business
    Education
    Forestry
    Home Economics
    Journalism
    Pharmacy

Chronological

The chronological or time pattern is a division telling us when events occur. This is a natural sequence for describing such subjects as the historical progression of an organization like the United Nations, an invention like the automobile, or the steps in a process. Here are two examples:

Early Development of the Automobile
  I. First self-propelled vehicle built in 1769
      A. Built in Paris by Nicolas Cugnot
      B. Driven by steam cylinders
 II. Internal combustion engine appeared in 1885
      A. Built in Germany by Karl Benz
      B. Design was three-wheel
III. U.S. inventors followed in 1890's
      A. Built by familiar names like Henry Ford and Ransom Olds
      B. Designs were open cars, steered by lever

Basic Steps to learning to Parachute
  I. Proper method to pack the chute
 II. Jumping from a four-foot stand for practice
III. Seven steps to follow from leaving the plane until the chute opens
 IV. Guiding the chute
  V. Landing with the chute

Spatial

Many topics lend themselves to some spatial arrangement. If you are explaining the layout of the front page of a newspaper, a Japanese garden, how books are arranged in a library, or the strengths of political parties in different sections of the country, you will find that answering the question "where" will be helpful to the audiences' understanding. For example:

Facet-cut Gems
  I. The following names of different parts of faceted gems help us understand the style of cut (such as the brilliant cut of a diamond).
      A. The large flat surface on top of the gem is called the *table*.
      B. Any one of the flat surfaces, placed on the gem by butting, is a *facet*.

C. The widest portion of the gem is called the *girdle*.
D. The portion above the girdle is called the *crown*.
E. The portion below the girdle is the *pavilion*.
F. The distance between the table and the *culet*, which is a small facet sometimes placed at the tip of the pavilion, represents the greatest depth of the stone.
G. The greatest expanse of the gem when viewed from above is the *spread*.

Topical

Perhaps the most widely used pattern of organization is the division of a subject into subtopics. This provides the speaker with a wide latitude of choices and enables one to incorporate other patterns within this framework. For example, in the following example the subtopics of Schweitzer as musician, physician, philosopher, and theologian can also subsume under these main points a chronological pattern, spatial, cause-effect and/or problem-solution sequences.

Albert Schweitzer: Greatness and Goodness
  I. His life as a musician
     A. His artistry on the organ
     B. Biography of Bach
 II. His medical missionary life at Lambaréné
     A. Medical experiences as doctor
     B. Raising money for the mission
III. His life as a philosopher and theologian
     A. "Reverence for life" concept
     B. His unorthodox Christianity

Cause-Effect

In informing and persuading, stating what has happened and predicting what will result is a frequently used method of dividing a speech. For example, a community votes down a school bond issue and the effect will probably be crowded schools, fewer teachers, and fewer courses the next year. Often this sequence is reversed and presented with effects described first followed by an explanation of the cause(s).

This pattern of reasoning is discussed in Chapter 6. To further illustrate cause and effect we present a skeleton outline below:

On Civil Disorders
  I. Patterns of disorder
    A. Pattern of violence and damage
      1. Major disorders
      2. Serious disorders
      3. Minor disorders
    B. Riot process
      1. Reservoir of grievances in the black community
      2. Precipitating incidents
  II. Basic causes
    A. Discrimination in employment and services
    B. Black migration and white exodus
    C. Black ghettos

Problem-Solution

One of the most frequently used plans, especially in persuasive speaking, is the problem-solution pattern. Here one recognizes, for instance, a need for change in the community and then presents a solution to the problem. For example:

Regulation of Guns in America
  I. Guns play an alarming role in crimes of homicide, suicide, armed robberies, and in accidents.
    A. The total number of victims of these crimes in the twentieth century is shocking.
    B. Last year's figures also dramatically illustrate this.
  II. Strict licensing of gun owners seems to be the best solution to gun control at the present time.
    A. States with stricter gun controls have a lower homicide rate per 100,000 people.
    B. Total removal of all firearms is not practical at this time.
    C. Stricter licensing is legal and constitutional.

PLANNING THE INTRODUCTION

Many speakers testify that once they are well into their speech, they have less difficulty with the rest of the speech. In the introduction the speaker can arouse interest in the topic, state and clarify the specific purpose, and create a climate for objective listening by the audience. The opening remarks also provide the speaker an opportunity to size up his audience so any necessary adjustments can be made in the prepared speech. There are a number of ways you can begin your speech.

Reference to the Occasion

Identification with the occasion and audience is one way you can begin the speech. Note how Dr. J. Martin Klotsche, Provost at the University of Wisconsin in Milwaukee, opens an Honors Convocation speech with reference to the occasion and audience, using two quotations.

> It is always a happy occasion when recognition is given to those who have shown superior achievement. It is especially gratifying to see those individuals of superior performance singled out for special recognition when talk far too often centers around the average and commonplace. I have never held to the idea that equality of educational opportunity and the education of the superior are mutually exclusive. It is possible, I believe, to pursue both objectives simultaneously. Yet there is an alarming tendency in our society to have excellence give way to normality, to have the average accepted as desirable, to have conformity disguised as adjustment, to glorify the mediocre and to ridicule distinction.
>
> Far too many of us are content with what others consider adequate. In fact, we have an almost frenetic resistance to anything that would set us apart from others. The old lady in Oklahoma was not too far out of character in declaring, "I ain't no better than anybody else but dang it, I'm jest ez good." Certainly we should all aspire toward something more than the ordinary. We should achieve more than the average. Goethe expressed it this way: "Was uns alle bandigt, das Gemeine"—"That which holds us all in bondage, the common and the ignoble." It is indeed fitting, therefore, that recognition in the form of this Honors Convocation be given to excellence and that certain ones be singled out for having placed the superior above the commonplace and distinction above mediocrity.[3]

President John F. Kennedy in a 1963 address at Vanderbilt University warmly refers to both audience and the multipurposed occasion after acknowledging the other dignitaries present.

> I first of all want to express my warm appreciation to the Governor and the Mayor of this state and city and to the people for a very generous welcome. And particularly to all those young men and women who lined the streets and played their music for us as we drove into the stadium. We are glad they are here with us and we feel the musical future of this city and state is assured.
>
> Many things bring us together today. We are saluting the ninetieth anniversary of Vanderbilt University, which has grown from a small Tennessee university and institution to one of our nation's greatest, with seven different colleges, and with more than half of its 4,200 students from outside of the state of Tennessee.
>
> And we are saluting the thirtieth anniversary of the Tennessee Valley Authority, which transformed a parched, depressed, and flood-ravaged

3. Dr. J. Martin Klotsche, "On Being an Educated Person," *Vital Speeches of the Day* 23 (August 1, 1957), p. 635.

region into a fertile, productive center of industry, science, and agriculture.

We are saluting—by initiating construction of a dam in his name—a great Tennessee statesman, Cordell Hull, the father of reciprocal trade, the grandfather of the United Nations, the Secretary of State who presided over the transformation of this nation from a life of isolation and almost indifference to a state of responsible world leadership.

And, finally, we are saluting—by the recognition of a forthcoming dam in his name—J. Percy Priest, a former colleague of mine in the House of Representatives who represented this district, this state, and this nation in the Congress for sixteen turbulent years, years which witnessed the crumbling of empires, the splitting of the atom, the conquest of one threat to freedom and the emergence of still another.[4]

Reference to Recent Incident

Since we tend to respond more readily to things familiar and near to us, reference to happenings in the immediate past awaken interest. In the following introduction by Henry Ford II, delivered at the twentieth anniversary dinner of the Advertising Council in New York City, he reaches overseas for his incident.

A recent event at Ford of Germany reminded me, most emphatically, that there are few things of deeper concern to American business today than the European economic unification movement.

What happened at our Cologne plant was nothing spectacular in itself. Some Italian employees at the plant wanted to get home to Italy for Christmas. A quick count revealed that there were not 100 or 500, but more than 2,700 Italians employed there, and special trains had to be scheduled to handle the load.

It was a small thing, but significant—one of thousands of events occurring daily in Europe that add up to something incredible—the beginning of the fulfillment of the Utopian vision of Jean Monnet and others: the unification of Europe.[5]

Reference to Preceding Speaker's Remarks

Student speakers can often adapt their introductory remarks so as to refer to what has been said or done in class. The following are typical possibilities:

"Monday, Sydney told us about some of the additives we find in our food. Today, I would like to explain some of the twelve food labeling actions recently announced by the Food and Drug Administration."

"Yesterday, Steve showed us some of the finer points of tennis. In

4. John F. Kennedy, "An Address by the President of the United States Commemorating the Founding of Vanderbilt University," *Vanderbilt Gazette* Vol. 2, No. 6, May 22, 1966, p. 2.
5. Henry Ford II, "New Directions in World Trade," Pamphlet, Ford Motor Company, 1962.

this speech I want to acquaint you with a lesser known cousin of tennis, a sport called racquetball."

"Jackie and I had not planned this, but I am sure that after just hearing her speech on mummification you will be properly prepared to accept testimonies of those who have seen ghosts, and the subject of ghosts is what I want to talk about today."

Reference to the Subject

Perhaps the simplest, easiest, and most direct method of approaching the audience is to get right into the subject itself. In most institutional, company, or governmental units that are assembled for the express purpose of being briefed on a particular subject—and the speaker is a co-worker or well-known superior—these audiences will expect few if any preliminaries. Mr. Erwin D. Canham, editor-in-chief of the *Christian Science Monitor* exemplifies this in a speech entitled "The Spiritual Revolution."

> The world in our time is full of triumph and of danger. But most of all it is full of a sense of spiritual confusion. My thesis today is that these three facts are directly connected:
> The triumph of our time is that of men's conquest of their physical environment, from the atom to the stars.
> The danger of our time is that the forces we have unleashed are not yet under control. Or, to put it another way, we have not yet learned individual and collective self-control.
> And the reason these elements are not under control is that we have generally failed to understand the nature, source, and significance of this revolution that is taking place in human thought and action.[6]

Use of Humor

The novice speaker is inevitably advised by some well-meaning friend to "warm up the audience with a joke" and will usually advise a popular joke book as ready reference. It is true that audiences do enjoy good humor but the chances of the inexperienced speaker getting Bob Hope responses from his opening store-bought gems are few. Recall the quotation of the old lady in Oklahoma used by Dr. Klotsche above. It set the scene for the subject with humor.

In the paragraph following President Kennedy's introduction, quoted above, he used a story which brought laughter and applause and warmed the audience to him.

6. Erwin D. Canham, "The Spiritual Revolution," (Boston: The Christian Science Publishing Society, 1966), pp. 1–2. Used with permission. ©1966 The Christian Science Publishing Society. All rights reserved.

> Nearly a hundred years ago Prince Bismarck said that one-third of the students of German universities broke down from overwork, another third broke down from dissipation, and the other third ruled Germany. I do not know which third of the student body of Vanderbilt is here today, but I am confident we are talking to the future rulers of Tennessee and America in the spirit of this University.[7]

When fun is poked at a traditional custom such as the commencement speech—especially at commencement and by the speaker—it is a good source of humor. Mr. Charles J. Scanlon, president of the Federal Reserve Bank of Chicago, did this in his address. "Economic Growth—The Common Goal," at the 102nd Commencement at North Central College in 1967.

> I am honored and flattered to be your commencement speaker. I must confess, however, I was even more honored before I decided to do some research on commencements and commencement addresses. Have you ever contemplated what an investigation of this kind would disclose?
>
> I discovered, for example, that not too many years ago the chancellor of the University of California stated, "The commencement speaker represents the continuation of a barbaric custom that has no basis in logic." This was followed by an article in *The New York Times* by the dean of admissions at Amherst College who indicated that the custom, if barbaric, nevertheless was widely adhered to. In the United States in the next month more than 2,000 colleges and universities, 25,000 secondary schools and an unknown number of junior high schools will stage commencement affairs for graduating students, complete with oratory largely uncomprehended.
>
> However, the author observed that the problem was really not serious. Surveys have shown that most members of a commencement audience cannot remember for any length of time who spoke or what was said. The article concluded that it was a great pity that these dramatic exhortations and moving revelations of life's mysteries rarely change any listener's life, attitudes or manners.[8]

Statement of Specific Purpose or Thesis

Somewhere in the introduction of your speech, a statement of specific purpose or thesis should appear. Students sometimes confuse the two terms because they are so similar. The purpose is a statement of what you intend to accomplish, whereas the thesis is a one-sentence statement which generalizes the content of your entire speech. However, the thesis may often be contained in the statement of specific purpose. For instance, your purpose might be, "I intend to convince the audience

---

7. John F. Kennedy, "An Address by the President. . . ."
8. Charles J. Scanlon, "Economic Growth—The Common Goal," *The Commencement and Baccalaureate Addresses* (Naperville, Illinois: North Central College, 1967), p. 4.

that the Electoral College should be abolished in favor of direct election by popular vote." Your thesis would be, "The Electoral College should be abolished in favor of direct election by popular vote." At other times the two will differ more, as in the following: Purpose—"I wish to explain the major variables in the communication process." Thesis—"The communication process is far more complicated than most people imagine."

Preview of Points

A device often recommended, especially for informative speeches and straightforward persuasive speeches, is a preview of points to be developed. Added to the specific purpose, this lays out the speech in an unmistakable design. Here is an example of a preview: "Today, I shall explain the three basic characteristics of the laser beam: coherence, single frequency, and intensity." It should be pointed out, however, that research is equivocal on results of the effect of previews of main points. In a study using audiotaped speeches, Vickery found that speeches with previewed and reviewed main points did not produce any higher retention scores on a multiple choice test covering all the material presented.[9] However, other studies by Thompson[10] and Ehrensberger[11] suggest that these repetitions do increase retention of main points. Certainly a summary of what will come later will aid audience understanding.

Finally, we note that all of these methods of introduction may be combined or adjusted. Adaptation depends on the kind of occasion and audience you confront.

PLANNING THE CONCLUSION

Ending the speech, like beginning it, can be crucial. Beginnings and endings are boundaries of a speaking situation which we tend to remember. The conclusion must do two things: (1) It must satisfy the logical requirements of the speech—to summarize, tie together loose ends, or provide a solution to the problem, and (2) it must also satisfy

9. James F. Vickery, Jr., "An Experimental Investigation of the Effects of 'Previews' and 'Reviews' on Retention of Orally Presented Information," *Southern Speech Journal* 36 (Spring, 1971), pp. 209–19.
10. Ernest Thompson, "Some Effects of Message Structure on Listeners' Comprehension," *Speech Monographs* 34 (March 1967) pp. 51–57.
11. Ray Ehrensberger, "The Relative Effectiveness of Certain Forms of Emphasis in Public Speaking," *Speech Monographs* 12 (1945), pp. 94–111.

the psychological requirements of an oral communication by reenforcing the listener's belief that the speaker fulfilled his purpose, by allowing the listener the enjoyment of seeing a communicator do an effective job, and by having a listener challenged to examine his beliefs or be spurred to some type of action. Several methods are available to the speaker to accomplish these purposes.

Summary

Main ideas are retained better if they are repeated near the end of the speech. We tend to remember what we hear last. This obtains especially if a presentation is long or complex. Avoid the hackneyed "In conclusion, let me say. . . ." Somewhat better is: "Let me summarize for you what I have said. . . ."

When concluding a persuasive speech, the speaker will appeal to the audience to agree with his point of view, reenforce an existing belief, or challenge the assembled group to act.

President Charles Anspach of Central Michigan University was trying to challenge a group of seniors with these closing rhetorical questions in his address "Would You Be Great?"

> "I hope the questions I now ask you will burn themselves into your memories. Would you be great? Are the people with whom you live and associate glad you are alive, and will they miss you when you are gone?"[12]

Illustration

Sometimes we can use an anecdote, parable, or illustration that succinctly explains or frames our speech purpose or the effect we want to leave on the audience. One of the authors concluded a speech on the economic plight of Greece with such an illustration.

> Just before we left Greece after our ten-month stay, a true story about nine-year-old Sofia came to us from the northern provinces and illustrated how far the rural areas have to go. Sofia was late for school and was scolded by her teacher. "Why were you so late?" she demanded. "I was waiting for our hen to lay an egg so I could sell it and buy this notebook to bring to school."
>
> The Greek's yearning for knowledge never ceases. Let us hope his economic condition will not make him wait too long to satisfy that yearning.

12. Charles L. Anspach, "Would You Be Great?" *Vital Speeches of the Day* 23 (August 1, 1957), p. 640.

Humor

A final method is the use of humor. (See also Chapter 13.) Appropriateness is the key here. If the audience has been listening intently to a serious speech, they begin to relax during the conclusion and are usually in a receptive frame of mind for a final light touch. A student concluded his thorough explanation of the complex subject of Rh incompatibility with this apt humorous quotation.

> I only hope I can leave with you the attitude once expressed by the world-famous physicist Enrico Fermi after he attended an important lecture. His words to the lecturer were as follows: "Before I came here I was confused about this subject. Having listened to your lecture I am still confused. But on a higher level."

OUTLINING

The purposes of outlining are three-fold: to encourage logical order in the development of ideas, to alert the speaker to gaps in reasoning, and to serve as a guide for working up key-phrase note cards.

Types of Outlines

We will describe just three types of outlines here. The first is the complete sentence outline or the *brief*. This is an exhaustive coverage of your topic in complete sentences with points fully subordinated to at least two ranks. This type of outline is sometimes used by debaters to assure their having all the arguments on both sides.

The second type is the outline with complete ideas. This resembles the brief, with complete sentences at most subheads (see sample outline at the end of the chapter). Its coverage is not as thorough as the brief, but it can be quite adequate for classroom speeches and will help you organize your materials.

The third type of outline is the key-phrase outline, and it is recommended for use by the speaker while delivering the speech. Usually put on 4 x 6 or 3 x 5 cards, the key phrases help jog the speaker's memory yet allow his speech to sound extemporaneous.

Division Into Three Parts.

The outline should be divided into three parts: introduction, body (or discussion), and conclusion. This follows an ancient tradition and reflects the basis of dividing almost any of life's activities or events into beginning, middle, and ending.

As has been discussed previously, the introduction may include a reference to the occasion or subject, provide a touch of humor, arouse interest, announce the purpose of the speech, give a preview of points to be covered, and so on. Suffice it to note here that the introduction might be outlined as follows:

I. (Attention material)   The price of meat is going up and the quality is going down.

II. (Specific purpose)   A possible solution is crossing a cow with a buffalo.

III. (Preview of points)   I will discuss past attempts at this cross-fertilization, present successes, and future problems.

The body, or discussion as it is sometimes called, contains the main points of the speech and must be covered if the topic is to be treated effectively. These will be subdivided until supporting materials sufficient to explain, prove, or stimulate are included. Though there is a sample outline on page 76, note that it does not include sufficient subordination for most speeches.

The conclusion gives the speech the ring of finality or successful resolution. As noted in the examples given previously, you will adapt the method to your speech purpose. In the outline, begin again with roman numeral I and write out the concluding remarks to ensure proper preparation.

Symbol System

In order to show the relative importance of speech materials, it is a common practice to use a number or letter symbol before each entry. Usually, a roman numeral identifies main points, capital letters subpoints, arabic numerals the third-level points, lower case letters for the fourth, and so forth. Two important rules to remember in using this system are that only one symbol should be used per point and that subordinate points should be indented. Note the errors in the specimen below.

Wrong

I. A learning golfer should know the three basic grips in handling his clubs.

Right

I. A learning golfer should know the three basic grips in handling his clubs.

A. 1. The overlapping grip is the first grip one should learn.
　a. Hold the club diagonally in the left palm, grip firmly with the last three fingers, and place left thumb slightly to the right.
　b. Then place the right-hand palm over the left thumb and a V-shape is formed.

A. The overlapping grip is the first grip one should learn.
　1. Hold the club diagonally in the left palm, grip firmly with the last three fingers, and place left thumb slightly to the right.
　2. Then place the right hand over the left thumb and a V-shape is formed.

One Idea Per Heading

Just as there should be only one symbol per idea, each unit in the outline should have only one idea per symbol. Observe how many units the following "wrong" paragraph contains.

Wrong

I. Since Consumer's Research has its own testing laboratories, it uses various methods to arrive at its findings; for example, some products are subjected to performance tests, such as shoes being put on mechanical feet which simulate walking.

Right

I. Consumer's Research uses various methods to arrive at its findings.
　A. It has its own testing laboratories.
　　1. Some products are subjected to performance tests.
　　　a. For example, shoes are put on mechanical feet which simulate walking.

Subordination

A prime benefit of outlining is to help see relationships between points. The principle of subordination means that one point is subordinate to another in a logical sense; it supports the point above it. To state it another way, since outlines are arranged deductively, main points are superior to subpoints which support them. One way to check the logical relationship between points is to put a connective such as *for, since,* or *for example* after the superior point. The higher ranked point will be a conclusion stemming from the points subordinate to it. Right and wrong relationships are indicated in the examples below:

Wrong

I. Judaism is a varied concept; there is, for example.

Right

I. Judaism is a varied concept; for instance, there is

A. Orthodox Judaism
B. Unorthodox Judaism
C. Conservative Judaism
D. Reformed Judaism

A. Orthodox Judaism
B. Unorthodox Judaism, including both
   1. Conservative Judaism
   2. Reformed Judaism

This is the deductive mode of subordination, but it can also be organized inductively. Subpoints can lead to the main points as follows:

    1. Conservative Judaism and
    2. Reformed Judaism make up
  A. Unorthodox Judaism, which with
  B. Orthodox Judaism combine to show that
I. Judaism is a varied concept.

Coordination

A corollary principle to subordination is that of making points coordinate or generally equal in importance. In the correct example above, Orthodox and Unorthodox are coordinate as are Conservative and Reformed. Another example showing coordinate division concerns constitutional powers.

The Balance of Governmental Powers
  I. Legislative Supremacy
 II. Executive Prerogative
III. Doctrine of Judicial Review

ADDITIONAL ORGANIZATIONAL AIDS

Since listening is hard work and perhaps is done without benefit of written supplements, the speaker can assist the audience, by adding to the principles and patterns already given, some further cues as to where he is going. Few things are as frustrating as being trapped into listening to a long speech whose rambling course is never clear. Ernest Thompson found in his research that the "addition of statements to highlight relationships among units in a speech can enhance comprehension. The value of transitions in oral communication has been supported empirically on two occasions."[13] We have already mentioned the use of preview and review of points as a method of reenforcing ideas. *Internal summaries, transitions,* and other *guideposts* are aids worth noting.

13. Ernest Thompson, *op. cit.*, p. 56.

Internal Summary

Most people absorb data better in shorter units. If you have a speech topic of special complexity or length, it would help if after a main point you summarize what that point said in brief, simple terms. President Donald C. Bryant of the Speech Communication Association utilized the internal summary in his presidential address in 1970. The first main point of his speech is quoted below followed by topic sentences of paragraphs which supported that point. The authors have italicized the last paragraph—the internal summary.

> ... Our first national organization ... was conceived in discontent, was gestated in rebellion, and was born in secession, in the years 1913 and 1914. ...
>
> Healthy discontent—and even unhealthy—is the fuel of change, and even of improvement. ...
>
> Our Associational forefathers wrought well. Over a couple of decades they brought into American education fresh prospects in the scholarship and teaching of public communication. ...
>
> In teaching, too, fresh developments began. ...
>
> *So the discontent, the rebellion, the secession of our founders—honor to them!—brought the positive achievement of which we are the legatees. It brought also, it seems to me, a perhaps less happy consequence.*[14]

Transitions

Transitions are bridges or connectives that get us from one point of fact to another, hopefully without interrupting the journey of the central idea on its way to the listener.

The example of the internal summary above includes the transition to the second half of the speech. You will hear it cast in various forms. One useful approach is found in the following example: "Having explained the need for more doctors, let me now consider the capacity of our medical schools to train them."

Guideposts

A final aid relies not so much on reference to substantive material in the speech as to directions you want to give the audience to help them follow the speech. One may be the simple *enumeration of points* as done by Henry B. duPont in the following:

> Everyone has his own list of "greatest inventions," and every invention has, I suppose, its partisans. My own list has three virtues to commend it.

14. Donald C. Bryant, "Retrospect and Prospect, 1970," *SPECTRA* 7 (February 1971), pp. 3–4.

First, it is brief; second, most of my selections are simple; and third, it is based not on scientific preeminence, but on the universal importance to our economic revolution.[15]

Or you may want to use rhetorical questions, i.e., questions which do not require an overt answer, to lead your auditors in a certain direction. Any device that signals the audience which direction you are taking and shows you are sensitive to their listening needs will enhance your speaking effectiveness.

SAMPLE OUTLINE

Title: The Characteristics and Uses of the Laser
General Purpose: To inform the audience of the laser.
Specific Purpose: To inform the audience of the unique characteristics of the laser and its widespread uses.

Introduction
  I. Since the invention of the laser in 1960 by a team of scientists at Hughes Aircraft Corporation, there have been thousands of uses discovered, ranging from cutting diamonds to delicate eye surgery.
 II. Today I shall explain the three basic characteristics of the laser beam: coherence, single frequency, and intensity.

Body
  I. The difference in ordinary light and laser light might be summed up in one word—coherence.
   A. In order to understand coherent light we must imagine ourselves walking into a dark room.
      1. Turn on an ordinary light and the entire room is lighted instantly.
      2. Now turn off the light and this time turn on a laser light.
      3. You will see that only a small dot will be lighted.
   B. This coherence is caused by laser light being emitted on the same frequency, in much the same manner as a radio station putting out sound waves on a certain frequency.
   C. It is this coherent quality of the laser that makes laser beam communication possible between the earth and the moon.
 II. The second characteristic of laser light is its single frequency.

15. Henry B. duPont, "The Greatest Invention of Them All," *Vital Speeches of the Day* 25 (July 15, 1959).

A. Since the beam is a single color, it will react only to that color.
   1. To simplify, let's think of a red balloon inflated within a clear balloon.
   2. When the red laser beam passes through the balloons it will react with the red and explode it while the clear balloon remains intact.
B. This fact has allowed surgeons to perform delicate eye surgery.
   1. The most common laser operation at present is to remove tumors from the retina of the eye.
   2. The tumors are heated and destroyed by the laser while the temperature of the surrounding tissue is changed very little and therefore remains unharmed.

III. Intensity is the final unique characteristic of laser light.
A. By increasing the power behind the laser and focusing the beam, an extremely intense beam can be formed.
B. This characteristic has already allowed scientists to bore holes in diamonds and weld metal alloys.

Conclusion

I. Now, let's review the characteristics of the laser.
A. First, there is coherent light that allows the laser to put out a powerful and useful beam of light.
B. Second, there is the single-color reaction of the laser beam that has been much help in medicine.
C. Finally, there is the intensity of the laser which may make it popular with the military.

II. These three characteristics may someday revolutionize our lives.
A. Maybe someday we'll sit in a dentist's chair and he'll use a laser beam on our teeth instead of a drill.
B. Dr. Kenneth Morris of Columbia University said "there is no theoretical limit to the power of the laser."

EXERCISES/ASSIGNMENTS

1. Examine two or three speeches from *Vital Speeches*. Does a clear pattern or organization emerge from each? Outline the one that is clearest to you. What aid has the speaker given to help the audience follow? Do you feel the speaker achieved his purpose?

2. Listen to a speaker in person or on television and analyze the organizational structure of the speech. Were the ideas presented clearly? How? What difference did the dynamics of the "live" speech versus the written speech in exercise 1 make?

3. What method would be most appropriate when organizing a speech on:
   a. How to Clean Up the Mississippi River
   b. Football, Canadian Style
   c. Planning a Trip to Europe
   d. The United Nations Building
   e. The Population Explosion
   f. Stock Car Racing
   g. Pop Art

4. The following scrambled outline is from a speech that could be entitled "The Traditional Classroom vs. the Open Classroom." Rearrange the points and subpoints into proper form

   The student feels as if he is an individual.

   The students can work in small groups and help each other solve their mistakes.

   The traditional classroom sets an environment in which students often lose their interest in school work.

   He achieves his goals by contributing his individual gains.

   The students learn about each other's interests by understanding the mistakes and corrections each makes in his school work.

   The teaching method and environment provide more achievement for students.

   The students feel as if they were just bodies occupying space.

   He doesn't just fill up the room.

   The student feels as if the teacher dictates to him and doesn't really care if he gains knowledge or not.

   The students are able to have more interaction.

CHAPTER 6

SPEECH CONTENT

$\mathbb{C}$ hapter 3 of this text took up how you, the speaker, should adapt to his audience and the occasion. Chapter 5 discussed the various ways you might organize your ideas. Chapter 4 presented ways and means of finding supporting material for your speeches. The present chapter takes up the question, "What kinds of things are said in speeches?" The central concern of this chapter is to detail the various kinds of speech content under the headings of personal assertions, supporting materials, and reasoning patterns.

PERSONAL ASSERTION

Speaking, whether "private" or public, is a very *personal* activity. In your speaking, you reveal yourself. Even though you appear to be speaking of "things" or "ideas" that exist apart from you, you are also talking about yourself. As you talk you reveal your evaluations, perceptions, opinions, prejudices, thought patterns, and knowledge; in short, you show your personality. As the Roman author Seneca expressed it almost 2,000 years ago, "Speech is the index of the mind."

Your own "index of the mind" will find its way into your public speaking mainly through the words you use to present your evaluations and understandings of the various aspects of your topic. Speakers, to be effective, cannot avoid expressing these evaluations and understandings. Thus Howard H. Callaway, former U.S. Secretary of the Army, in helping to open the United Way drive in Atlanta, gave his own assessment of his duty as regards the new "volunteer army":

> The . . . great challenge is to make the volunteer Army work. Now there are people within the Army, and friends of the Army outside, who are seriously confused about the issue of the volunteer Army. I know they're confused because they ask the wrong basic question. They are still asking, "Should we have a volunteer Army, or should we have a draft?" That question has been answered for us. We have a volunteer Army; we have no draft. The right question now is, "How can we make the volunteer Army a success?" I can assure you, the Army's friends and critics on Capitol Hill agree that we will not get a draft unless the volunteer Army fails miserably, and I don't expect that to happen.[1]

1. Howard H. Callaway, "The Volunteer Army: Its Success Depends on You." *Vital Speeches of the Day* 39 (November 1, 1973), p. 35.

Although Mr. Callaway's speech is peppered with facts, statistics, and other supporting materials, his *personal assertions* permeate his speech. His words convey the hopes, convictions, and observations which stem from his unique position as civilian head of the U.S. Army.

Some speeches contain very little *but* personal assertion. Usually such speeches emanate from well-known speakers discussing well-known subject matter, as when Adlai E. Stevenson delivered the eulogy at the Washington, D.C., memorial services praising Sir Winston Churchill after his death in 1965. Stevenson did not bother citing the facts, the biographical data of England's wartime leader; rather he plied his considerable oratorical skill to express what he considered the very essence of Churchill's greatness:

> Contemplating this completed career, we feel a sense of enlargement and exhilaration. Like the grandeur and the power of the masterpieces of art and music, Churchill's life uplifts our hearts and fills us with fresh revelation of the scale and the reach of human achievement. We may be sad; but we rejoice as well, as all must rejoice when they "now praise famous men" and see in their lives the full splendor of our human estate.
>
> And regrets for the past are insufficient.... Churchill, the historian, felt the continuity of past and present, the contribution which mighty men and great events make to future experience; history's "flickering flame" lights up the past and sends its gleam into the future. So to the truth of Santayana's dictum, "Those who will not learn from the past are destined to repeat it," Churchill's whole life was witness. It was his lonely voice that in the thirties warned Britain and Europe of the follies of playing all over again the tragedy of disbelief and of unpreparedness. And in the time of Britain's greatest trial he mobilized the English language to inspire his people to historic valor. It was his voice again that helped assemble the great coalition that has kept peace steady throughout the last decades.[2]

Here is one well-established statesman praising another. But, were Stevenson some relatively little-known person, or the subject of his discourse some obscure and unheralded anonymity, it would be necessary for the eulogizer to supply a great deal more specific factual information. And this point exemplifies the basis for the sometimes wide divergences in the ratios between *personal assertion* and *supporting material* one finds in speeches.

When the speaker possesses a large amount of personal prestige with his audience, he will rely more on his own personal assertions for much of his speech content. When the President of the United States speaks on "The State of the Union," his audience will accept many of his ideas because he is, after all, in a position to know what he is talking

2. As quoted in *The Washington Post*, January 29, 1965, p. A5.

about. When CBS executive Frank Stanton discusses the broadcasting industry, we are ready to believe his personal assertions because of his known expertise in the field.

Of course, there are other reasons why some people seem to have little in their speeches other than personal assertions. It is far less work to "talk off the top of one's head" than it is to dig into the library for the specific supporting material needed to induce acceptance of arguments. And teachers of public speaking have little patience with those who do not do their research, with those who apparently feel that preparing a good public speech requires less work, proportionately, than preparing oneself to become good at anything else, such as creative writing, playing the trumpet, or painting a portrait.

When the speaker does not possess much personal prestige with his audience, such as when he is inexperienced or unknown, or is speaking on a subject in which he is not an expert, he will need a greater amount of specific support for his assertions if he is to be believed. By citing evidence secured from trustworthy sources, he can establish himself as knowledgeable, if not "expert." By citing consonant opinions from experts whom the audience *does* accept, he may borrow their credibility. Certainly, the speaker lacking intrinsic prestige *must* exercise a higher ratio of support to personal ideation, especially in short speeches, than does the speaker of considerable repute.

The assertion immediately above is bolstered by empirical research in the speech communication field. A number of experimental studies on the use of evidence in speeches exist. These studies are reviewed and summarized by James McCroskey,[3] and they point consistently to the same conclusion: the addition of "good evidence" to a speech delivered by a speaker with high *ethos* (i.e., "source credibility") does not add noticeably to the speaker's persuasiveness. But when the speaker is low in ethos originally, the use of good evidence *does* enhance his persuasiveness.

SUPPORTING MATERIALS

Before considering the various types of supporting materials, let us turn our attention to the components of an argument as defined by many texts on logic. An *argument* consists of two parts: there is a conclusion, or generalization, and there is a "reason why" the conclusion or generalization, either explicit or implicit, is asserted. Professor James N.

3. James C. McCroskey, "A Summary of Experimental Research on the Effects of Evidence in Persuasive Communication," *Quarterly Journal of Speech* 55 (April 1969), pp. 169–76.

Holm says that speeches are made up of such "arguments," which he calls *speech units,* and he defines one as consisting of a conclusion, or application, plus the information needed to make the reason for the conclusion clear to the hearer.[4] To say, "We need a new school because the present structure is a firetrap," is a complete argument, or speech unit. "We need a new school" is the conclusion; "the present structure is a firetrap" is the reason why.

Occasionally the "reason why" for an assertion is one or more citations of supporting material. In this chapter we will consider eight specific kinds of supporting materials: facts and statistics, examples, comparison and contrast, testimony, repetition and restatement, definition, description, and wit and humor.

Facts and Statistics

These are widely available in library materials, books, magazines, and newspapers. Facts and statistics not only serve to "prove" the conclusions you draw in your speech, but, if specific and accurate, they will add credibility and interest to your speech. When Catherine May, Congresswoman from the state of Washington, argued that the American farmer was not responsible for high food prices, she used specific factual and statistical information. Rather than simply *assert* that American farmers were guiltless in this regard, she hit hard with specific proof of a factual nature:

> Disregarding for the moment the fact that more than 25 percent of the market basket contains items other than food, let's examine some of the valid examples for the upward surge of retail prices.
>
> The facts show that our fondness for highly processed snacks has increased by 68 percent over a decade ago. Although this may seem to be a minor item in the family budget, it actually has taken on more than a minor role.
>
> Potatoes can be cited as an example of this trend, although by no means is this item unusual. For whole potatoes, farmers receive from one and one-half cents a pound up to three cents—depending upon area and supply situation. At the supermarket, potato chips sell for well over one dollar a pound, and instant mashed potatoes would run seventy-four cents per pound.[5]

Does not such specificity evoke more interest, and does it not make a stronger case for the farmer than merely asserting that he is not

4. James N. Holm, *Productive Speaking for Business and the Professions* (Boston: Allyn and Bacon, Inc., 1967), pp. 420–23.
5. Catherine May, "The American Farmer," *Vital Speeches of the Day* 36 (August 1, 1970), p. 626.

to blame for high food costs? Ms. May used further factual and statistical information to explain who was and who was not making all the money from the production and sale of food:

> Looking at the "big picture" of America's food bill, the facts show that of the $60.6 billion difference between the amount farmers received for food products in 1968 and the amount consumers paid, labor costs accounted for $27.3 billion. Other major components were packaging—$7 billion; transportation—$4.6 billion; and corporate profits *before* taxes—$3.6 billion.
>
> Although profits are often blamed for rising prices and expenditures for food, they obviously are a relatively small percentage of total marketing costs. Net profits of leading retail food chains average a little over one percent of sales, declining generally during the past few years. Net profits for food manufacturers in 1969 averaged about 2.5 percent of sales.[6]

The facts and statistics you use in your speech should be as specific as possible, except when using quite large numbers. It is usually better to "round off" large numbers, because your listeners must comprehend what you say immediately—they cannnot "play back" what you have just said. So, instead of saying, "So far this program has cost nine million seven hundred thirty-two thousand nine hundred sixty-eight dollars," you should say, "So far this program has cost just under ten million dollars."

The facts you use should come from sources that are competent observers, intellectually honest, and as free from deliberate bias as possible. They should be based upon observations made by reporters who had suitable opportunity to make the observations and the ability to observe and report objectively.

When using statistics, it is good to remember the dictum that statistics can certainly be used to deceive, a theme inherent in the title of Darrell Huff's delightful and informative book, *How to Lie with Statistics* (New York: W. W. Norton & Co., 1954). Also remember: the problem with statistics is that they can lie *with such precision!* You want to use statistics truthfully. Before using statistics in your speech, ask yourself several questions about them. Were these statistics gathered by an impartial source, or by someone with "an axe to grind"? Did they gather these statistics with sufficient rigor and scientific method to assure their truthfulness? Do the statistics present a complete enough picture to warrant the conclusion drawn? Can alternate conclusions be drawn from the same data? Are the statistics supported (or refuted) by other kinds of evidence? Remember, numbers can be tricky. Mr. Huff's book is strongly recommended for any speaker using or any listener hearing statistics.

6. *Ibid.*, pp. 627–28.

Examples

Examples are generally considered to be of two kinds: *illustrations* and *specific instances*.

Illustrations are detailed narratives exemplifying some point. There are two general types: the *factual* and the *hypothetical*. The factual illustration is a true explication of actual events. For instance, Phyllis Jones Springen, speaking on "The Dimensions of the Oppression of Women," used a factual illustration early in her speech:

> We find laws which are a sort of "back-handed compliment" to women. She is supposed to be of a higher order of virtue than the male. For example, many states require that a woman convicted of a crime be sentenced differently and generally more severely than a man. Right here in Pennsylvania in the Daniels case a woman was convicted of robbery and sentenced a maximum of four years. Then someone discovered a state law requiring different sentences for women, and she was given ten years instead of four. The conviction was finally overturned by the Supreme Court, but laws are still on the books in other states which require different sentences.[7]

Hypothetical illustrations are detailed narratives, not of some event that has happened, but of events which could or might happen. Heather S. Kleiner used three such hypothetical illustrations to show some of the inequities from which women suffer under present laws.

> 1. You and your wife and your children have lived all your life in Georgia, gone to school here, paid taxes here, served on juries here. Your daughter marries a University of Georgia student who comes from Florida. She decides to attend the university and, to help the young couple out, you agree to pay your daughter's tuition. You will be required to pay higher out-of-state rates because in Georgia, a wife's legal domicile is automatically her husband's. In this case, your Georgia belle is considered a Floridian.

> 2. A young husband, a Vietnam veteran, returns to Georgia to face life in a wheelchair. His wife has been supporting herself more than adequately as a model. There are no children. The couple decides on a divorce, at which time the financial settlement gives nothing to the handicapped husband. Under Georgia law, alimony can only be awarded to a wife by a husband.

> 3. A teen-aged girl must leave high school when she becomes pregnant. She goes on the welfare rolls to support her child. She would like to join the WACs to become a data processor but is denied enlistment on two counts: lack of a high school diploma or its equivalent and presence of a dependent. Her brother, also a high school drop-out, not only can join the Army, but also can receive a high school education while serving.[8]

7. Phyllis Jones Springen, "The Dimensions of the Oppression of Women," *Vital Speeches of the Day* 37 (February 15, 1971), pp. 265–66.
8. *Athens* (Ga.) *Daily News*, January 24, 1973.

Illustrations properly chosen can be a most powerful form of support. Illustrations make concrete the operation of some abstract idea. The late William Norwood Brigance, a highly respected speech teacher, asserted that illustrations were probably *the* most useful form of supporting material with a general audience. Syndicated columnist Jenkin Lloyd Jones, who has spoken in all our fifty states, agrees:

> Skilled speakers go easy on abstractions and heavy on specific example. Unless an audience is constantly dragged back to a world it knows and understands it will drift off. Jesus understood the power of parable, and Abe Lincoln often made a political point leap to life by beginning: "There was an old farmer down in Sangamon County....[9]

Specific instances may be thought of as *brief* examples. Specific instances, usually used several at a time, one after another, must be instantly recognizable or else self-explanatory. As with illustrations, they lend an aura of concreteness and reality to an abstract idea. For instance, Dr. L. M. Skamser, when urging members of the Northeastern Poultry Producers Council of the necessity of adopting innovative ideas (or, what Dr. Skamser calls *radicalism*), first defined radicalism and then gave instances of what he meant:

> **Radicalism: movement away from the usual or traditional.**
> **Norman Thomas made his first race for the presidency of the United States, on the Socialist ticket, in 1928. He made his last effort in 1948. Early in 1975, he announced he was through running. His traditional, radical platform, he said, had either been enacted into law by others or was contained in the platforms of the major parties.**
> **Henry Ford, radical, brought the automobile within reach of the average man. Wilbur and Orville Wright, radicals, put man into the air. Stokstad and Jukes, radicals, put aureomycin into poultry and livestock feeds. Dr. Zindel, whom you heard this morning, is a radical.... **
> **Radicals are people who make things happen.[10]**

Note that Dr. Skamser's last reference to a specific "radical" was to Dr. Zindel, a man not universally known like Henry Ford or the Wright brothers, but well known to his specific audience, as were Stokstad and Jukes.

CBS executive Frank Stanton, in a 1973 speech, used specific instances to impress his audience with the growing problem of governmental suppression of what he considers freedom of the press:

> **... there are more pressing matters and one, particularly, would seem to lay special claim to our attention this morning. That subject is the dis-**

9. Jenkin Lloyd Jones, "Short Course in Public Speaking," *Greenville* (S.C.) *News*, November 28, 1970. Copyright, General Features Corporation. Reprinted with permission.

10. Dr. L. M. Skamser, "Radicalism." Quoted by permission of *Vital Speeches of the Day* 40 (January 1, 1974), p. 189.

maying and very serious assault that has developed, in the courts and elsewhere, against newsmen's rights and the public's right to receive an unrestricted flow of information.

Consider just this sample of recent events:

Amid a flurry of subpoenas and contempt citations, four newsmen have gone to jail in the past few months for refusing to hand over unpublished information to courts or grand juries. One of them, William Farr of Los Angeles, has only recently emerged from prison after almost seven weeks behind bars.

At least a half-dozen other newsmen across the country now face jail sentences for defying court orders to break confidences or for insisting on publishing information about criminal cases that judges did not want published.

The U.S. Supreme Court in the so-called Caldwell case has narrowly held that the journalists have no general First Amendment right to resist answering material questions put to them by grand juries.

Earlier, a Congressional committee, using its subpoena power, attempted to force CBS to deliver outtakes and other materials concerned with but not broadcast in "The Selling of the Pentagon." The Justice Department sought, and for a time succeeded in obtaining, prior restraint against the publication of the Pentagon Papers. Most recently, the Administration has announced that in consideration of legislation to stabilize broadcast license renewal it will expect network affiliates to "jump on" their networks with respect to alleged bias in network news and public affairs broadcasts.[11]

Although illustrations and specific instances can support well through their ability to concretize the abstract, one should carefully consider any example before using it in his speech. Examples should be true, certainly; but they should also present a fair picture of what they are supposed to exemplify. It would help if they are recent. Also, you should use enough examples so that they will warrant the conclusion you draw.

Comparison and Contrast

Comparison and contrast are occasionally used together but more often are used separately as supporting material. Comparisons, sometimes called "analogies," are used to show similarities; contrast is used to emphasize differences.

The use of comparison is usually for one of three reasons: to compare something meaningless with something meaningful, to compare something unknown with something known, and to compare some-

---

11. Speech presented at the 28th Annual Georgia Radio/Television Institute, University of Georgia, January 24, 1973. Quoted by permission of Mr. Stanton.

thing new and "suspect" with something old and "acceptable."

Almost any large quantity or large number is practically meaningless to the ordinary "man on the street" who seldom if ever deals in large quantities or numbers. It is practically impossible for most of us to really comprehend so enormous a sum as a billion dollars, or the distance in miles from our earth to the nearest star, *Proxima Centauri* (25,000,000,000,000 miles). In order to facilitate the understanding of such sums and distances and ages we might use a comparison, using a different scale, one that can be better grasped, as the editors of the *Guiness Book of World Records* did. They wished to compare the tenure of man on the planet earth to the history of the earth itself.

> If the age of the earth-moon system (latest estimate at least 4,700 million years) is likened to a single year, Handy Man (earliest known man) appeared on the scene at about 8:35 p.m., on December 31, Britain's earliest known inhabitants arrived at about 11:32 p.m., the Christian era began about 13 seconds before midnight and the life span of a 113-year-old man (see Oldest Centenarian) would be about three quarters of a second.[12]

Groups formed to protest military spending often attempt to point out the enormity of the cost of war materiel by the use of comparison; they compare the money spent on military hardware to what could have been bought with it otherwise:

> SANE, an antiwar group in Washington, says one Main battle tank costs $600,000 which would provide full-time psychotherapy for 171 drug addicts for one year.
>
> One B1 giant bomber costs $25 million, which SANE says would build fifteen fifty-bed hospitals.
>
> One aircraft carrier costs about a billion dollars, which could build 67,000 low-cost housing units with two bedrooms each.[13]

Phyllis Jones Springen explained something *unknown* in terms of something *known* to her audience by comparing the condition and treatment of women in our society to that of the American black:

> . . . as in the Negro problem, most men had accepted as self-evident the doctrine that women had inferior endowments in most of those respects which carry prestige and power in society. (About the only thing not said about women is that they all have rhythm.)
>
> . . . as the Negro had his "place," so there was a "woman's place." The myth of the contented woman who did not want suffrage or civil rights had the same social function as the myth of the "contented Negro."

12. Norris and Ross McWhirter, eds., *Guinness Book of World Records* (New York: Bantam Books, 1971), p. 20.
13. *Family Weekly,* January 21, 1973, p. 14.

> Her education was first neglected then changed to a special type to fit her for her "place". . . .
> The same cycle is still present in 1970.[14]

Most people have a tendency toward conservatism, especially when a new idea or plan of action is suggested. They accept the present way of doing things, no matter how faulty it may appear to be, rather than accept some "radical" new technique or policy. In addition, when they encounter any "new" phenomenon, they tend to be perplexed.

The use of comparison can aid in promoting needed change. A program of federal grants to public schools may be feared as "federal aid to education" that will lead to a "government-controlled curriculum." Fear might be dispelled by comparing such grants to other *accepted* instances of federal aid to education which have not led to government-controlled curriculum. One could point to the G.I. bill's educational benefits, the national hot lunch and milk program, or the granting of land by the federal government for the building of state universities.

Many people were quite disturbed by disorders on college campuses in the U.S. As Sydney J. Harris reminds us, the campus riots of the 1960's constituted no unique event in our history. He points out that Columbia University, in 1811, experienced the "riotous commencement" at which a student was denied his diploma because of an inflammatory address he made. "His classmates pushed him back on the platform, the provost called the city marshal, but students overwhelmed the police, the faculty was put into full flight and students held possession of the church where the commencement took place." Further:

> In 1851, the University of North Carolina had an enrollment of 230; during the year the faculty dealt with 282 cases of delinquent behavior. In 1841 Yale students defeated New Haven firemen in a brawl, destroying their equipment. In 1807 at Princeton half the student body was suspended. Twenty years later the University of Virginia was the scene of student riots, with armed and masked students patrolling the campus. College presidents were shot, stabbed and bombed; a Yale professor armed himself with two pistols for an entire summer. Student unrest is as old as the earliest of medieval universities.[15]

Knowing the long history of such disturbances may not make campus riots acceptable, but at least comparison of recent riots with those long past may tend to allay the terror we feel which might arise from their seeming newness.

14. Phyllis Jones Springen, *op. cit.,* p. 266.
15. Sydney J. Harris daily column, *Athens* (Ga.) *Daily News,* January 30, 1973.

The comparisons discussed so far have been what we might call *literal* comparisons or analogies. Literal comparisons are those which argue that, since two or more phenomena are alike in certain known respects, they should be alike in other, unknown respects. But to compare two things which are not really comparable in content or in principle is to make a *figurative* analogy, and figurative analogies do not prove anything, although a figurative analogy may be useful for clarifying or for emphasis. Consider the statement, "Instead of spending over two and one-half billion dollars on Skylab we may as well have thrown that money down a rat hole!" The comparison drawn does not disprove the worth of Skylab, but it certainly clarifies and emphasizes the speaker's feelings.

Therefore, when considering whether to use a comparison in your speech, ask yourself if the things being compared are really comparable. Are the similarities significant? Do they have a considerable *number* of similarities? Are there any significant differences between them? If so, the analogy is much weakened. Analogy is discussed in more detail later in this chapter as a link between one's supporting material and the conclusion to be drawn from it.

Contrast is a strong means of support to emphasize differences by juxtaposing two ideas or sets of figures for all to see clearly. It is used often and effectively by members of the women's liberation movement to show how women are unfairly treated as contrasted to men. Ms. Springen, previously quoted in this chapter, makes her audience acutely aware of the different status of men and women in the U.S.:

> Let's look at the economic discrimination in detail. We find it appalling. Let me give you some figures from the most recent Department of Labor Fact Sheet on the Earnings Gap and from the April 1970 Report on the President's Task Force on Women's Rights and Responsibilities. The median wage or salary income of a woman who worked full-time in 1968 was only 58.2 percent of the male's. The gap has widened 5.7 percent since 1955. There is a far more economic discrimination by sex than by race. The median earnings of white men employed full-time is $7,366, of Negro men $4,777, of white women $4,279, of Negro women $3,194.... Women scientists and engineers are paid $2,500 to $3,000 a year less than men.
>
> An infuriating example of unequal pay for equal work concerned a New Jersey manufacturer. Their chief financial officer was a woman paid $9,000 a year. When she left, they had to pay a man $20,000 to do her job. When he left, they hired another woman at $9,000. When she left, they hired a man at $18,000....
>
> A recent study (at Columbia University) was done of 195 males and 25 females on their faculty who had received their Ph.D.'s in the 1960's. Over 50 percent of the 195 males had received tenure at the rank of associate professor or above. None of the 25 females had. One had received tenure at the rank of assistant professor.

> In 1969–70 30 percent at the instructor level at Stanford were women;
> 1.6 percent of the full professors were. At the University of Michigan 40
> percent at the instructor level were women; 4.3 percent of the full profes-
> sors were. . . . the median annual salary for women who finally make full
> professor was over $1,000 less than the men's.[16]

Comparison and contrast *can* also occur together: The driver is safer
when the roads are dry; the roads are safer when the driver is dry.

Testimony

Testimony is a technique which can both help you prove a point and
provide a kind of borrowed prestige as when you quote reputable and
respected authorities. You have probably used testimony in term
papers and perhaps in speeches, as in the following:

> There seems to be a general tendency for people to begin their adult lives as lib-
> erals and idealists, but wind them up as conservatives and realists.
> Clarence Darrow, that giant of American trial lawyers, put it this way: "At
> twenty a man is full of fight and hope. He wants to reform the world. When he's
> seventy he still wants to reform the world, but he knows he can't."
> Ralph Waldo Emerson expressed the idea more poetically: "We are refor-
> mers in spring and summer; in autumn and winter we stand by the old; refor-
> mers in the morning, conservers at night."
> The late Prime Minister of England, Benjamin Disraeli, is supposed to have
> explained this metamorphosis that parallels the aging process: "Any man of 20
> who is not a liberal has no heart; any man of 40 who is not a conservative has no
> head."

Although most students would be aware of the usefulness of testimony as corroboration, many may not have thought of two other uses
for quoting others: saving time and adding spice to the speech.

If you should prepare a speech for or against the government's
funding of a complicated technological project, such as the new B1
bomber or an antiballistic missile system, you would find early in your
research that the technical arguments for and against the project are
complicated, varied, and difficult to understand and present. In a short
speech you will not have sufficient time to present all the technical arguments on the practicability of the hardware involved. To save time you
can quote several *experts* who will be acceptable to your audience on
whether they believe the project is feasible.

Quotations, especially of a literary nature, can do much to add
spice and interest to your speech. A great deal has been written on
most subjects, and perhaps you can find someone who has spoken or

16. Phyllis Jones Springen. *op. cit.*, p. 266.

written about your topic in a vivid and brilliant manner. A high school exchange student from England gave a short speech explaining to her American classmates the fierce loyalty and love her countrymen have for their native land. She concluded with an apt quotation:

> I could do no better in describing how the people of my country feel toward England than by reciting the few words in the hearts of most Englishmen, first penned by Shakespeare to describe our island home:
>
> *This royal throne of kings, this scepter'd isle,*
> *This earth of majesty, this seat of Mars,*
> *This other Eden, demi-paradise,*
> *This fortress built by nature for herself*
> *Against infection and the hand of war;*
> *This happy breed of men, this little world,*
> *This precious stone set in the silver sea.*

Finding apt literary quotations to add sparkle to one's speech should be no real chore. Anyone who does much writing or speaking should regularly consult some reference book of quotations, such as *Best Quotations for All Occasions*, edited by Lewis C. Henry. Each quotation is listed under the topic to which it applies; the topics are arranged alphabetically. So, if you are preparing a speech urging upon your audience some diet or exercise plan in order to improve their health, you might look up "Health" in the book and find that you would like to quote the old Arabian proverb, "He who has health has hope, and he who has hope has everything." Turning to another, related topic, "Body," you may find that you will want to quote Sir Francis Bacon: "A healthy body is a guest-chamber for the soul; a sick body is a prison."

Repetition and Restatement

These may strike one as more a stylistic device than a means of "support" or proof. But each can be used to reinforce your points. Repetition, of course, is the reiteration of the same words; restatement is usually the repeating of the same idea but in different language.

Repetition is widely relied upon by advertisers to implant into our minds their "Unique Selling Propositions," USP's as they are called in the trade. These are the slogans or sayings or mottoes regarding particular products which they hope, through large doses of repetition, will create in their audience members a constant, positive image of the products: "Coca-Cola: the real thing"; "You're in good hands with Allstate"; "All you need to know about insurance is State Farm";

"Budweiser, the king of beers"; "When you're out of Schlitz, you're out of beer"; "Pepsi beats the others cold."

In his impressive speech before a huge outdoor throng in August 1963, Dr. Martin Luther King, Jr. coupled the repetition of the ringing phrase with restatement of his phrase, "I have a dream ...," "I have a dream ...," "I have a dream. ..." If you have not heard this speech, you should make every effort to find a record or tape and observe Dr. King's application of many of the principles discussed here.

Definition

As a technique, definition is often useful as "proof" for some controversial conclusion. The U.S. for years kept Mainland China out of the United Nations partly because we argued that, "by definition," that country did not fit the U.N. charter's requirement for membership: a "peaceable, peace-loving nation." More often, however, definition is used to explain, in other than a dictionary sense, what a complex concept is and/or is not. For instance, Major James N. Rowe, a prisoner of the South Vietnamese Viet Cong for 5 years, escaped to tell his story to the officers of the U.S. Army General Staff and Command College at Leavenworth. During this speech he defined what he meant by "sacrifice" of one U.S. prisoner for another during the ordeal:

> When you see an American prisoner giving up his meager ration of fish, just so another American who is sick can have a little bit more to eat, that is sacrifice. Because when you don't have anything, and you give it up, or you have very little and you give it up, then you're hurting yourself, and that is true sacrifice. That's what I saw in the prison camp.[17]

Description

When it is especially vivid and image-producing, description can be powerful and sometimes is the only kind of supporting material that is effective in achieving results—especially on themes that have exhausted all other forms of support without success.

Take the theme of driving safely. We have all heard the statistics: the thousands killed, the millions injured, the billions of dollars lost through accidents. We have been "sloganeered" to the point of "overkill": "Slow down and live," "arrive alive," "drive defensively," "watch

---

17. James N. Rowe, "An American Prisoner of War in South Vietnam," as quoted in Will Linkugel, R. R. Allen, and Richard Johannesen, eds., *Contemporary American Speeches*, 3rd ed. (Belmont, Calif.: Wadsworth Publishing Co., 1972), pp. 57–58.

out for the other guy," "the life you save may be your own." Yet we speed merrily on our way, murdering over 55,000 of our fellow Americans each year—more than the number of Americans we lost in the entire Vietnam conflict. The statistics, the slogans, the lectures seem to do little good.

But law enforcement officials believe that an article originally written for the *Reader's Digest* in 1935 is effective in making motorists into safer drivers. They have distributed over five million reprints of this article, written in the belief that what each motorist needs "is a *sustained* realization that every time you step on the throttle death gets in beside you, waiting for his chance." It builds this sustained realization almost entirely through description. Some excerpts:

> If you customarily pass without clear vision a long way ahead, make sure that every member of the party carries identification papers—it's difficult to identify a body with its whole face bashed in or torn off. The driver is death's favorite target. If the steering wheel holds together, it ruptures his liver or spleen so he bleeds to death internally. Or, if the steering wheel breaks off, the matter is settled instantly by the steering column's plunging through his abdomen. . . .
>
> Overturning cars specialize in certain injuries. Cracked pelvis, for instance, guaranteeing agonizing months in bed, motionless, perhaps crippled for life— broken spine resulting from sheer sidewise twist—the minor details of smashed knees and splintered shoulder blades caused by crashing into the side of the car as she goes over with the swirl of an insane roller coaster—the lethal consequences of broken ribs, which puncture hearts and lungs with their raw ends. The consequent internal hemorrhage is no less dangerous because it is the pleural instead of the abdominal cavity that is filling with blood. [18]

James Farmer, a one-time head of the Congress of Racial Equality (CORE), in a 1965 attempt to explain the black riots of the previous summer, utilized his recognized oratorical prowess at description.

> People ask me why the senseless, futile riots of last summer, in that long hot summer. The answer is simple, crystal clear: the unemployed youth who rioted, 16–21, were empty-pocketed, far too hot to be up in the stinking flats, running from rats and chasing cockroaches. They toil in the streets, building up in frustration and anger, feeling they have been expelled from society; feeling as Richard Wright put it in one of his characters from *Native Son,* Bigger Thomas, "Sometimes I feel I'm on the outside of the world looking in through a knothole in the fence." And that I think was the feeling of most of these youngsters, hot—their frustrations joining hands and congealing into a hard mass of counter-hate, they struck out blindly, futilely, senselessly.

18. Excerpt from ". . . and Sudden Death," by J. C. Furnas, *Reader's Digest,* October 1966. Copyright 1935, 1945, and 1966 by the Reader's Digest Association, Inc.
19. Speech by James Farmer at Colorado State University, as quoted in Donald Smith, "Social Protest . . . and the Oratory of Human Rights," in *Today's Speech* 15 (September 1967), p.5.

Wit and Humor

Frequently authors of the printed word use wit and humor as elements of support. However, until recently there has been much theorizing but very little empirical research into the communicative impact of humorous stimuli. But the past few years have seen a small but growing number of such research studies.[20] These studies point tentatively to the following conclusions about the use of humor and wit as communication in speeches:

1. Relevant humor inserted into a speech will generally cause the audience to "like" the speaker better.
2. Despite the fact that an audience may like a speaker more who uses humor, the humor seems not to affect that speaker's persuasiveness.
3. The addition of humor to an already interesting speech does not seem to add heightened interest to the speech; humor added to a dull speech will heighten that speech's interest rating, but audiences will still not learn any more from the speech as a result of the higher interest.
4. Satire may be entertaining without being persuasive, probably because many people fail to perceive the serious message embedded in the satire.

It would seem, then, that the student speaker would be well-advised to avoid the exclusive use of satire; he could profitably use apt and relevant humor in his speeches to add interest and enhance his personal image.

REASONING

As stated earlier, an argument, or speech unit, consists of two parts, a conclusion or assertion plus a reason in support of that conclusion. The support for the conclusion might be another conclusion, but if it is, that conclusion also must be supplied with support. Conclusions can be used to support other conclusions in a chain-like sequence of several steps. Eventually, of course, conclusions must be supported with some form of supporting material, as defined earlier. We now take up the ways of *linking* or *connecting* conclusions and their support in order to make whole arguments—what we call reasoning.

20. An annotated bibliography of such studies is provided in Chapter 13 of Jeffrey H. Goldstein and Paul E. McGhee, eds., *The Psychology of Humor* (New York: Academic Press, 1972). A shorter, annotated bibliography, limited to studies of humorous stimuli as communication, is Charles R. Gruner, "An Annotated Bibliography of Empirical Studies of Laughter-Provoking Stimuli as Communication," available through the Speech Communication Association in microfische from the ERIC system and abstracted in the August 1973 issue of *Research in Education.*

Argument and Probability

Before detailing the various patterns of reasoning, a brief discussion on the nature and use of probability in argument is in order. When we give speeches to persuade, for the most part we are talking about probabilities, not certainties. It is useless to argue verifiable certainties. If you and I disagree, for instance, on which is the world's longest river, we could simply look it up in the record book. But suppose you and I disagree over whether Lee Harvey Oswald assassinated John F. Kennedy alone or with the help of conspirators? A considerable amount of investigation has gone into trying to discover just how this event, witnessed by hundreds of people, some of whom were photographing it, actually occurred. And today there are substantial numbers of people who are not satisfied with the conclusions of the Warren Commission Report. Why? Because there is simply not enough solid evidence available to establish absolute certainty in the minds of everyone. We can therefore only argue that, based upon the evidence that we *do* have, it is more (or less) *probable* that Oswald killed the President alone and unaided. We can argue that a "negative income tax plan" will more equitably and inexpensively meet the needs of the poor, but the only way we can know for certain is to adopt it and try it out. We must gather our evidence and employ our reasoning abilities to demonstrate what is or is not *probable*.

Generalization through Induction and Deduction

Writers dealing with the reasoning process generally differentiate between "induction" and "deduction," though actually reasoning is a continuing process which includes both. While it is helpful to define each separately in order to better understand how reasoning works, this is more appropriate for a textbook on logic or argumentation and debate than for one on public speaking.

Induction is the process of reaching a general conclusion or generalization from several examples or cases. This is arguing from the specific to the general. Much of our learning is done inductively. A child touches a hot stove and it hurts, strikes a match and is burned, reaches out to grab the gas space heater and is told "No! Hot!" Thus, by a number of specific experiences with hot stimuli, the child learns a generalization: "Things that are hot will hurt you." All of us by the time we get in high school or college have developed inductively definite conclusions or generalizations about numerous factors. What conclusions come to your mind when you hear the following words: person with long hair, college professor, person over fifty years of age, big business,

Republicans, and America? There are many ways you could have developed generalizations about these and other subjects (by listening to one you consider an authority; by scientific investigation, etc.). But you also learn about life inductively. If, for example, a person who fishes a lot goes to a lake he has never been to before, where will he fish? More than likely his fishing behavior will reflect the generalizations he has formed inductively from long years of fishing. His generalizations might include: "Persons who fish near the bank where there are dead trees and stumps will catch fish." This generalization may have been learned from the following specific experiences:

INDUCTION
{
1. Fished in lake in Georgia near the bank where there were dead trees and stumps, and caught six nice bass.
2. Fished in lake in California while on vacation near the bank where there were dead trees and caught one ten-pound bass.
3. Fished in lake in Tennessee while at my brother's home near the bank around some old logs and caught eight beautiful bass.
Generalization: Persons who fish near the bank in a lake near dead trees and stumps will catch bass.

Of course there are variables other than the locale and condition of the place where you fish: proper fishing equipment, method of using the equipment, time of day, temperature of the water, etc. The fisherman would also have generalizations about all of these.

Deduction is reasoning which goes from the generalization to a specific instance; you apply your general conclusion concerning a category or family of items to a specific member of that group. For example you may have concluded that "Frankenstein monster movies are great." This is a generalization concerning a category of movies, i.e., those which have Frankenstein in them. Now when you find that a new Frankenstein monster movie is coming to town, you *deduce*: "This particular Frankenstein movie will be great." When we diagram how deductive reasoning works it looks like this:

DEDUCTION
{
Generalization: Frankenstein monster movies are great.
Identify a Member of This Category of Movies: "Frankenstein and the Computers" is a new movie which is coming to town.
Application of Generalization: "Frankenstein and the Computers" will be a great movie.

As stated above, inductive/deductive reasoning in a public speaking situation is one continuous process. Deduction begins where induction leaves off. How did the movie goer arrive at his generalization concerning Frankenstein movies? Early in life he saw a movie about Frankenstein, and enjoyed it. Later he saw a second and considered it great entertainment. Later he saw a third, a fourth, etc. Each experience was fun. So, inductively (through specific experiences) this person *induced* a conclusion about this category of movies. He would not recall every event in every movie; what he remembers is what he generalized about each movie: "It was great." Now he has stored in himself this generalization, and when he reads in the newspaper that a new movie, "Frankenstein and the Computers," is coming he applies that stored conclusion about all Frankenstein shows to this coming attraction. We can diagram the entire inductive/deductive process as follows:

INDUCTION
1. "Frankenstein and the Snakes" was a great movie.
2. "Frankenstein goes to the Movies" was frightening, but also wonderful entertainment.
3. "Frankenstein's Twin" was as good as the other two.

DEDUCTION
Generalization: Frankenstein movies are great.
Identify: "Frankenstein and the Computers" is just out and is coming to town next week.
Application of Generalization: "Frankenstein and the Computers" will be great.

Note how the "generalization" is the end of inductive reasoning and the beginning of deductive reasoning. The generalization is part of both kinds of reasoning. Thus, you will be using in your speaking a combination of induction and deduction by which to argue from what we call "argument from generalization." (Be certain you review Chapter 3—on occasion and audience—to see how deductive reasoning works in a speech.) You have a responsibility to make your reasoning clear to your audience, and you also have the responsibility to present *sound* reasoning. How can you check your reasoning from generalization for clarity and soundness?

First, your specific items of evidence from which you draw your generalization ought to be acceptable to your audience—they should be clear, believable, recent, and truly representative of the conclusion which you draw. In order to make them acceptable to your audience you may have to document them, by telling where they came from or who published them, for instance.

Second, your items of evidence should be numerous enough to

allow the inferring of the conclusion you draw. Don't become guilty of overgeneralizing. Of course, it isn't possible to cite *every* item of evidence and so, in a sense, you must always overgeneralize somewhat. But at least, do not fall into the "I know a man who" type of overgeneralizing ("I know a welfare cheat who has enough money to drive a Cadillac. That's welfare for you!")

Third, any items of evidence contrary to your conclusion must weaken it. If you are arguing that the cost of living will go up next year because it has gone up in most of the past few years, your conclusion seems probable. But if the cost of living has actually gone down in some of these years, it is possible that it might go down next year, too. Negative instances reduce generalizability. Exceptions do not "prove" rules; they tend to negate them.

Analogy

The idea of analogy, or comparison, has already been treated briefly in this chapter as a supporting material. The basic, underlying logic of arguing from analogy is that, since two objects, concepts, or ideas are alike in certain known respects they ought to be alike in certain as-yet-unknown respects. This is the logic that might prompt you to argue that your state is very much like that of Nebraska in population, geography, and other aspects and thus, if your state should adopt the Nebraska-type unicameral legislature, it would be as successful as it has been in Nebraska.

The above example is that of a literal, or factual, analogy. It compares two or more things that are actually comparable, that are in the same class of phenomena.

An analogy comparing things which are alike *in principle* is also a valid literal analogy. Robert Henderhan, in a speech prepared for a convention of educators, expressed his dismay at certain kinds of undisciplined and "modern" education through this device. His thought is paraphrased as follows:

> So much of this "modern" education is conducted the way some unthinking parents try to teach their children to swim, and with much the same results. These parents simply throw their kids into the deep end of the pool. And what happens? Some very few drown, some other very few learn to swim quite well, but most just learn to float on their backs.[21]

---

21. Gathered aurally from Mr. Robert Henderhan as he prepared his paper for presentation in Columbus, Ohio, July 1962.

The test of whether an analogical bridge between support and conclusion is valid is the extent to which the things being compared are really alike. To the extent that they are *not* alike, to that extent is the analogical bridge weakened. For instance, it has been argued that so-called "right-to-work" laws have been enacted in several states without doing damage to labor unions, and that, by analogy, they could be adopted elsewhere with the same results. But opponents of such laws point out that the states adopting them have been mostly Southern and Midwestern agricultural states, and that adopting right-to-work laws in the industrialized states of the Northeast would greatly cripple unions. In other words, they argue that those states adopting right-to-work laws are not substantially the same as states without the law. As noted earlier, the figurative analogy has no value at all in *proving* links between support and conclusion, if the two things are not comparable.

Argument from Cause

"Accidents do not happen; they are *caused*," reads a once-popular safety slogan. Its purpose was to remind people that accidents have definite causes, causes which can be removed or circumvented, they do not just "happen" due to capricious, uncontrollable "fate."

Scientists take the view that all phenomena are due to cause-effect relationships. It is their task to discover these causal relationships, categorize and test them, then publish and teach them. Scientists do not accept the explanation that a particular event simply "happened." For every effect there is causation. The task is to isolate it for testing.

In the task of isolating causes the physical scientist has the advantage over the social scientist. The chemist can predict perfectly that when he mixes hydrogen and oxygen in certain amounts their reaction will cause the formation of water. But an economist can recommend a 10 percent income tax surcharge to cause the economy to cool down and a year after its adoption remain quite unsure of exactly what effect the surcharge had on the economy. A psychologist propounding learning theory can explain the results of a learning task experiment as caused by reward, or reinforcement; a Gestalt psychologist might claim that the same learning was caused by "sudden insight." Each would have a difficult time proving his case to the other.

You too will use argument from causation in your speeches, because people tend to think in terms of causes and effects. And, if you are to show in your speeches how to solve problems, you will need to point out causes of problems, so that elimination of these causes can be offered as the means of solving the problems. There are three general patterns of argument from cause: from causes to effect, from effect to causes, and from effect to effect.

The argument which one hears so often about the lack of suitable censorship of books, magazines, TV, and movies is usually one of causes-to-effect. The proponents of stricter censorship point primarily to the causes: the number of violent incidents in a normal week's television programs; the "girlie" magazines and pornographic books on the newsstands; the nudity and licentiousness of our motion pictures. They then argue that these "causes" *must* have some dangerous *effects* upon our young or upon society. Perhaps they quote the "rising crime rate" as proof of the effects.

The effect-to-causes pattern is the reverse of the above. The effect is noted or explained, and the proof—explanation of causes—comes afterward. Jenkin Lloyd Jones, previously quoted, used this pattern to explain the fall of Rome:

> **Alaric's Goths finally poured over the walls of Rome. [effect] But it was not that the walls were low. It was that Rome, itself, was low. The sensual life of Pompeii, the orgies on Lake Trasimene, the gradually weakened fibre of a once-disciplined people that reduced them at last to seeking safety in mercenaries and the payment of tribute—all these brought Rome down.[22] [causes]**

Let us look at an example of effect-to-effect reasoning. Some teachers of foreign languages have argued that students who take foreign languages also do well in English courses. Therefore, they reason, taking a foreign language "causes" success in English. Opponents of this point of view argue that one is not a cause of the other, but that a common cause is responsible for both. Do students with poor ability or low interest in language do well in English and also elect to take a foreign language? Hardly. But people with high ability and high interest in language do. Thus, students get good grades in English (effect) because of high ability and interest in language (causes) and also enroll in foreign language courses, in which they do well (effect). Thus, such effect-to-effect reasoning is actually effect-to-cause-to-effect.

The very idea of causation is, of course, completely inferential. No one has ever seen "a cause." It is possible to *infer* that a particular event, or several specific events *caused* another particular event, but it remains just that—an inference. The inferential nature of causation renders it more of a verbal or mental construct or abstraction than an actual entity. And in making these inferences, there are several pitfalls we should all try to avoid.

22. Jenkin Lloyd Jones, "Who is Tampering with the Soul of America?" *Vital Speeches of the Day* 37 (January 1, 1962), p. 180.

For instance, we need to try to avoid the fallacy of *post hoc ergo propter hoc* (after this, therefore because of this) which is so prevalent. The post hoc fallacy assumes that just because A happens before B, A must be a cause of B. For instance, Chanticleer the rooster noticed that shortly after his early-morning crowing the sun would rise; he therefore assumed that his crowing caused the sun to rise. Since Herbert Hoover was elected President of the U.S. in 1928, and the entire world plunged into a disastrous depression in 1929, Mr. Hoover accumulated most of the blame for the depression. "Night air" was once believed a cause of yellow fever in the tropics, because it was frequently noted that persons coming down with the disease had earlier taken a walk at night (in the mosquito-laden night air).

Avoid the fallacy of attributing a single cause to a single particular effect, because, in the realm of human actions especially, almost no effect can be attributed to a single cause. Keep in mind the idea of *multiple* causation, emphasized in this chapter by the frequent use of the word "causes" (in the plural). For example, in 1948 the polls predicted the election of Thomas E. Dewey as president of the U.S. over incumbent Harry Truman. Newspapers which headlined Dewey's victory were prematurely printed. But Harry Truman stayed in the White House until 1952. Was there a single cause of the unexpected victory? Some people would say that the 1948 polls were not scientific. George Gallup said they stopped polling too soon. The Democrats might say that the people "came to their senses" at the last minute. The Republicans might say that the Republicans were overly optimistic and did not work hard enough at getting out the vote. Speech teachers sometimes claim that Truman's last week or two of persuasive personal speaking on tour won enough converts to push him into the victory column. Astrologers might claim that the position of the stars and planets prevented the Dewey victory. One observer thought that Dewey's appearance being likened by a waggish columnist to "the bridegroom on the wedding cake" caused his defeat. There may have been several hundred causes which produced the Democratic victory.

These three reasoning patterns—generalization, analogy, and causal relations—are the three basic patterns of reasoning with which you will be most concerned as a speaker and as a person. Some writers insist upon the existence of other distinct types, such as "reasoning by comparison" and "classification." But reasoning by comparison can be easily subsumed under *analogy,* and "classification" is quite similar to generalization, as it is defined here.

In light of the explication here that the usefulness of a reasoning pattern is in its providing a link or connection or bridge between the support and the conclusion of an argument, two other types of reasoning patterns ought to be mentioned. You will not generally find these classified as types of reasoning in logic texts, but they are certainly given space and attention in speech textbooks. They *are* patterns of thought; perhaps not "logical" thought, but certainly patterns of "rhetorical" thought. They are reasoning from *authority* and reasoning from *motive.*

Authority

In discussing testimony above as a form of supporting material, the use of testimony, or authority, for "proof" was discussed only briefly. A fuller treatment of it has been saved until now.

The general idea, of course, is quite simple. In a persuasive speech you want to induce belief or action. In order to do this, you draw certain conclusions for your audience. They may accept these conclusions simply because you say so, because they accept you as a credible speaker and believe you. But if you are not a highly credible speaker and the audience is not apt to accept your conclusions, you can enhance acceptance of the conclusions by quoting the testimony of others whom the audience *will* consider credible: *There seems to be a general tendency in people to accept the conclusions of those whose authoritativeness and character they accept.* A substantial number of experimental studies of speaker credibility point to the fact that the italicized sentence, above, states a conclusion of law-like consistency.[23] Thus, this audience willingness "connects" your specific testimony to the conclusions you draw from it.

Motive

There exist human motives common to all people which can be used as links between support and conclusion, and if appeal to one of these motives is the reason why an auditor accepts your conclusion, we can think of "reasoning by motive." Inducing people to see their dentist regularly through the motive of fear of dental caries or to purchase a new car through the motive of "keeping up with the Joneses" would be examples.

23. For instance, see James C. McCroskey. "An Introduction to Rhetorical Communication" (Englewood Cliffs, N.J.: Prentice-Hall, Inc., 1968), Chapter 4, "Ethos: A Dominant Factor in Persuasive Communication," and Kenneth Andersen and Theodore Clevenger, Jr., "A Summary of Experimental Research in Ethos," *Speech Monographs* 30 (1963), pp. 59–78.

"Outlining" Reasoning Patterns

The concept of how various reasoning patterns act as bridges or links between support and conclusion can perhaps be best demonstrated spatially.

Link	*Support*	*Conclusion*
Generalization: Induction. Reaching a general conclusion from several examples.	Senator X favors expanded social security benefits. Senator X favors a negative income tax. Senator X favors expanded medicare and medicaid, etc.	Senator X favors federal spending programs that benefit low-income citizens.
Generalization: Deduction. Concluding about a particular case by applying a general principle or conclusion.	The possibility of human error precludes the impossibility of accidents in industrial/mechanical undertakings.	Oil spills from drilling off the New England coast cannot be ruled out.
Analogy. Entities alike in certain known ways may be alike in other, unknown ways.	New York's laws about firearms have not significantly curtailed crimes involving guns.	Los Angeles could not reduce its gun-related crimes by adopting laws like New York's.
Cause-to-Effect: Concomitant variation. When the values of two qualities vary together, they are linked by some aspect of causation.	There are strong statistical correlations between cigarette smoking and lung cancer.	Cigarette smoking is a cause of lung cancer.
Authority. Audiences will perceive journalistic experts as highly credible.	Journalist Herbert Matthews wrote: "In my thirty years on the *New York Times* never have I seen such a big story so badly handled [by the government] as the Cuban [Bay of Pigs] story."	The Cuban story was handled poorly by the government.

Motive. People desire economic security.	A sound life insurance program provides both a savings plan and economic protection of the family upon the loss of the breadwinner.	Family breadwinners should maintain a sound program of life insurance.

SUMMARY

This chapter has taken up the various content categories of speaking, personal assertions, supporting materials, and reasoning patterns. Another topic related to speech contents is *visual aids*, which you will probably want to use in at least some of your speeches. The visual aid is a *medium* for presenting speech content and is discussed in Chapter 7.

EXERCISES/ASSIGNMENTS

1. Go to *Vital Speeches* or to *Representative American Speeches* and, using recent speeches, find and evaluate examples of the following kinds of supporting material: statistics, examples, comparison, definition, and humor.

2. Select a subject and demonstrate how inductive and deductive reasoning can be used to explain that topic. For example, how could those processes be used to explain "how to be a successful fisherman" to an audience of experienced fishermen?

3. Consult a standard book of quotations such as Bartlett's *Familiar Quotations* or Henry's *Best Quotations for All Occasions.* Suppose you would want to give a speech on "Censorship." Are there any useful quotations you might use for such a speech in the book?

4. While researching a speech on "Health Insurance," you find that the average cost per patient for a day of care in a hospital was $11.09 in 1947, $30.19 in 1959, $81.01 in 1970, and $106.14 in 1975. How would you use these statistics in your speech?

5. You wish to impress upon an audience the wealth of the country's private enterprise economy. You know that in December of 1972 the total estimated assets of U.S. corporations (excluding banks, savings and loans associations, and insurance companies) was 561.2 billion dollars while their total liabilities were 224.4 billion dollars. How could you make these large figures more meaningful to your audience?

6. Make a list of mottoes, USP's, rhymes, and jingles you have learned through repetition of them through the mass media.

CHAPTER 7

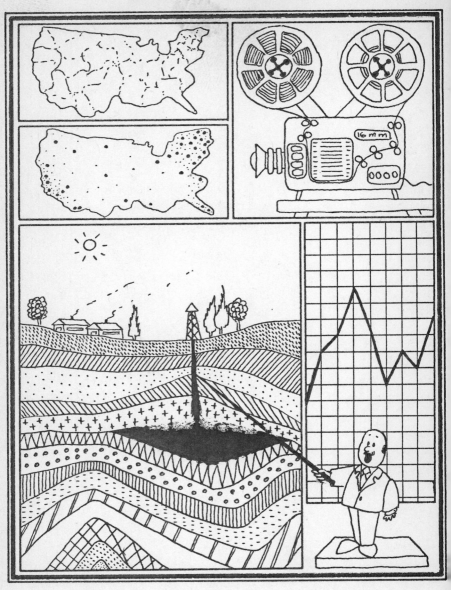

USING VISUAL AIDS

In 1962 Soviet Russia began constructing ballistic missile sites in Cuba, just a few short miles from the U.S. President Kennedy clamped a quarantine on Cuba and explained the tense situation on nationwide television. A debate then ensued in the United Nations, with world opinion in the balance. The U.S. representative, Adlai E. Stevenson, debated the Russian Ambassador Zorin. In one of his speeches he presented positive proof that missile sites were, indeed, being built on Cuban soil. The proof was a series of before-and-after aerial photographs. The use of these photographs was convincing proof to the other diplomats of Russia's perfidy.[1]

One need not literally accept the old dictum that "one picture is worth a thousand words" in order to realize the value of visual aids in certain circumstances. Could you successfully communicate by words alone what a circular staircase is, or would a model of it help you explain it better? Could you explain the working of the electric motor better with or without a large cutaway drawing of one? The point to be made here is that you should try to use visual aids to explain or prove your point whenever they are available and when they will be more useful than mere words.

PURPOSE OF A VISUAL AID

What *are* visual aids? They are anything that your audience will perceive visually and will *aid* them in understanding (or believing) the points you want to make in your speech. For instance, a blown-up reproduction of Form 1040 for reporting income tax would be useful if you are explaining how to fill one out. If you wished to teach your audience how to read the stock market report in the daily paper, a portion of the data from the paper transferred to poster board would be highly useful. You could better explain your community's budget by using pie charts of

1. The entire speech with the visuals used appears in Linkugel, Allen, and Johannesen, *Contemporary American Speeches*, pp. 93–100.

109

income and outlay. You also could teach an audience emergency first aid by using demonstrations which they could follow visually.

Skilled speakers know that they can enhance the persuasiveness of their arguments with visual materials. Speakers have emphasized their concern over industrial pollution by using pictures of smoke-belching factory stacks and thick smog. And the danger of high-speed automobile driving has been accented by speakers' use of vivid pictures of what happens to automobiles and people when speed combines with carelessness.

ADVANTAGES OF A VISUAL AID

If the resources are available, slides can be shown with the aid of a slide projector, snapshots or pictures from books, magazines, or news-papers with an opaque projector, or large transparency materials with the highly flexible overhead projector. Even the blackboard, if used skillfully, can enhance your ideas pictorially. However, few people ever use the blackboard well; the person who really cares about getting his points across with the aid of visuals will be well advised to avoid the blackboard in favor of making up his visuals ahead of time on some sort of poster board. Several types of such visuals have been found to be useful.

Unfamiliar mechanical operations are especially difficult for an audience to conceptualize and, therefore, to understand. Such under-standing is greatly enhanced by a well-made drawing such as that being used by the girl in Figure 1. Would it not be difficult to explain the sub-ject of that speech to an uninformed audience without some sort of pic-torial representation? Figure 2 shows a cutaway drawing of two types of radio transformers. Such a visual aid would be almost mandatory in a speech explaining how radio transformers operate.

Figure 3 is an "exploded" drawing. This is the kind of visual aid with which such magazines as *Mechanics Illustrated* and *Popular Mechanics* have made successful do-it-yourselfers out of thousands of amateurs. Figure 4 shows two "pie chart" or circle graphs which, a thor-ough study has indicated, are "read *most* accurately when used ... to compare parts to a whole."[2] Figure 5 is an example of the popular bar graph which one important study at Wisconsin indicated is equal to the circle graph for presenting percentage data. The study also showed that

2. Lewis V. Peterson and Wilbur Schramm, "How Accurately Are Different Kinds of Graphs Read?" *Audio Visual Communication Review* 2 (Summer 1954), p. 188.

Figure 1. *Speaker Using Poster Board Visual Aid*

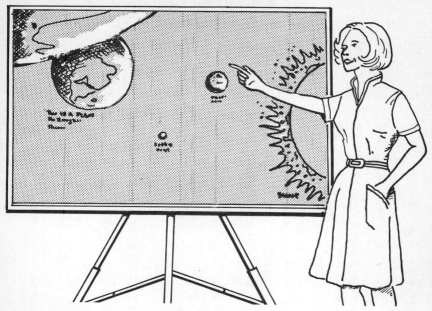

Figure 2. *Representative i.f. Transformer Constructions*

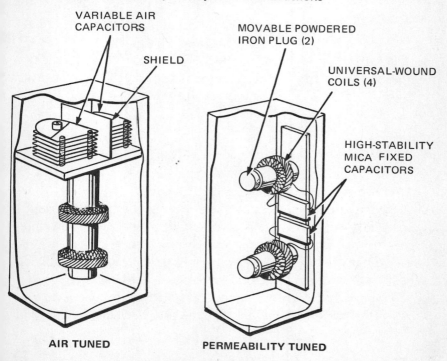

AIR TUNED   PERMEABILITY TUNED

Figure 3. *"Exploded" Drawing of an SVEA 123 Stove*

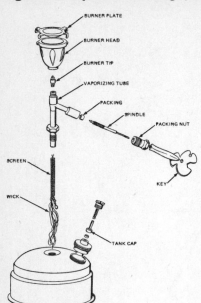

Reproduced from EMS Catalog, 1971–1972, by permission of Eastern Mountain Sports, Inc.

the bar graph, whether the bars were horizontal or vertical, was superior to line graphs for evaluating and comparing specific quantities.[3] However, for showing a trend over time, or for showing how trends compare or contrast (when the remembering of specific quantities is not the goal), the multiple line graph such as that in Figure 6 will be as good or better.

USING VISUAL AIDS SUCCESSFULLY

Although the use of visual aids can help your speech to evoke greater interest and understanding, it is quite possible to achieve just the opposite. Mostly through lack of advance preparation, many speakers waste their audience's time. Further, they bore, exasperate, even anger their audience through inept handling of their visual materials. Therefore, the following suggestions are offered, based upon the experience gained by the authors from sitting through and evaluating hundreds of such speeches.

3. Hugh M. Culbertson and Richard D. Powers, "A Study of Graph Comprehension Difficulties," *Audio-Visual Communication Review* 7 (Spring 1959), p. 109.

Figure 4. *"Pie Charts" Showing Average U.S. Federal Budget, 1967–70*

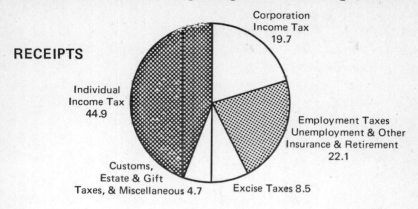

RECEIPTS

Corporation
Income Tax
19.7

Individual
Income Tax
44.9

Employment Taxes
Unemployment & Other
Insurance & Retirement
22.1

Customs,
Estate & Gift
Taxes, & Miscellaneous 4.7

Excise Taxes 8.5

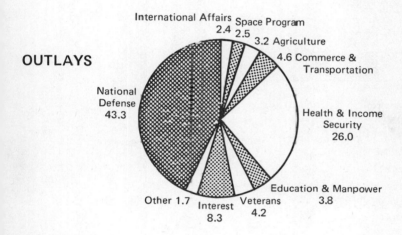

OUTLAYS

International Affairs Space Program
2.4 2.5
3.2 Agriculture
4.6 Commerce &
Transportation

National
Defense
43.3

Health & Income
Security
26.0

Education & Manpower
3.8

Other 1.7 Interest Veterans
8.3 4.2

Make Sure That Your Materials Are Large Enough to be Seen

This suggestion may sound too elementary even to be mentioned, but many speakers will troop to the front of the room expecting the people in the back row, perhaps thirty or forty feet away, to clearly see a 3 x 5 snapshot, a miniature hand-held model, or a pale, pencil-drawn chart. With all charts, graphs, and such aids this admonition includes making your lines dark and heavy enough to be seen easily. Test your materials to be sure they are large enough and your lines dark enough. Stand them up as far from yourself as the farthest audience member will be sitting. See if *you* can see them clearly. And you should remember that color-coding different parts of your visuals adds to clarity and interest.

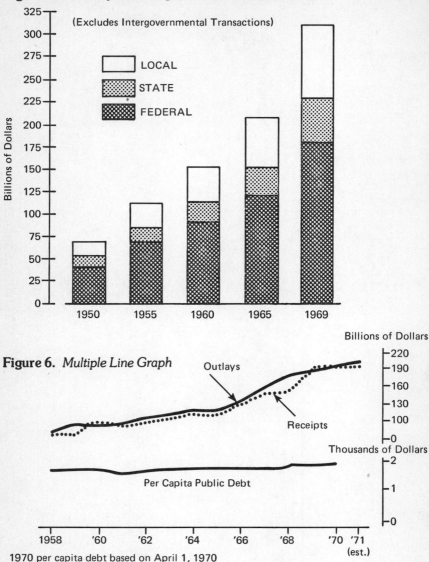

Figure 5. *Bar Graph Showing U.S. Federal Expenditures*

Figure 6. *Multiple Line Graph*

1970 per capita debt based on April 1, 1970
opulation; all others, July 1 estimated population

Keep Your Visuals Simple

Do not try to crowd a great many details into any one visual. Then speaker and audience alike can maintain a focus of attention on the same point at the same time in an orderly, chronological manner. If you use a visual aid such as that shown in Figure 7, you run the risk of losing the full attention of your audience to the complexity of the data.

Figure 7. *Example of Too Much Detail for a Speech Visual Aid*

Reactance

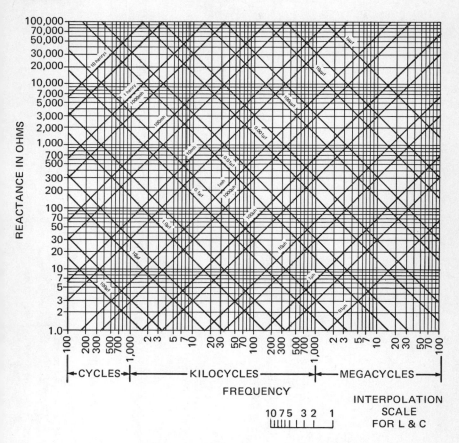

Reproduced from *The Radio Amateur's Handbook.* 1961, 38th edition, by permission of the American Radio Relay League, p. 35.

This urgency for simplicity is probably the most persistent and consistent one in the entire field of audio-visual materials. A recent government-sponsored summary of research in this area reports several studies recommending simplicity of presentation in the use of visuals.[4] For instance, it states that, in presenting material graphically, "In all cases, it was noted that the simpler the presentation, the more likely it was to be readily understood and remembered."[5] Simplicity is even

4. Mary C. McCormick, Robert M. W. Travers, Adrian P. Van Mondrans, and Frank E. Williams, *Research and Theory Related to Audiovisual Information Transmission,* Interim Report on U.S. Department of Health, Education and Welfare, Office of Education Contract No. 3-20-003 (University of Utah: Bureau of Educational Research, 1964), p. 2.23.

5. *Ibid.*

more important, apparently, than is "realism." A study of the use of visuals in teaching knot tying found that "the presence of hands are not important for demonstrating knot tying but may interfere with learning. The findings suggest that demonstrations should include only the basic elements of what is to be demonstrated," The authors of the monograph point to the reason why simplicity is probably so important:

> ...the rate of assimilation of material is an important factor to take into account. ... The data suggest that the information processing system of the human learner is a limited capacity.... It may well be that simplicity of presentation is necessary for effective learning because the learner has a limited capacity to utilize information. A source of information has generally a vastly greater capacity for transmitting information than the human learner has for receiving.[6]

Further implications of this limited capacity of humans as information processors will be brought up in Chapter 9.

Talk to the Audience, Not the Visual Aid

With your chart set up or your demonstration material in your hands, don't yield to the temptation to keep your eyes on the visual aid. Look at and talk to the audience, even though you are nervous. We have all seen speakers (and professors!) who look at and talk at everything *but* the audience, and we may not have appreciated the reason for this speaker indirectness. The tendency to avoid looking at an audience is an adaptation of the inherent urge to flee a source of discomfort. If you must point to your visual, look at it and do so, then fix your finger or pointer there and turn and speak directly to your audience.

Don't "Play With" Your Visual Aid

In your early speeches you will naturally be a bit nervous, but don't distract your audience with unnecessary fidgeting. An audience of a speech on golf will divide its attention if the nervous speaker endlessly swings the club. Speakers who slice the air and jab, sword-like, with their sharp pointers likewise are likely to teach little, as are those who perform shaky calisthenics or isometric exercises with the pointers as they speak. Your audience will pick up and reflect as much nervousness as you demonstrate, through the process of empathy, so keep your audience comfortable with a minimum of fidgeting.

6. *Ibid.*, p. 2.111.

Show Your Visual Aid Only When You Are Using It

This admonition includes two points: first, bring out your aid only when you are ready to use it; and second, put it out of sight when you are through with it. Don't let an unused visual aid, such as a chart or graph or an intriguing-looking piece of exotic equipment, distract from the point you are making. Keep small objects in a sack or box. Have a blank piece of poster board to place over charts when not using them, or else turn them to the wall. Keep large objects covered with a sheet or blanket until time to use them, then re-cover them.

Rehearse Realistically with Your Visuals

Rehearse under conditions which are as close as possible to those under which you will give the actual speech. The history of student speakers giving "visual aids speeches" is rampant with failure to communicate because this suggestion was not heeded. Charts which were beautifully clear in the tiny dormitory room have turned up hopelessly small for the large classroom in which the speech was actually delivered. Embarrassed speakers have strained mightily, but unsuccessfully, to thumb-tack their visuals onto impenetrable hardwood blackboard frames. Speakers with borrowed projectors have realized too late that the projector they planned to use is a model which they do not know how to operate. Tiny, 100-watt projectors will cast pictures too pale and washed out to see in a room with deficient shades, while a 500-watt machine would be adequate. Vacuum-cleaner demonstrations have failed because ancient classroom building wiring delivered less than full voltage. Your only protection against these catastrophes is planning and preparation.

Projectors Present Extra Hazards

Most projectors have a motor-driven fan to cool the projection bulb. It will make a steady noise. As a speaker, you will have to remember to speak a little more loudly, over the hum of that motor. Of course, you will have to know how to operate the projector, or else arrange for someone else to do it. But consider what would happen if your projection bulb burned out in mid-demonstration. So always have a spare bulb on hand. It is a simple thing, but be sure there is an electrical outlet where you will need one. If not, arrange to have an extension cord available. Note the seating arrangement.

Will there be heads in the beam of the projector? Can the seating arrangement be changed easily, or should you use a projection table that puts the projector's beam above the audience's heads? A little planning ahead can save a great deal of trouble and embarrassment.

Do Not Have the Audience Pass Things Around

Remember, the point of public speaking is that everyone is to focus his attention on the same point at the same time. To have the audience pass objects around is to invite chaos in this regard. Several years ago a coed gave a classroom speech on the Hawaiian Islands, which she had recently visited. She wanted to impress the audience with the beauty of the islands, so she handed a stack of snapshots to the left and another stack to the right. All during her speech people were looking at pictures, whispering, turning, squeaking their chairs, and dropping and picking up pictures from the floor. They were *not* listening to the speaker. Her flustered facial expressions showed she realized how little attention she was getting from her audience.

It is all right, of course, to let the audience have handouts that are all alike and that will not be passed around. For instance, a girl once handed out an envelope to each classmate. She then instructed them to open the envelope, take out the button, the square of cloth, the needle, and the thread, and she then proceeded step by step to teach the class to sew on a button. Other students have dittoed or Xeroxed small copies of their charts, instead of making one large one, and handed these out. An additional advantage accrues from this practice. The audience can carry away the information for future reference.

Although misused visual aids can create atrocious problems, properly used aids can aid communication tremendously. Consider the following summary statement on graphics by a trio of audio-visual experts:

> Graphics continue to occupy an increasingly important place in our world today. They provide assistance in building more effective communication, particularly when masses of otherwise complicated statistical data or relationships are involved.
>
> Both teachers and students need to be familiar with the principal characteristics and unique advantages of using cartoons, posters, graphs, charts, and diagrams.... Very often ... students increase their own ability to communicate effectively and economically—helping others to "see what they mean."[7]

7. James W. Brown, Richard B. Lewis, and Fred F. Harcleroad, *A-V Instruction: Methods and Materials.* 2nd ed. (New York: McGraw Hill, 1964), p. 386.

EXERCISES/ASSIGNMENTS

1 Find a visual aid suitable for a speech to be given in your classroom and an aid which would be unsuitable. Explain why one should be used and the other should not be used.

2. Look up the table, "Safety Record: World Scheduled Airlines," on p. 215 of the 1974 *Official Associated Press Almanac.* What kind of graph could you draw that would best present the "Fatality Rate (per 100 million Pass. Mi.) from 1950 through 1972?" Would such a graph make the information more understandable than an oral presentation alone?

3. Borrow a slide projector suitable for presenting slides during a speech. Turn it on, stand next to it, and talk in your normal conversational voice. Do you feel that your "normal" conversational voice has to be increased in volume?

4. Go to your library and find any one of a number of textbooks on audio-visual aids. Leaf through the book and see how richly it is illustrated. There will probably be a chapter or section on "how to make your own visual aids" inexpensively. Read it.

CHAPTER 8

SPEAKING DELIVERY

We have talked about purposes of speaking, ideas and materials to speak about, and ways to organize them. We must now consider the means by which to share those ideas.

When the famous orator Demosthenes was asked what the three most important aspects of speaking were, he is reported to have replied, "Delivery, delivery, and delivery!" As one who had suffered vocal delivery problems, his emphasis was understandable. He knew as we do today that the most brilliant content and organization may be wasted by inept delivery, yet many speakers, in their sincere belief that the idea is the most important ingredient in a speech, will somehow short-change themselves in their training of voice or body. As Lord Chesterfield put it, "Words were given us to communicate our ideas by; and there must be something inconceivably absurd in uttering them in such a manner as that people cannot understand them or will not desire to understand them."

Marshall McLuhan, a spokesman of the electronic age, would agree as he quotes Frendhman Bernard Lam who wrote in 1696, "A discourse cannot be pleasant to the hearer that is not easie to the speaker; nor can it be easily pronounced unless it is heard with delight."[1] But he would go further and say the medium itself—television, the spoken word in face-to-face communication, or the like—is a message itself. After being inundated with the print media and the unresponsiveness of the printed page, McLuhan sees the reemergence of the oral communication tradition as vital to societies maintaining their equilibrium since the world has become a "global village."[2]

If the medium of oral communication is indeed part of the message, we need to take a closer look at delivery. Modern communication researchers confirm the desirability of effective delivery. In his summary of such research studies, Wayne Thompson commented, "Every study of the relation of delivery or any of its aspects to some desirable

1. Marshall McLuhan, *Understanding Media* (New York: The New American Library, 1964), p. 34.
2. *Ibid.*, pp. 23–35.

outcome arrives at the same conclusion: good delivery does matter."[3] This means, among other things, that delivery affects comprehension and persuasiveness significantly.

What we are trying to balance here are the ends and means of speaking. To reach the desired ends, verbal and physical means must be selected which communicate one's intended meaning. How you achieve this is the concern of this chapter.

PRINCIPLES OF DELIVERY

Effective delivery helps the speaker to achieve the goals of most communicative acts. It does this because of the principles of *artful artlessness* and the *conversational mode*.

By artful artlessness we mean that a speaker has so woven his vocal elements and body movement into the fabric of his speech that the audience is not consciously aware of those aspects of delivery. Think of the most effective speakers you have heard. The chances are that you were not aware of a speaker such as Dr. Billy Graham stabbing the air with Bible in hand, because it fit in so well with what he had to say. This kind of presentation is artful because it results from training and experience; it is an art, not a science. It is called artlessness because like all good art, it is concealed, appears natural.

The second principle which helps the speaker become effective is that speaking in a *conversational mode* creates a receptive climate for good communication. The conversational mode suggests at least three things: a high sense of communication, concentration on meaning while speaking, and use of oral style. First, how do you achieve this high sense of communication? Nothing can replace *motivation*. In early America it was the circuit riding preacher who was "pressed down, and running over" with his subject. Today, if you are "turned on" by a topic, the sparks may well jump to the audience. But do not be deceived. Inspiration will not replace perspiration. As enthusiastic as you might be about your subject, if you start too late and leave too little time for final polish and rehearsal, you may well deliver an undigested, dull list of points in a desultory manner. So care enough to prepare enough.

Also, one of the most difficult things to convince beginning speakers is that they are not "giving a speech" but "communicating ideas."

3. Wayne N. Thompson, *"Quantitative Research in Public Address and Communication"* (New York: Random House, 1967), p. 83.

The assignment to give a speech somehow suggests more of a performance, both to the speaker and to the audience, than a sharing of ideas. Vice President Nelson Rockefeller's chief speech writer illustrates how this can be true outside the classroom as well. He describes how sometimes prepared speeches in a campaign would not be read at all.

> These were the frequent occasions at which the Governor was thoroughly at home with the subject or when he sensed a prepared text would anaesthetize the audience. The Governor would open saying "I've got a wonderful speech here, and for the purposes of the press, I stand on every word of it. But, I think I'll just talk to you." This approach usually got a warm crowd response since it allowed the audience to feel an intimate rapport with the Governor without some unseen literary spectre interfering.[4]

We cannot deny the public presentational aspects of speaking carry with it some characteristics of a performance. But your *primary* mind set toward such an assignment should be "I want to communicate this idea to that audience," or in Governor Rockefeller's words, "I'll just talk to you."

Second, if you concentrate on meaning while you are speaking, you will more likely achieve a conversational mode. This follows from wanting "to communicate ideas." You cannot just parrot a magazine article read the night before a presentation on the urban transportation problem, for example, and convey its significance and urgency. You might find yourself reading boring figures and using evaluation lines such as "It's absurd for all these single passenger car commuters to pollute our cities" with the same inflection as the daily reporter uses to read off stock quotations. This is not to say that you should even be thinking "Now, I should increase my volume and pitch on the word 'absurd' for better emphasis." You would not do that in animated conversation. But if you found the facts, integrated them into main ideas, talked with friends, let the speech material incubate a couple of days, and rehearsed several times with different wording, then at the moment of utterance your conclusions will be communicated as sincere conviction.

A final characteristic of the conversational mode is oral style. This topic will be taken up in more detail in Chapter 9. Suffice it to note here that using short sentences, personal pronouns, contractions, and the like will keep your presentation from having a stodgy, written quality.

4. Joseph Persico, "The Rockefeller Rhetoric: Writing Speeches for the 1970 Campaign," *Today's Speech* 20 (Spring 1972), p. 60.

While you will want to follow certain principles in developing your delivery, at the same time you can cultivate a manner of presentation which best suits you. Some speakers appear to be successful with a relatively formal presentation. Others prefer many gestures and a highly spirited delivery. There is no one best formula.

J. C. Penney, founder of the chain store which bears that name, impressed a reporter, Ralph McGill, by his sincerity. Although Mr. Penney seemingly disregarded many of the usual rules of delivery, his deep conviction and integrity came through to his audience. This example is cited, not because we recommend that you try speaking without preparation and discipline, but to demonstrate the importance of enlightened sincerity for your topic and audience:

> Mr. Penney, who is a man of 75 years, slight and gray, stood and began to fumble for words. It was this which first attracted me. "What," I said to myself, "doesn't he know it by heart? Hasn't he got it all down like the rest of them, X plus Y equals Z?". . . He talked awkwardly as I have ever heard a man talk, yet he was convincing as orators rarely are. He was not glib. His joke was not too well told. He fumbled around, finding his way through his thoughts. Finally he got going. It was a rambling story of a man (himself) who began with poverty and became wealthy through initiative and hard work. It was the story of a moral man. . . . He never avoided God. He was not hostile. He was just a sojourner and a seeker. He didn't have any answers. He didn't have any formula for me or anyone else. . . . He didn't make the mistake which, in my opinion, is the mistake of so many who preach, talking in generalities. . . . Mr. Penney held his audience still and quiet because he was completely and humbly sincere. . . . It was a unique meeting. Men who have heard hundreds of "inspirational" talks, dozens of glib and cheery leaders and who remembered not a word they said, will remember for a long, long time the deeply moving and completely sincere, awkward, halting talk of a humble man.[5]

THE VOCAL CODE

When we speak we actually give two speeches, one with the voice and one with the body. We need to be sure the verbal and the nonverbal are sending the same signals. Considering verbal behavior first, recall how many times a day you use it, probably in informal situations.

In the discussion above, a conversational mode, reflecting a variety of vocal elements, was recommended for speaking to groups. What those desirable elements are, how speech is produced, and what pro-

5. Ralph McGill in the *Atlanta Constitution*, February 24, 1950.

gram of improvement you may initiate is our next concern. Your voice should acquire the following characteristics:

1. Loud enough to be heard.
2. Intelligible so as to be understood.
3. Flexible enough to give intended meanings.
4. Pleasant to listen to; a clear tone and sympathetic quality.

To learn how to achieve these minimal vocal attributes, we need to review the steps in the physical production of speech itself.

THE SPEECH PROCESS

Speech sound is a by-product of organs which serve another physiological function. Thus, we call speech an *overlaid process*. The lungs and nasal cavities, for example, are for breathing; our teeth, which help form "f's" and "v's," are for mastication. The speech process can be compared to musical wind instruments in which air is blown over a reed which vibrates, as do the vocal folds in the larynx, and is amplified in the tubes and bell. Let us look now at the four parts of speech production: respiration, phonation, resonation, articulation.

Respiration

Breathing itself is a vegetative process and strangely enough the chief organ involved in the process, the lungs, is entirely passive in the respiration cycle. It is the diaphragm, a tendonous sheath separating the heart and lungs from the digestive organs, that coordinates with the rib muscles and abdominal muscles to press upon the lungs and provide air pressure against the vocal bands setting up the next step, phonation.

Phonation

Once the breath stream is forced through the trachea, it sets the vocal folds in the larynx vibrating producing an initial sound. This is phonation. The larynx consists of muscles and cartilage and serves two purposes. It allows air but not food into the lungs and allows the vocal folds to open and close.

The space between the vocal folds is the glottis. The leaf-like appendage above the glottis prevents foreign matter from entering the larynx and windpipe and is called the epiglottis.

Resonation

The sound produced at the phonation stage must be amplified. This amplification and enriching process is resonation. The sound waves emitted by the vocal folds are reenforced by the three resonating cavities—the pharyngeal, nasal, and oral. After the vibrations originate in the glottis, sympathetic vibrations are set up in these three areas and, as molecules bump one another much like freight cars bumping, the energy is passed along. Each cavity has a natural vibration rate and, when vibrating air with the same frequency meets it, the original vibrations are strengthened or amplified. This is why you may notice opera singers or cheer leaders open their mouths more than ordinary speakers or singers. They are seeking the richest, amplified tone that their natural resonators can provide.

Articulation

Amplified sound is still not "speech." It must be modified or shaped to form the variety of sounds which make up our particular spoken language. That modification of sound is called articulation. The articulators are the lips, tongue, teeth, soft palate, and jaw. Their job is to modify the air stream in some way—to stop and explode it as in the sound "p," to create a friction-like "s" as it passes out of the mouth, or perhaps to allow a voiced lateral alveolar sound like "l" to continue though the tongue has partially stopped the stream of air. The twenty-five consonants of the English language all result from having the air stream modified in some way. (The number of consonants will depend on the phonetic system used.)

VOCAL ELEMENTS

The sound which emerges from the above four-step process has the characteristics of pitch, volume or loudness, and quality or timbre. We would add a fourth vocal element—rate.

Pitch

Physically, pitch refers to the fundamental frequency of the vibrations of the vocal folds, i.e., to the number of openings or closings of the folds per second. Psychologically, we perceive pitch on a scale from low to high. It is affected by the mass, length, and tension of the folds. The more the tension and shorter the length, the higher the pitch will be. Conversely, the less tension and longer the folds, the lower the pitch will be. For example, the mean frequencies of males aged 8, 10, 14, and 18 are, respectively 297, 270, 242, and 137 cycles per second. You can see that the male voice drops about an octave between the ages of 10 and 18 due to the natural growth of the vocal folds.[6] The average fundamental frequency for females is 256 cps, (middle C on the piano).

Volume

If pitch refers to frequency of vibrations of vocal folds, volume or loudness means mainly *intensity*. This is the relation between amount or distance traveled by the vibrating vocal folds and the frequency of vibration. *Amplitude* is the distance that a wave impulse oscillated. We perceive this as loud or soft. Though loudness is determined partly by the vigor in which we expel air from the lungs through the trachea into the larynx, we have noted above that the resonators reenforce the sound as well.

Quality

Physically speaking, it is easier to define what quality is not. Heinberg says that "Voice quality refers to those characteristics of voice which prevail regardless of the vowels or syllables uttered, the frequency or intensity of the sound produced, or the rate of speaking."[7] Quality can be said to be the "relation between the native character of the vocal bands, the degree of complexity of vibration, and the action of resonators. [It is] the complexity of a wave's form."[8] Subjectively, quality identifies for us the uniqueness of a voice, tells us whether it is pleasant or unpleasant. It is that characteristic which helps us differentiate the trumpet from the French horn in the brass instrument family. In the human family, we identify brothers or sisters by similar "qualities" of voice. We may call them rich or thin, nasal or denasal, guttural, strident, harsh, hoarse, husky, or the like.

6. Paul Heinberg, *Voice Training for Speaking and Reading Aloud* (New York: The Ronald Press Company, 1964), p. 183.

7. *Ibid.*, p. 152.

8. Donald C. Bryant and Karl R. Wallace, *Fundamentals of Speaking,* 4th ed. (New York: Appleton-Century-Crofts, 1969), p. 251.

Rate

Rate represents the time element in the speech process. How fast or slow you speak will determine whether your speech is intelligible, interesting, and emphatic. This time element of speech can be broken down into *duration* and *pause*. In duration, sounds are being emitted, while pause indicates absence of sound. Though research results on rate vary, the following conclusions may be made.

1. College students reading aloud vary considerably in rate, with the middle two-thirds of this population ranging between about 155 and 185 words per minute. These limits come close to limits judged most effective, though a rate as low as 140 is acceptable for some persons.
2. Speaking rate is slower than reading rate and has a wider range for the middle two-thirds of the college population. You'll find yourself in this group if you speak extemporaneously at a rate somewhere between 135 and 183 words per minute.
3. Longer and more variable pauses and phonations of greater variability in duration distinguish trained from untrained speakers.
4. Syllable duration is significantly correlated with intelligibility when communication takes place in noise. Moreover, longer syllable duration distinguishes good from poor communication. However, if rapid speech becomes necessary in some circumstances, contextual clues may compensate for misarticulated and misheard message elements.
5. Increased duration is one of the most frequently used techniques to achieve vocal emphasis. Time factors also help to distinguish portrayals of different emotions.[9]

In addition, to pause before presenting a statement in an extemporaneous informative speech has definite retentive value.[10] While the speaker needs to be judicious in the use of the pause, research does indicate that listeners remember more from statements where the speaker has paused than where there were no pauses.

ARTICULATION

As noted earlier, articulation refers to modifying the air stream into sounds. When the lips stop the air and then suddenly release it, we hear a "p" or "b." If sounds are carelessly produced, indistinctness will

9. Theodore D. Hanley and Wayne L. Thurman, *Developing Vocal Skills,* 2nd ed. (New York: Holt, Rinehart, and Winston, 1970), pp. 149–50.
10. Ray Ehrensberger, "An Experimental Study of the Relative Effectiveness of Certain Forms of Emphasis in Public Speaking," *Speech Monographs* 12 (1947), pp. 94–111.

result. One critic of speaking in the United States has written, "Americans—perhaps because they have become deranged by the babble of so many parochial tongues—have always been the most lingually sloppy and tone deaf peoples on earth. Listening to them talk, particularly after one has been away from the country long enough to have stopped taking the sound for granted, is like listening to parrots just coming out of ether."[11]

We like to think of words as precision tools. It would be absurd to us to have a surgeon buy an expensive scalpel but not have it sharp before an operation. Yet we go to school for twelve years using oral language as our primary means of communication but still in too many cases allow our articulators to be dull. We develop lazy lips, an idle tongue, or an iron jaw which result in what has been called "slurvianism," as in *Unine Stays Gumm't* for *United States Government*. An extreme example of slurvianism is illustrated in the story of a teacher who taught her class the Longfellow poem that begins "Lives of great men all remind us." She noticed one little boy who seemed to be echoing the words rather peculiarly, so she wrote them down as he said them, thus: "Liza Graham, Allry Mindus, Weekend Maker, Liza Blime . . . Andy Parting, Lee B. Hindus, Footprint Johnny, Sanzer Time." The little fellow thought she was calling the roll.

PRONUNCIATION

If articulation is the physical production of speech sounds, pronunciation refers to correct, preferred, or acceptable ways of saying words. Since we have nothing comparable to the French Academy which rules on correct pronunciation for Frenchmen, we have to rely on some other standard of correctness. The standard used by most authorities is the current, cultivated or educated usage.

How shall we handle this in our land of varied dialects? We first should recognize the three major dialect areas in the United States, the region south of the Ohio River and the Mason-Dixon line and including eastern Texas and southeast Oklahoma (Southern speech); the area east of the Hudson River generally excluding New York City (Eastern speech); the rest of the United States (General American). Within these areas, you should be able to recognize the acceptable standard of the educated person, especially for public speaking presentations. We

11. John W. Aldridge, "In the Country of the Young, Part II," *Harper's* (November 1969), p. 103.

know there will be local dialects which require special handling, such as Charlestonese which might say, "braid—what you make to-est from, to go along with beckon and a-igs for brake-fuss." Or New Yorkese, which might identify "annoys" as the woman who checks your pulse in the hospital, or the word "fusel" as in "Fusel go by my house, I'll go witcha." If you know you will stay within your dialect area for the rest of your life, you will have little need to be concerned about being understood. You may have discovered already, however, that several of your classmates talk differently and with the continued mobility of the population, the audiences to which you will be speaking upon graduation may well reflect a cross-section of the country's speaking population.

Be especially attentive during this course, then, to variations in dialect. Listen to network radio and television announcers and note why it is they are easier to understand than other speakers. If you discover words pronounced two different ways, consult an up-to-date dictionary for the preferred pronunciation. One dictionary, *A Pronouncing Dictionary of American English* by John S. Kenyon and Thomas R. Knott (G. and C. Merriam Co., Springfield, Mass., 1953,) gives the pronunciation of all three dialect areas where there is a difference. Standard dictionaries will cite General American or Standard English as the basis for preference.

PLAN FOR IMPROVEMENT

To improve vocal skills takes a specific program which will include three steps: awareness of the problem, analysis of the problem, and practice.

Awareness of the Problem

By this time in the course you may have already had your attention called to some aspect of voice that needs attention. You may well have defended your manner of speaking, saying, "But this is the way I've always talked." Perhaps a tape or video-recording may have sounded the alarm as you protest, "I don't really sound like that, do I? But it's so 'country.'" Or, it may have been a high school teacher, a 4-H leader, or parent who didn't understand some word and wanted you to "speak up." As suggested above under pronunciation, you can gain awareness by careful listening to effective radio or TV speakers. Broaden this by listening critically to campus speakers or instructors, and decide how the effective communicators achieve their goals by the vocal code.

Analysis of the Problem

Once you are aware that some problems exist, you need to assess which should take priority. Your instructor may well have noted what should be worked on first. It may help to probe the cause of your problem. Can you not be heard because of improper breathing to support your tone? Do you speak much too fast in a subconscious attempt to get through? Listen again to some effective speakers and try to discover how they handle the problem.

Practice

If change is to take place, practice makes it happen. You can expect it to be slow, for these are habits of a lifetime. And since vocal improvement is only part of the total program, you will have to be motivated to work on your own. Further improvement may have to come in advanced, more specialized courses. For now, concentrate on one problem at a time. Use the exercises at the end of the chapter. Ask your instructor for others. Seek out a tape recorder or the speech laboratory to record and play back until you hear some differences. Exaggerate where possible; you will discover limits you didn't know you had. In pitch, work for at least an octave, an eight-step range, in a given sentence. In volume, unless you are dropping the voice for a particular effect, project loudly and clearly to the person on the back row, using the diaphragm for good breath support. In rate, adjust to the difficulty and nature of the material, but use the normal rate of about 160 words per minute, increasing it for appropriate narration and slowing down for main points, reiteration, and the like.

When speaking, concentrate only on ideas you are communicating. If you have exaggerated some pitch variety in practice, some should carry over. You should not have to think about particular word emphasis at this point. If there has been ample rehearsal, the weight of the idea should motivate the vocal musculature to produce the desired emphasis.

PHYSICAL CODE

Not only do we transmit meaning orally, but we also communicate nonverbally. In fact, it is impossible not to communicate something even when silent. Sigmund Freud once wrote: "No mortal can keep a secret. If his lips are silent, he chatters with his fingertips; betrayal oozes out of him at every pore."[12]

The study of body language has been labeled "kinesics," and has been investigated by persons such as R. L. Birdwhistell and A. E. Scheflen. Researchers tell of the importance of body communication but warn "that we must not try to tie up specific posture changes to specific vocal statements. We should beware of deciding that one postural shift always means this, another always that. 'The meaning or function of an event,' Scheflen explains, 'is not contained in itself, but in relation to its context.' A shift in posture means that something is happening. It does not always tell us what is happening. We must study the shift in relation to the entire incident to find that out."[13]

How shall we communicate most effectively with our bodies? Here again we need to be artful without calling attention to the art. Hamlet would advise us, as he did the players, to "suit the action to the word." To use the physical code takes a sense of fitness for the audience and occasion. Ideally, the speaker will be energized to communicate an idea whose time has come. There should be a certain rhetorical restlessness in the speaker like the thoroughbred who can't wait for the starting gate to open. John F. Kennedy exhibited many of these qualities in his historic campaign of 1960.

> If Kennedy's use of his voice was something less than an asset, his physical presence on the speaking platform was, by-and-large, in his favor. After first-hand observation. Haberman noted the "appeal about him" and how "he gave an impression of caring mightily—not simply about himself—but about an idea that was external to him." And my notes throughout the campaign underline this same infectious energy: physically, he looked, acted, and talked in a vigorous way. Indeed, so much so that during the televised speeches of October 31 and November 4, 1960, Kennedy's characteristic jabbing of the lectern with his index finger came over the microphone as a heavy "thump-thump." But on other occasions, said *Time* magazine, there was less confidence, especially when he was waiting his turn to speak on the stump: "He fidgets with his coat buttons, smooths his hair and swings his right foot restlessly. A gesture of extreme agitation; a desperate fingering at his necktie, reserved for the approach of Indians bearing war bonnets, nuns, or other disconcerting greeters. He obviously has a New England reticence about himself, is unwilling to surrender some recess of his privacy."[14]

The physical code can be treated in four areas, facial expression and eye contact, posture, body movement, and gestures.

12. Quoted in William D. Brooks, *Speech Communication* (Dubuque, Iowa: Wm. C. Brown Company, 1971), p. 112.

13. Quoted in Julius Fast, *Body Language* (New York: M. Evans & Co., 1970), p. 128.

14. James G. Powell, "Reactions to John F. Kennedy's Delivery Skills during the 1960 Campaign," *Western Speech* 37 (Winter 1968), pp. 62–3.

Facial Expression

Since attention is directed at the source of speech, facial expression becomes an important part of conveying ideas. We get an idea of how important when we consider speakers such as President Franklin D. Roosevelt who was immobile from the waist down.

> His broad, friendly smile and his highly expressive countenance were important assets to Franklin Roosevelt as a speaker. His mobile face could reflect a wide variety of reactions. It "changed expression with the quickness and sureness of a finished actor's. It was amused, solemn, sarcastic, interested, indignant. It was always strong and confident and it was never dull."[15]

Facial expression is one of the first cues to the audience that you want to speak to them, that you appreciate their presence, and that you are concerned about your topic. It can suggest friendliness or indifference, alertness or lethargy, poise or uncertainty. One of the best ways to engage the audience's attention is through eye contact. This helps generate the circular response that takes place between speaker and listener and is the hallmark of the heightened sense of communication. Bishop Fulton J. Sheen used his deep-set eyes to great advantage. One writer wrote,

> His personal magnetism is contained not only in his voice but also in his eyes. Undoubtedly they are one of the most remarkable pairs of eyes in America. He creates the impression of not only looking at you but through you. They seem to possess a hypnotic power which is emphasized under the television lights.[16]

Look at your listeners as if you were conversing just with him or her. But staring too long will make the person uncomfortable. Include all of your audience in your visual contact as the speech moves along, but do not sweep the audience like a searchlight and not really see anyone. Watch for reactions by individuals. Let this feedback tell you if they are bored or confused. Ask yourself should you pause and amplify a technical point or repeat materials they apparently did not understand? A visual reading of your audience will aid your speech and demonstrate that you care about them. Of course, appropriate behavior (such as eye contact) will depend on the cultural patterns of a particular country.

15. Ernest Brandenburg and Waldo Braden, "Franklin D. Roosevelt," in *History and Criticism of American Public Address*, ed. by Marie Hochmuth (New York: Longmans, Green, & Co., 1955), p. 516.
16. Nelson Hart, "Bishop Sheen's Television Techniques," *Today's Speech* 20 (September 1962), p. 20.

Posture

Posture communicates attitude just as facial expression does. The round-shouldered slump with weight resting mainly on one leg may feel relaxed to you but may translate to the audience as slovenly indifference. As a basic posture, work for a straight but not rigid stance with legs slightly apart, so that you have a working base from which to move in any direction. The speaker should always suggest *alertness* through his posture. If he *is* mentally alert, thinking the thoughts, and also keeping the audience in mind as he says the words, he will both *be* and *look* alert.

Body Movement

Movement can help the speaker, speech, and audience. It can relax the speaker by helping him dissipate some of the excess energy which has built up. It can aid emphasis in the speech through its use on transitions to main or subpoints or by head or body emphasis in description or narration. It can be a boon to an audience by helping sustain attention and creating empathy. It attracts attention as a camper's movements attract a deer. Empathy is created when the audience "feels in" with what the speaker is conveying. If the student speaker is recounting a foxhole experience and ducks his head as he recounts the experience of bullets going over, his audience may well duck too.

The most important thing to remember about movement is that it should be motivated. Random pacing will distract as much as immobility will bore. Accept the fact that beginning speakers do not use much movement—unless they have built it into their rehearsal and it becomes habitual.

Gestures

A specific kind of body movement is the gesture. Starting with the principle of motivation just mentioned, we stress that any hand or arm gestures should be coordinated with the ideas to be shared. We are familiar with the gestural signs of baseball umpires and coaches, traffic policemen, and the like. Speakers also employ many nonverbal signs which are widely recognized. They have been conveniently divided into *conventional* and *descriptive* types. Under conventional gestures, the speaker may divide, point, clench his fist, count on his fingers, give or receive, reject, or caution.

While conventional gestures may be used by most speakers at one time or another and elicit a traditional response, descriptive gestures are usually initiated by the speaker to clarify or enhance an explanation, description, or narration. You may suggest size, shape, or speed of an object and, as in body movement, you will help the speech, the audience, and yourself.

KINDS OF DELIVERY

Speeches are delivered in several ways according to the kind of preparation and the occasion. We shall consider manuscript reading, memorized, extemporaneous, and impromptu speeches.

Manuscript Reading

One of the methods of delivery used by many public speakers is to read from a prepared manuscript. Public officials who will be "on the record" want to be sure of what they said. Papers delivered at professional meetings, especially of a technical nature, will usually be presented via a manuscript. Whenever a speaker is restricted by time limits, the manuscript helps him control that factor. The manuscript, then, has the advantage of being a reliable source for the record, it assures accuracy, and it gauges the speech for time.

As attractive as these advantages are, reading from a prepared script is hazardous. First of all, the speech may *sound* as if it is being read. There are few effective oral readers. Secondly, physical activity is limited. Eye contact suffers, and arm and body movement is restricted. Finally, adaptability is difficult. One of Senator Talmadge's speech writers relates that when he was governor of Georgia,

> ... he had been in the habit of delivering his speeches from the news releases with appropriate interpolations on the spot. This particular time, however, he read his speech verbatim and it came out something like this: "The Fish and Game Commission's budget will be increased this year, Governor Talmadge announced today. ..." After this experience, Mr. Talmadge had regular speech manuscripts prepared.[17]

If you must use a manuscript, incorporate an oral style so that you can seem as communicative as possible. Provide for pauses in which you maintain eye contact, and rehearse until you can read whole lines at a time.

17. Interview with William Burson, February 1964.

Memorized

Though less popular than in former times, the memorized speech or portions of one may be needed on occasions. Shorter speeches for presenting awards, delivering eulogies, or performing rituals in the church or synagogue are effective when memorized. Also, memorizing becomes part of a political candidate's stock-in-trade. The speech writer for a nationally known southern governor candidly related, "You can't get our governor to read or check over any speech or draft until minutes before he is set to give it. He is more effective when he has given the same speech several times and gives one without a copy of the speech off-the-cuff, after memorizing parts of it."[18]

By memorizing you can achieve accuracy, predictable timing, and have complete physical freedom. Your greatest risk is loss of memory and a memorized style. Actors, of course, face this problem as a professional fact of life. They do create the "illusion of the first time" for parts they may have played a hundred times, so it can be done successfully. If public speaking is not your profession, however, you had best not rely on this method for long speeches. Besides the other drawbacks, it would be too time consuming.

Extemporaneous

Extemporaneous has come to mean carefully prepared but spontaneously delivered in the speech communication field. It is the method recommended for most speaking assignments by most speech authorities. It provides several advantages over other methods. (1) It enables the speaker to make changes as he goes along, adjusting to conditions as they arise. Late developments may necessitate toning down, rearranging, or cutting out parts of what he planned to say. In speech classes, it may be what a previous speaker has said. (2) It allows physical freedoms. The speaker can heighten his sense of communication by more direct eye contact, freer movement, and gestures. (3) It gives the speaker confidence. Legible, well-organized note cards should eliminate the fear of forgetting, as is the case with the memorized speech, or losing your place or missing an important word in the manuscript speech.

Even this recommended procedure has limitations. Unless severe discipline is used in rehearsal, time limits may seldom be honored. This

---

18. Dwight L. Freshley, "Gubernatorial Ghostwriters," *Southern Speech Journal* 31 (Winter 1965), p. 100.

is why some speakers write out their entire speech, practice from a manuscript for timing, then put the speech on note cards and try to approximate the written speech very closely to stay within the time allotted. Another deficiency of the extemporaneous method is the general imprecision of language. The person who has not developed an effective vocabulary may have to settle for the cliche. Fragmented sentences that are acceptable in conversation will be left hanging when the speaker is up there alone.

To use this method most effectively, the following suggestions might be useful. (1) Start early and prepare thoroughly. A late start might leave you time to get ideas down but rob you of precious rehearsal time in which you make those crucial decisions of what to leave in and what to take out. If you haven't made those decisions, during the speech you may include all manner of materials that "come to you." The result could be distracting digression or unnecessary amplification.

(2) After you have made the complete sentence outline, you will need to remember enough of it to deliver it smoothly. Different speakers have different techniques for achieving this. Some have to write out the entire speech before they make an outline. Others put down a few key words and rehearse from them. When Dr. Norman Vincent Peale was asked, "How do you fix in mind the sequence of ideas in a speech?" he replied, "I 'picturize' the outline rather than 'memorize' it. . . . Usually when someone speaks of memorizing an outline, he means that he learns verbatim the precise wording. What I do is to 'picture' in my mind the sequence and relationships of the major and minor points."[19]

(3) For practice and delivery purposes, the use of note cards (3 x 5 or 4 x 6) is highly recommended. Be careful not to put too much on each card. Key words should be enough to remind you of main and subpoints. For the sake of accuracy you will want to write out statistics and quotations. Make no attempt to hide the cards. In fact, the audience will be pleased you have them. It relieves them of anxiety that you might forget. In addition, quoting authorities or statistics from cards tends to give more credibility to what you say.

(4) Practice aloud, standing, and in front of a friendly listener at least once. Though you will go over the speech enough to become comfortable with the material, don't rehearse so much that the speech becomes stale. Use words that are comfortable for you. Rehearse with an audio- or videotape recorder if possible.

19. Eugene E. White and Clair R. Henderlider, "What Norman Vincent Peale Told Us about His Speaking," *Quarterly Journal of Speech* 40 (December 1954) p. 415.

Impromptu

Impromptu speaking is unpremeditated, without rehearsal, off-the-cuff. For a practice exercise in speech communication classes, you may be handed three topics, asked to choose one, and given a minute or two to prepare. Even with this short notice you will try for a coherent presentation with some primary emphasis and discernible pattern of organization. The topic may lend itself to problem solution, advantages-disadvantages, local, state, or national, economic, political, and social, or some similar broad pattern. Jot down a few words you can amplify. At least use an introduction, body, and conclusion, trying not to ramble or end with "Well, I guess that's all I have to say." Comment briefly and confidently.

Delivery, then, is an indispensable part of the speech process. It can determine in large part whether you achieve your purpose. After diligent research and appropriate outlining of a worthy topic, it makes good sense to provide the most effective means of presenting it.

EXERCISES/ASSIGNMENTS

1. Tape record a five-minute speech of your own and analyze your strengths and weaknesses using the principles in this chapter. Are you loud enough to be heard? (Don't cheat by turning up the volume!) Is your tone pleasant to listen to? Objectively ask yourself: Would I like to listen to that voice for fifteen minutes? If the answer is "no," ask the instructor for some help in the speech lab on developing better resonance. Do you have some variety in pitch? See if you can pick out the range on a piano.

2. Record the following passage. It contains all the sounds in the English language. Do you have difficulty in producing any sound? Have your instructor listen to double-check.

   "It is usually rather easy to reach the Virginia theatre. Board car number fifty-six somewhere along Churchill Street and ride to the highway. Transfer there to the Mississippi bus. When you arrive at Judge Avenue, begin walking toward the business zone. You will pass a gift shop displaying little children's playthings that often look so clever you will wish yourself young again: such things as books and toys, and behind the counter, a playroom with an elegant red rug and smooth shining mirrors. Beyond this shop are the National Bank and Globe Garage. Turn south at the next corner, the theatre is to your left."

3. The following passage contains many troublesome articulation and pronunciation problems. Look up the pronunciation of those words you're not sure of.

The election year is exciting all right. From February to November, candidates become national figures. They need only to wave "Hello" to a gathered company of visitors and recognition is immediate. Naturally, the quantity of speeches given by candidates for president is great, even into the hundreds.

The campaigns are actually pretty grueling and usually everybody involved gives up his comfortable routines for the time being.

The juvenile delinquency problem in many places is a lamentable one. Statistics showing the steady increase in teen-age crime substantiate the idea that this is a national problem. Some maintain that teen-age behavior is infantile; others insist that it is barbarous or even heinous at times; all agree that it is more than mischievous.

That their behavior has not always been decorous is agreed. When they organize their spare time around the nucleus of the gang, violent actions sometimes occur. Irreparable harm results with harrassed and grievous parents paying the consequences.

The problem is one for genuine concern and is not to be laughed at with irrelevant remarks. It will take all our strength to guarantee a solution to the problem. However, research shows there have been comparable bad boys in history; perhaps they just didn't get the column coverage in the Daily Gazette.

4. If you have student acquaintances from different parts of the country, listen to key words that identify their region. For example, notice how eastern New Englanders and southerners differ from the general American region in pronouncing the words *forest, orange,* and *horrid;* also *hurry* and *carry.* You are no doubt familiar with southerners and eastern New Englanders dropping their "r's" in "for" and "farm." And the famous southern drawl is not much more than making two sounds out of one (walk becomes "wa-ook"). What words of yours do these acquaintances ask you to repeat?

5. If your instructor has indicated you have limited effectiveness in your use of the vocal elements of pitch, rate, or volume, check out a voice and diction text from the library and practice the appropriate exercises.

6. People-watching is a favorite pastime. At the intermission of a play, waiting for a bus or plane, where you're out of earshot, observe how people communicate with their bodies. What moods do the actions convey? Can you guess the content of their animated gesticulation? What does the space between the communicators tell you? Check your conclusions out with a fellow observer if possible.

7. Prepare a three- or four-minute report on a topic of interest to you and present it in the following ways: read from a manuscript, deliver it extemporaneously, and memorize the speech.

erır supe uueritureantur, con a p
ilec s acc et s a
rε6 si ogi h b arna e
m o escensus tus c bur pab
ica atra erat, iati erias milites
m daan m xus umani
ante ab i p n a tritur. ic
na on ılt p tu lu R pe u ie s-
itio us occ D ti
Ari ed

epr
cogitare gu
imere erant. De
pe one omn m s utis
c su us
primis bus quibus haberi s
et de trib
nfer t. Is temp er Ravennae
Pro n betur extra urbe
udat; 'pias suas ponit legi
es eque sse persu
austus Sull

, reliquae no
minum cum ea legion
qui jubet. Eo L. Caesar a
ompeio ad eum privati officii n
tumeliam vertat. Semper se reipu
tudium et iracundiam suam reipubl
ejusdem generis addit cum excusatione
m commemorasse demonstrat. Quae r
vellet ad eum perferrentur, petit
parfo labore magnas controv
ιese se quod

USING WORDS TO COMMUNICATE

$\mathbb{A}$s the reader gazes at this page at this moment he sees black marks surrounded by white space. He recognizes these black marks as *words* because he has been taught to so recognize them. He seriously began to learn to recognize black marks on paper as words about the age of five or six years; however, he began to use words orally even sooner. At about the age of two years most of us have a vocabulary of between 200 and 300 words, and because we used and recognized words at such a very early age, we very seldom ask ourselves the question, "Just what *is* a *word?*"

HOW WORDS WORK

Defining Words

What is the nature of a word? What is its function? To what useful purposes can a word be put? What are the limitations to the usefulness of words?

The answer to the question, "What is a word," is seemingly quite simple. It *seems* simple because it can be phrased in a very short sentence. But, as we shall see, the answer has some important and complicated implications for the effective use of words as communication. To put it briefly, *a word is a symbol*—something which "stands for" or "substitutes for" something else. The flag of the United States of America is a symbol. It "stands for" our country. A coin is a symbol. A quarter has very little inherent value in and of itself, but it can be exchanged in a store for a product because it "stands for" a certain amount of what we agree is "purchasing power." A map is a symbol. It represents, or "stands for," a certain amount of geographical territory.

Using Words Effectively

What is it, then, that words stand for? Again, the answer can be phrased, quite simply, although the answer has a host of important implications.

Words are used to stand for anything that human beings can perceive or conceptualize.

In general, the word "referent" is used to denote what a particular symbol refers to or stands for. The referent for many nouns is an object. The word "apple" refers to or stands for red or yellow edible pome (fleshy) fruits which grow on trees of the family *Malaciae*. Other nouns refer to referents more abstract in nature. The word "love" refers to a complex, complicated state of psychophysical symptoms, mental sets, attitudes, and so forth. The usual referent for a verb is an activity, action, or state of being. The verb "fly" refers to the activity of moving through the air without support. The referent to "is" is usually some state of existence ("is fat," "is alive," "is reading"). Adjectives and adverbs usually have as referents some abstract and generally arbitrary quality. The word "fast" refers to a speed of movement which exceeds other speeds of movement classified as more "slow." The referent for "simple" is some arbitrary point on a continuum that extends between "complex" and "simple."

Words are like any other kind of symbol. To be used effectively, they must be used accurately. In a sense, we exchange words in our communication much as we exchange coins in our financial transactions. Suppose I say to you, "Fine day, isn't it?" You reflect briefly on my words, quickly check the meteorological situation, agree that the temperature, humidity, wind direction and intensity, and absence of clouds meets your concept of "fine day," and respond, "Yes, sure is."

Like maps, words to be useful must accurately reflect "the territory" they purport to represent. If you should habitually and incorrectly use the word "mushrooms" when the referent is actually what we call "toadstools," someone is apt to be poisoned. To label what your friend considers one of his "unfortunate mistakes" as a "dishonest act" may irreparably damage your friendship.

Words may symbolize different things to different people, and so care must be taken in choosing words. To a poverty-stricken unemployed person living in one of our rural or urban slums, poorly educated and from a broken home, the red white and blue of the stars and stripes may symbolize all that is ugly in his life. In contrast, to the "middle American" who has grown up in an atmosphere of successful competition in education and the business community, our flag might well stand for all the good things democracy has to offer. By the same token, the word "home" probably means, to your instructor, where he goes home to dinner at the end of the school day; whereas to the college student "home" may mean to some other town or city, where his or her parents live, where one goes when college recesses for Christmas or for summer vacation.

Principles to Remember

Now consider several implications, when choosing words for a public speech, that can be drawn from what has been said about the nature of words.

   1. *Meanings are in people, not in words.* The word "apple" means nothing to someone who has never experienced one. We can explain that an apple is a roundish, generally sweet, red or yellow edible fleshy fruit which grows on trees. Our apple-illiterate may, then, begin to conceive of *some* meaning for the word "apple," depending upon his past experience and knowledge of roundness, sweetness, redness and yellowness, fleshiness, etc. But his "meaning" for "apple" will be far different from that of most of us who have actually eaten apples.

   2. *Words do not transmit meaning; they merely "stir up" meanings already present in people.* If people to whom you are speaking have little or no meaning for the words you use, or, because of their different backgrounds, experiences, perceptions, and motives have *different* meanings for your words, communication will be difficult. (See Chapter 3.) In the years of big-time radio there was an action-drama police program called "Gangbusters." The show opened with a loud, fast "signature" including sirens, screeching tires, and the rattle of machine gun fire. From this developed the expression, "He comes on like 'Gangbusters'!" which means that he "comes on strong." The expression would have little or no meaning for those too young to have experienced the old radio show, but it would have instant and fairly standardized meaning for its devotees.

   3. *The speaker must choose words he thinks his listeners will understand.* That is to say, the speaker should abandon plans to use any pet phrases or favorite words or any erudite-sounding words he feels may dazzle but not enlighten his audience.

ACHIEVING CLARITY

The author of a famous book on style[1] might offer three rules for good writing: (1) Be clear. (2) Be clear. (3) Be clear. This emphasis on clarity in writing should be even further emphasized for the *spoken* word. For, if a *written* message is not clear, it can be reread—several times if necessary. Difficult or obscure words in that written message can be found in

---

1. William Strunk, Jr., *The Elements of Style* (New York: The Macmillan Co., 1959). It is alleged that Professor Strunk, exceedingly spare with his prose, repeated each of his specific dicta in the classroom three times.

dictionaries; obscure place names and other elements of the message can be looked up in encyclopedias. But not the spoken message. It has been said many times that "Written style must be ultimately intelligible, but spoken style must be *instantly* intelligible." To achieve clarity, one must consider its four elements: concreteness, simplicity, precision, and appropriateness.

Concreteness

This element should be considered as the relative opposite of *abstractness.* For instance, if you wish to be concrete rather than abstract, don't say, "The man walked into a building." What *kind* of building? Did he walk into a church? A synagogue? A mansion? A hut? A firehouse? Be specific. Would you say the man *went* down the street? Or that he "sped?" Or "dashed?" Or lurched, staggered, crawled, skipped, or cycled?

Concreteness adds detail, which produces interest in your comments. Compare the following statements:

> Some time back, when I was out West, I was walking along when I came across this cloth bag.

> During Christmas vacation, 1967, I was strolling along Market Street in San Francisco, when I looked down in front of me to discover a green bag with the name of the U.S. Mint on it.

Does not the second and more concrete statement evoke more interest than the collection of abstractions above it?

Simplicity

Simplicity in word choice is to be preferred over its opposite, all other things being equal. Granted, sometimes complicated or technical words are necessary in order to be concrete and specific, but do not use large words just for the sake of using large words when smaller ones will suffice. You need not say "he returned to his domicile" when "he went home" would do. A World War II directive to Washington, D.C., offices regarding blackout instructions concluded with directions for "terminating the illumination." A reporter figured out that this meant "turn out the lights."[2] A "jargoneer" might say, "And initiate protective measures to safeguard us against activities or tendencies that are antisocial." Jesus said it more simply: "Deliver us from evil."

2. Arthur Edson, "Terminate the Illumination"? Simple: "Turn Out the Light," *Lincoln* (Neb.) *Sunday Journal and Star*, May 16, 1965.

Precision

Precision in choosing words is often a special kind of concreteness, discussed above. Other times it is simply choosing a word that will not have several meanings. For example, syndicated columnist James Kilpatrick once complained that his editors changed some of his copy, and for the worse.[3] Mr. Kilpatrick had used the phrase, "Over the past fifteen years," meaning the "immediate past fifteen years in time." The offending editors substituted "last" for "past." Mr. Kilpatrick groaned in print that "last" can have any one of three meanings. "Last" can be "final" (the last rose of summer, fight to the last man). It can mean a time certain, such as last week or last March. Or it can mean "most recent," as in the last few minutes. The reader may experience a brief moment of "flickering ambiguity" in determining which of the three meanings of "last" is intended, Kilpatrick writes. But had they left the word "past" in his phrase, they would have left untouched a word which has only one meaning in that context. The ambiguity would not have had a chance even to flicker.

Appropriateness

A criterion of clarity, appropriateness, if not used by the speaker, can cause him to "lose" his audience. When speaking before friends and classmates the speaker can use relatively informal language. Relevant and nontrite slang can be used, for instance. On the other hand, a grandiose and overly formal style might well sound pretentious and "phony" to your peers. To begin a speech in class with, "Mr. Instructor, fellow classmates of the University of _____, friends ..." might draw smiles or smirks. On the other hand, in a more formal situation, such an opening would be appropriate. For a ceremonial occasion, such as a valedictory speech at the June commencement, such a formal salutation would sound perfectly correct, but slang expressions and "common" words like "wallop" and "lousy" would have little place.

ACHIEVING VIVIDNESS

Your language can be concrete, simple, precise, and appropriate and still not cross the interest threshold of your audience. What you might

3. James Kilpatrick, "An Editor Has the Last Word," *Athens* (Ga.) *Daily News*, December 22, 1970.

require to jolt your audience into awareness is language more vivid than normal. For instance, political extremists use extremely vivid language to capture the public's attention. *Time* magazine once reviewed, in a rather satirical manner, two books on the language of the "New Left," meaning Students for a Democratic Society and their like-minded friends. *Time* indicates that one lesson those on the New Left seemed to have learned is:

> Keep in mind that the primary purpose of words is not to express meaning but to pump adrenalin. Use active, blood-tingling verbs like "smash" or "liberate." If anybody disagrees with you, call him imperialist, authoritarian or at least manipulator for the power elite.[4]

Colorful and Personalized Words

While your authors cannot ascribe to this advice sarcastically offered by *Time,* it is true that vivid language often achieves the best results. This conclusion is substantiated by research on the relative effectiveness of various styles of advertising. Carroll J. Swan[5] offers a number of cases in which the more vividly worded ads, those which were more personally tailored to the "you" in the potential readership, were more successful in actual tests. For instance, an ad headline for a Legal Almanac Series was more effective with direct address to the reader: It began, "DON'T BE YOUR OWN LAWYER—But You Should Know 'YOUR LEGAL RIGHT,'" and was superior to the less personal headline, "AN ANNOUNCEMENT OF INTEREST TO THE READERS OF THIS NEWSPAPER ENABLES YOU TO KNOW 'YOUR LEGAL RIGHTS.'" Research with ads for "Self-Seal Envelopes" resulted in advertisers choosing one with a lady saying, "I avoid licking glue . . . and so can you . . . with SELF-SEAL. . . ." A Welch's Grape Juice ad beginning, "On our 80th anniversary we are offering you . . .," was superior to one beginning, "We are playing host to the nation on our 80th anniversary. . . ." A deodorant ad headlined by the catchy "Torrid test in Palm Springs proves . . ." drew more requests for free samples than more unctuous headlines. The Arthur Murray dance program ad headlined with "It's Amazing! It's Sensational! It's Exclusive!" was more successful than one headlined with the blander, "How to become a popular dancer. . . ."

Apart from colorful and personalized words, another technique of vividness involves the use of figures of speech. They are discussed next.

4. "Jeers or Jeremiahs?" *Time* (January 5, 1970), p. 58.
5. Caroll J. Swan. *Which Ad Pulled Best?* Printers Ink Publishing Co., 1951.

Figurative Language

Life in general and speech making in particular would seem monotonous and dull if either were one fact piled atop another. The speaker who would keep his audience alert and make his appeals vivid uses figurative language. And what is figurative language? It is nothing more than reality with a bit of "art" added to it; it is "reality plus." And figurative language is not a novel, strange, or exceptional form of language even for a beginning high school or college public speaker. Most slang can be considered figurative language: "reality plus art."

Consider an example. To say, "John is asleep" is to make a clear statement of fact. But this fact can be expressed by two slang expressions current (at this writing) among today's youg people by adding a bit of art to the fact. One can say, "John is piling up the Z's" or "John is flaked out." Of course, when using slang, you must be aware of the transient nature of the medium. Slang comes into and out of vogue, sometimes abruptly. In the youth of the authors of this book the slang expression would have been, "John is sawing logs."

One must be careful when using figurative language, of course, because by "adding to" reality you may add something that will be misunderstood, and perhaps even resented. It is widely believed that George Romney's statement that he was "brainwashed" by our own military officers in South Vietnam during the war there caused him to lose (or at least damaged his chances of winning) the Republican nomination for President in 1968. And the author of the movie imaginatively (and figuratively) entitled, "I Am A Camera," left himself wide open for the most critical and shortest movie review in history: "No Leica."

Do not rely too heavily on figurative language in your speeches. Treat it and figures of speech (and humor) as you would spices on the dinner table—sparingly. The spices make the meal taste better, but are certainly not the whole meal.

Simile and metaphor. These are perhaps the most popular figures of speech, as each is a kind of comparison. Simile is the weaker, using the words "as" or "like," whereas a metaphor's strength tends to more firmly join the two concepts. You are using metaphor when you say, "He had muscles of steel." "His muscles were *like* steel" is a simile.

Epigram. Another type of catchy comparison is the epigram, which often employs plays upon words and is usually intended to be witty. "Wooden legs are not inherited, but wooden heads may be," is an epigram. Several years ago there seemed to be a good chance that Congress might pass a bill allowing an increase of 10% in the moisture content of canned hams. The bill was stopped cold by a congressman's epigram that what Congress was actually considering was a bill to allow meat companies "to sell water at ham prices."

Allegory.   A comparison that is quite extended is often called an allegory. One dictionary gives *Pilgrim's Progress* as an example of an allegory. One example from the realm of public speaking is known to this author. In 1963 CBS television did a one-hour program entitled, "The Strange Case of the English Language." One section of the program ridiculed then-Congressman Gerald Ford when he compared President Johnson to a ship's captain who was not doing a good job of running the ship. He referred to Mr. Johnson's throwing his minor officers overboard, complained that he needed to get to the bridge and set a proper course away from the rudderless meandering which the ship of state was presently following, etc. CBS remarked that the comparison went on for so long the audience became seasick. Beware of such extended comparisons.

Personification.   This is the device of attributing human characteristics to inanimate objects or other nonhuman entities. "Genius abhors fetters; its wild blood makes it difficult to tame," ascribes human-like traits to an abstract idea (genius). Joyce Kilmer poetically wrote of a tree "lifting her leafy arms to pray."

Analogy.   Mentioned in Chapter 6, analogy shows resemblance in some particulars between things otherwise unlike. Abe Lincoln's advice, "Don't change horses in the middle of the stream," meaning "Don't change presidents in the middle of a war," is an example.

COMPARING ORAL AND WRITTEN STYLE

Students of language have long contended that there are definite differences between the style used in good spoken discourse and that used in good written discourse. In fact, over two thousand years ago Aristotle wrote in his *Rhetoric* that, "It should be observed that each kind of rhetoric has its own appropriate style. The style of written prose is not that of spoken oratory. . . . Both written and spoken have to be known."

In Theory . . .

Gladys Borchers summarized what Aristotle and subsequent writers specified as the differences in the two styles which should exist:

1. In oral style the sentence should be shorter.
2. There should be greater variety in sentence structure in oral style.
3. Sentences are less involved in structure in oral style.
4. Personal pronouns are more numerous in oral style.
5. Oral style requires more careful adaptation to the speaker.
6. Oral style requires more careful adaptation to the audience.
7. Oral style requires more careful adaptation to the occasion.
8. Oral style requires more careful adaptation to the subject matter.
9. Fragmentary sentences may be used in oral style.
10. Slang may be used in oral style.
11. Contractions are used more often in oral style.
12. Oral style is more euphonious.
13. Indigenous language should be more predominant in oral style.
14. Repetition is more necessary in oral style.
15. Concrete words should be used more often in oral style.
16. Effusive style or copiousness is more predominant in oral style.
17. Vehement style is more predominant in oral style.
18. The rhythm of oral style is different from the rhythm of written style.[6]

Dr. Carroll C. Arnold has said that it makes a difference, an important difference, when you are composing a message for a listener rather than a reader. A listener has three requirements that a reader does not: "time to review, 'catch up,' reflect and take instants of rest." He also requires "constant refreshment of interest," and "obvious distinctions between most important and less important ideas."[7] Dr. Arnold gives a list of differing characteristics which readers and listeners look for in writing and speaking:

When Reading We Look For:

1. Printed signs pointing to main thoughts and showing how they're related (capital letters and terminal marks, paragraph indentations, numerals, extra spaces or other symbols identifying major subdivisions, etc.).

When Listening We Look For:

1. Repetitions and statements that tell us to take special notice of this or that.

6. Gladys Borchers, "An Approach to the Problem of Oral Style," *Quarterly Journal of Speech* 22 (February 1936), pp. 114–17.
7. Carroll C. Arnold, "Reader or Listener? Oral Composition," *Today's Speech* 13 (February 1965), p. 6.

2. Good form: neatness, helpful punctuation and paragraphing, conventional grammar, etc.

2. Behavior showing that the speaker is educated, trustworthy, and really means what he says: appropriate dress and manners; grammar suited to who he is and who we are; the kinds of pauses and emphases that show he's thinking about *us*; movements, gestures, words that set ideas apart and help us understand them better.

3. Ideas that are worthwhile for anyone who may pick up the writing, whether today or in the future.

3. Ideas that are worthwhile to *us*, right *now*.

4. Pleasing ways of saying things whether through unusual use of words and sound combinations or special forms of composition like poetry.

4. Memorable ways of making things clear through unusual uses of words and sound combinations that seize our attention or by special forms of composition like bits of poetry, other quotations, etc.

5. Descriptions and narrations we can linger over with pleasure or read several times, getting new pleasure each time.

5. Descriptions and narrations that put instantly before our eyes the kinds of pictures that clarify or prove.

6. Reasoning that's logical enough to stand up under careful reexamination.

6. Reasoning that's sound and convincing when you hear it once.

7. Evidence, in the writing, that the writer understands the kinds of people he writes about.

7. Evidence, in both what the speaker says and the way he says it, that he knows his subject.

8. Evidence, in the speaker's manner and in what he says, that he understands not only the kinds of people he talks about but understands *us* as well.

9. Evidence, in what the speaker says and in his manner, that he has *our* interests at heart.

10. What the speaker says, and the way he says it, must be consistent with what we already

know about him and with the
kinds of relations we have had
and are having with him.[8]

Research Findings

The findings of objective research in general tend to support the theoretical differences proposed between written and oral style. Borchers[9] analyzed 20,000 sentences of famous speakers who also wrote considerably. Some of her findings, paraphrased, are:

1. The oral style contained fewer declarative, loose, and compound sentences and more imperative, interrogative, and exclamatory sentences.
2. The written style adapted more to particular audiences and occasions.
3. The oral style contained more first and second pronouns than the written.

Gibson, Gruner, Kibler, and Kelly[10] analyzed the extempore speeches and formal essays of students at two colleges. They found that the speeches contained shorter sentences, smaller words, more "personal sentences" (direct address), more "personal words," and a smaller vocabulary (indicating more repetition) than did their essays.

Horowitz and Newman[11] studied the written and oral outputs of college students. Their results confirmed that oral style uses a smaller vocabulary (more repetition) and that oral style is much more spontaneous, whereas written style is more careful, deliberate, and efficient.

DeVito has examined the written style of professors' published work and those same professors' extemporaneous comments about those publications and concludes:

Among those features found more frequently in one mode of communication than the other are the following: (1) Speech contains more easy, short, and familiar words, more personal pronouns, and more function words—words which indicate grammatical relations rather than make reference to the real world as do nouns, verbs, adjectives, and adverbs. (2) Speech contains fewer different words. (3) Speech contains more self-reference terms, more allness terms such as *never, all,* and *always,* more pseudoquantifying terms such as *many,*

8. Ibid., pp. 6–7.
9. Borchers, "An Approach to the Problem of Oral Style," pp. 114–17.
10. James W. Gibson, Charles R. Gruner, Robert J. Kibler, and Francis J. Kelly, "A Quantitative Examination of Differences and Similarities in Written and Spoken Messages," *Speech Monographs* 33 (November 1966) pp. 444–51.
11. Milton Horowitz and John B. Newman, "Spoken and Written Expression: An Experimental Analysis," *Journal of Abnormal and Social Psychology* 68 (1964), pp. 640–47.

much, and *very,* more qualification terms such as *but, however,* and *although,* and more terms indicative of consciousness of projection such as *it seems to me* and *apparently.* (4) Speech is less abstract than writing, containing more concrete verbs and less abstract nouns than does writing. (5) Speech contains more verbs and adverbs whereas writing contains more nouns and adjectives.[12]

In Practice ...

The one practical implication of all this research should be obvious. Oral style does differ from written style, and the speaker should recognize this. He should speak in oral style and write in written style and not vice versa. The speaker should follow the dictum of the late William Norwood Brigance: that one should consider public speaking a kind of enlarged conversation, and that a speech should never resemble "an essay on its hind legs." Speak with the natural rhythm of conversation; use shorter, sometimes incomplete sentences; use more personal pronouns, especially of the first and second person; refer to and adapt to your specific audience and occasion; use shorter, more common words, and repeat statements; speak more spontaneously than you write.

Although the extemporaneous method of speaking, as defined in this text, is the mode of public speaking preferred by most speech teachers *and* audience members, it is necessary, especially on some formal occasions, to have a written manuscript from which you must read your speech. The danger in this practice is that the speech will be composed primarily in a written style and will thus sound like "an essay on its hind legs,"—pompous and overly pretentious. To prevent this, after properly outlining the speech and before it is written in final form, you should compose it orally, sentence or paragraph at a time. Then the orally composed speech sections should be written down.

EXERCISES/ASSIGNMENTS

1. When a speaker is asked to submit his speech for publication in an anthology, why is he likely to prepare a different version from that actually given orally?

12. Joseph DeVito, *The Psychology of Speech and Language* (New York: Random House, 1970), p. 11

2. Prepare a three-or four-minute (written/oral) analysis of the language in Abraham Lincoln's "Gettysburg Address." Did he use an "oral" style or a "written" style? Was the language appropriate for the occasion?

3. In what way, if any, is public address literature?

4. Stating only the facts, write a paragraph on any topic of interest to you. Now write it again and use language which, because of its vividness, makes the paragraph more interesting.

5. Look up the word "defenestrate." Find its origin from the Latin. Walk up to one of your friends or classmates and ask him/her, "Have you ever defenestrated anyone?" Observe his/her reaction (to the connotation due to the sound). Later, explain what you mean. Do the same with "absquatulate." For the latter, you may have to use the *Oxford English Dictionary*.

6. Write down a one-sentence definition (your own) of the words "wit" and "humor." Write a short paragraph depicting what you feel are the differences between the two concepts. Now look up each in the *Oxford English Dictionary*. Do the origins and developments of the meanings of the two words tend to support your own definitions and perceived differences?

7. Below is a report of an employee accident written by a supervisor. Rewrite it to make it clearer, as did the employee's oral report (below and upside down).

   "Employee failed to withdraw digit due to failure in accurately estimating self-activated drawer closure speed."*

8. Consider the statement, "She has a *good* smile." Look up "good" in an English thesaurus and substitute several different synonyms for "good" in the sentence. How does each substitution affect the *meaning* of the sentence? Do the same with the sentence, "The tension in the Middle East results from a very *bad* situation."

*slammed a file drawer on his finger

CHAPTER 10

INFORMATIVE
SPEAKING

$\mathcal{A}$s we become proficient in our area of specialization or assume positions of increased responsibility, we shall be called on more and more to convey to others information we have acquired," writes Roger P. Wilcox of the General Motors Institute.[1] And it would be difficult to over-emphasize the importance of one's ability to impart information. Prospective teachers spend years in training and practice. Governmental agencies spend hundreds of thousands of dollars to discover the most efficient techniques of communicating skills and knowledge to trainees. Even the Boy Scouts, in their leader training program, are emphasizing "GGI ability"—the skill of "Giving and Getting Information."

CHARACTERISTICS OF AN INFORMATIVE SPEECH

The effective speech to inform should have four characteristics: (1) contain new and useful information for its audience; (2) be organized so as to enhance audience learning of the information; (3) present information in a manner which appeals to the audience, and (4) contain elements which will make the audience *want* to learn the information in the speech. Let us consider each of these characteristics in turn, though not necessarily in their order of importance.

Communicating New Information

If a speech "to inform" contains no information *new* to the audience, it does not perform the function of *informing* at all. In the spring of 1973 a young man in a class of one of the authors gave a speech on "how to find and check out a book from our college library." This speaker conveyed no new information whatsoever to this particular class. They knew it already.

1. Roger P. Wilcox, *Oral Reporting in Business and Industry* (Englewood Cliffs, N.J.: Prentice-Hall, 1967), p. 6.

If the information in your speech is not somehow *useful* to your audience, that speech might more properly be considered a speech to *entertain* or to *interest*. And often whether your speech is more to inform or more to entertain is a matter of degree. For instance, suppose you have been lucky enough to have been able to travel to Europe and have a goodly collection of colored slides as a result of that visit. If you chose to speak about the more unusual "adventures" you had during your trip, showing slides of the magnificent Alps, Place Pigalle, the Eiffel Tower, Big Ben, etc., you would probably please your audience by helping them to pass the time during your speech rather pleasantly. Of course, in a way you are "informing" them of your trip to Europe, also, but the speech has more of an *entertainment* than an *informative* function. You could increase your speech's informative value by giving it a focus, for instance, famous sculpture, birthplaces of historical figures, or one specific cathedral you found especially fascinating. Even a speech on the practical aspects of a trip to Europe, including the least expensive or most rewarding methods of travel, how to deal with local authorities, where help can be secured if necessary, would be more *informative* than a reciting of your adventures. The speech to inform ought to instruct, not merely help an audience pass the time pleasantly.

Organizing Informative Ideas

New and useful information can be learned more easily when it is organized in a meaningful pattern and the pattern is discernible to the audience. One of the clearest conclusions to be drawn from educational research is that organization is important to learning. As three educational psychologists summarize it:

> Schooling is more efficient when learning is well-organized and there is a psychologically sound basis for materials, methods, and processes of instruction. So strong is the tendency to learn in an organized way that even when material is presented in a disorganized or relatively meaningless fashion, pupils tend to develop an organization of their own.[2]

Two excellent companion studies testing the hypothesis that well-organized speeches to inform convey more information than the same speeches *not* well-organized have been conducted by Ernest Thompson.[3] Each of the studies confirms the advantage of the well-organized over the poorly organized speech to instruct.

2. Glenn M. Blair, R. Stewart Jones, and Ray H. Simpson, *Educational Psychology*, 2nd ed. (New York: The Macmillan Co., 1967), p. 236.
3. Ernest C. Thompson, Jr., "An Experimental Investigation of the Relative Effectiveness of Organizational Structure in Oral Communication." *Southern Speech Journal* 26 (Fall 1960). pp. 59–69, and "Some Effects of Message Structure on Listeners' Comprehension," *Speech Monographs* 34 (March 1967), pp. 51–7.

Presenting the Informative Speech

Just because the information of your speech is important to the audience and is well organized does not mean that your speech to inform will be received favorably. The speech must also be delivered to maximize learning. The delivery of an informative speech should be as appealing as possible—enjoyment increases learning. You, the reader, can attest to the ease with which appealing material is learned compared to the difficulty of learning unpleasant material from your own experience as a student. For the public speaker the implication is clear; you should try for the most appealing and pleasant delivery you can muster. A number of experimental studies in public speaking demonstrate the help which good delivery will provide for informative discourse. You would be well advised to reread Chapter 8 on delivery at this point.

Motivation of the Audience

Another well-established conclusion of educational research is that people learn best when they are motivated to do so. The informative speaker will tailor his information to make his audience *want* to learn it. A wealth of educational research shows that an appeal based upon *utility* is an important factor in the learning and retaining of information:

> There is a large body of convincing evidence which shows how poorly students retain information which is not related to significant problems and which has a low degree of internal relationship. In contrast, results obtained with well-organized and meaningful materials may show actual gain rather than decrease with a passage of time. Meaningful learning may suffer only slightly with a passage of time.[4]

In the introduction the speaker should point out the importance his information will have for the audience and then continually relate his subject matter to their needs, wants, and desires throughout the speech.

As stated in Chapter 5 two of the functions of a speech's introduction are: to state the speaker's thesis or purpose, and to provide listeners with "interest material" or a "rationale" for paying attention. Can you make the point that your speech will save them time or money? Will your speech make them more attractive to the opposite sex? Will it provide insights to make their lives more meaningful? But let's examine some examples of speech topics for which you might be

4. Blair, Jones, and Simpson, *Educational Psychology*, p. 236.

able to develop a reason your audience could perceive as pertaining to their interests.

Speech Topic	**"Reason" to Give Audience**
The historical facts that inspired Tennyson's "Charge of the Light Brigade"	Did you know that the man after whom the "cardigan" sweater was named was a principal character in the battle that inspired the poem, "Charge of the Light Brigade"? The other facts about that battle enhance one's appreciation of the poem . . .
Special library indexes	If you knew how to use *Psychological Abstracts, Sociological Abstracts,* the *Education Index,* and a few other special indexes in our library, you could not only enhance your knowledge on a variety of topics, but could higher-grade term papers and speeches.
How to identify counterfeit money.	If you can spot phony $20.00 bills, you can prevent some serious dollar losses.
Artificial respiration	You never know when you might be able to save the life of an almost-drowned friend or relative.

So the effective speech to inform presents new and useful information, well-organized and pleasantly delivered in such a way that the audience will want to learn from it. But there are several well-established conclusions regarding *how people learn* to which the speech to inform should adhere.

HOW WE LEARN

Three principles of learning that have been proven in a number of educational experiments are that people learn best when information comes in small amounts, is repeated often, and comes after the general principle or generalization which it explains or to which it pertains.

Introduce Small Amounts

From your own experience you know that learning is best when it comes in small amounts. You need time to receive, digest, mull over, perhaps put into practice a bit of information. If you are inundated with fact upon fact upon statistic, each more or less unrelated to the other, the mind boggles. Your speeches to inform in class will probably be quite short, as speeches go, perhaps between two and four or five minutes long. You cannot pack into those few minutes too much information or you will produce what information theorists call "information overload" or "channel overload" which will completely befog the minds of your audience. So you must narrow your topic, select only the pertinent points to present to your audience, and then use them in following the advice of the next paragraph.

Repeat Often

A famous American company that produces canned soup has, at this writing, an advertising campaign on radio in which, in a particular ad, a company representative calls a housewife long distance and either asks her to sing the company's advertising "jingle" or else plays one of their other "jingles" with the name of the advertised soup's brand name deleted. In the latter case, the housewife is asked to supply the deleted brand name. The housewife's success in answering the representative's query is rewarded with a case of the product. Occasionally some housewife who is called must fail to answer properly, but those answers are never played on the air. The many who do answer correctly owe their free case of soup to one facet of the soup's advertising: constant repetition.

Advertising, with its repetition (occasionally ad nauseum) is the one most flagrant example of communication which succeeds because of sheer reiteration. The careful and dedicated speaker to inform will learn from his professional communicators: Do not hesitate to repeat your salient points of information several times during your speech.

Stress the Principle

People generally learn better when they are first taught the *principle* involved in what it is they are learning. One classic experiment performed to test this hypothesis involved the ability of boys to hit underwater targets with air rifles and darts. One-half of the boys were taught the *principle* of light refraction as it passed from air to water; the other half were not. They all were given the task of trying to hit the target as the water depth was systematically varied. The boys taught the principle of light refraction scored much higher than the boys not so taught.

Petrie came to much the the same conclusion with regard to informative speaking after examining all the available experimental studies of the phenomenon. He concluded that, "generalizations or major ideas are better comprehended and retained than are details or specifics and that the better developed the generalizations are, the better they will be retained. . . ."[5]

Petrie's conclusion bolsters a particular belief of the authors, that, *informative speaking should be limited to messages which depend for their effectiveness more on the learning of a few general principles than on the remembering of an accumulation of specific bits of information.* If it is necessary for your audience to remember a large number of details, you should ditto, mimeograph, photocopy, or reproduce them in some written or printed form and distribute them. But repeating a long list of specific facts to remember or actions to take will quickly overload your audience's capacity to absorb data. Almost every autumn some young man in a speech class will present a speech on "Twenty-two Helpful Hints for Wintertime Driving." It is impossible for anyone with less than total recall to remember twenty-two items of information from a five-minute speech. But most listeners could remember two well-developed generalizations such as (1) winter requires that your car be in tip-top condition, and (2) you must drive with much more caution and patience in winter than in summer.

Using these two generalizations as the main ideas around which to arrange the details of the speech will aid the audience's learning tremendously, for it provides two *principles* for taking a number of separate actions. And, to quote from the three educational psychologists referred to earlier, *"Ability to apply principles,* solve problems, and interpret experimental data are examples of the kind of activities which *are very resistant to the ravages of the forgetting process."*[6]

A simple illustration may further clarify the usefulness of knowing the principle involved in learning. When the writer of this chapter was a Boy Scout working on his Second Class rank, he was faced with learning the side of a tree on which grows the most moss. Knowing this, a Scout could find his directions even if lost and without a compass. One learns that the moss grows mostly on the *north* side, then a few days later one would not be sure; he would re-learn that it was the north side, and in a week or two forget it. He was afraid he would not be able to keep the item of knowledge memorized until he got to the Board of Review. Then the patrol leader explained one day that the *reason why*

---

5. Charles R. Petrie, "Informative Speaking: A Summary and Bibliography," *Speech Monographs* 30 (June 1963), p. 80.

6. Blair, Jones, and Simpson, *Educational Psychology,* p. 236.

moss grew most readily on the north side of most trees is that it is the side which receives the least *sun*. And we all know that "the grass grows best where there is the least traffic." Learning this principle insured that the scout would never again forget why the most moss is usually on the north side of the tree. Furthermore, applying this principle, another perplexing discrepancy became clear. On some trees, moss grows equally well on *all* sides of a tree, the explanation being, of course, that the trunks of such trees are constantly in the shade.

The above paragraphs should not be misunderstood as contradictory to the advice of Chapter 6, that the speech should be rich with detail. The speech to inform *should* contain specific and concrete details, but not as ends in themselves. Some details should be used to explain, exemplify, and amplify the few main ideas or generalizations that the speaker is trying to put across, but if many details are necessary for the information to be useful, they should be distributed in written form for later referral.

KINDS OF INFORMATIVE SPEECHES

Practically any speech contains "information," even speeches to persuade and, as mentioned earlier, speeches to interest or entertain. In fact, some speeches "to inform" actually are intended to persuade, as when Pentagon speakers dispense information which it is hoped will promote good will toward the armed services. But the concern of this chapter is with speeches whose sole or major purpose is that the audience learn information. The most prevalent types of speeches to inform are those that explain *processes, products or services, organizations,* and *concepts.* The oral report is a distinct type of speech to inform and is considered separately.

Speech to Inform on a Process

A *process* is a series of individual events which together make up some sort of meaningful whole. To explain a process in a speech is to *tell how.* Among speeches to inform on a process are found speeches on how to do something, how something is made, how an event occurred, or how something evolves into something else. Some examples of topics for speeches to inform on processes appear below:

- Navigating an airplane by radio ranges
- How to refinish antiques

- How to do decoupage
- How tornadoes are formed
- Making maple sugar in Vermont
- Cooking without a stove
- What makes an airplane fly?
- Applying artificial respiration
- The minting of coins
- Transmitting photographs by radio
- Sailing a boat against the wind
- How your liver works
- How to tie three useful knots
- How to sew on a button

Usually the main ideas of a speech to inform on a process are arranged in chronological order. Occasionally such a speech may be arranged in a topical order. For instance, a speech on counterfeit money might be organized using the following points: paper quality, ink quality, and printing workmanship.

Speech to Inform on a Product or Service

A speech to inform on a product may describe *what* but may also be much like the speech on a process and explain *how*. For example, in a speech on the Primus model 8R camping and backpacking stove you would want the audience to see it so you could emphasize its small size and light weight for backpacking. But you might also want to show the audience how it works—the steps of unfolding, filling, priming, lighting, and using it to boil water. Ours is a gadget-oriented culture and new products are constantly coming to us from the assembly lines. If you discover some new or unusual product that would be useful and may still be unknown to your audience, it would make a timely and practical speech topic.

An explanation of some useful but little-known service can also make an effective speech to inform. For instance, students do not realize that many college libraries, even their own, have an inter-library loan system whereby a student can obtain a book or periodical otherwise unavailable. Knowledge of this service and how it operates could be extremely useful for a college student. Some possible topics for speeches to inform on a product or a service are:

- The Time-Life Record Club
- The new self-sealing freezer bags
- Services offered by radio WWV, National Bureau of Standards

- The new Polaroid SX-70
- The electron microscope
- Devices to make your home secure
- The Cost Comparer (for shopping economy)
- The newest man-made fabric
- The Wankel engine
- The radial tire
- Epoxy glue
- Citizen-band radio
- Car burglar alarm
- The miniature hand-held calculator
- What Social Security does for you
- A portable camp kitchen
- Using the ERIC system to research your topic
- A waterproof two-man tent weighing less than four pounds

Speech to Inform on an Organization

Americans are probably the most organization-joining group of people on earth, and you undoubtedly have information on one which your audience lacks. A speech to inform on an organization is usually designed to explain *what,* but it may also be involved with *how* (how the organization operates, serves its members, and so on). The essential task of the speaker is to cover those aspects of the organization that will be of interest and use to his audience. If discussing Rotary International you might tell your student audience of the overseas scholarship program which it sponsors. In discussing the local credit union you might stress how one may join and what benefits it provides members. In a speech on an unusual organization such as the Liars' Club of America you might concentrate solely upon the reason for its existence. Choose your topic not just to fulfill an assignment but one which will be relatively unfamiliar to your audience. And pick for your main points only those aspects of the organization that relate to your audience's interests and needs.

Speeches to Inform on a Concept

Speeches explaining concepts basically answer the questions of *what* and *why.* They seek to explain by defining the concept from a cause-effect or theoretical standpoint and may also point out practical implications. For instance, a speech may explain the principles of optical illusions, then explain how these principles can be employed in the design and patterning of clothing to make the wearer appear taller or shorter, fatter or slimmer. A theoretical explanation of the hydrological cycle may be used to explain why your community has had so much (or so little) rain. You might give a speech explaining how the ionosphere affects electrical radio waves and use this to show why reception of radio broadcasting at night differs from daytime broadcasting.

Following is a short speech on a concept—one theoretical explanation of how life originated on this planet. It was given in a speech class at the University of Georgia in July of 1973 by Miss Cindy Kenyon, and is re-created in written form from her original outline with her permission. It is offered here as a model speech to inform and demonstrates several features of good informative speaking.[7]

The Origin of Life
by Cindy Kenyon

Back in the days of big-time radio there was a popular dramatic show called "I Love a Mystery." It was aptly named, because all of us do, indeed, love mysteries. The unknown and the hidden are inherently fascinating to the mind of man. Today, I would like to discuss with you one mystery which has captivated man's fascination for as long as men have lived on this earth. I want to talk about the origin of life itself.

As you know, there are two forms of interpretation as to how life began on this planet. One is theological or religious and relies upon the idea of a supreme being creating life. The other form is scientific and employs known principles of physical laws. And, according to the Encyclopaedia Britannica at least, the theological explanation in its most general form does not necessarily conflict with the scientific form. Well, it is this scientific form that I am going to discuss. Specifically, I hope to explain to you today first, what scientists believe about the origin of the earth itself and its atmosphere; and second, I'll show you how such early conditions could give rise to very basic components of living cells, and therefore life.

The origin of the earth has long been debated. This is pretty natural, since no one was around to record the event or to take pictures of it. But scientists in many specialties, including geology, astronomy, anthropology, botany, and biochemistry now tend to agree on many of the issues. They agree, for instance, that it all started between four and one-half and five and one-half billion years ago. And I think you'll agree the four and

---

7. Reconstructed from a speech by Cindy Kenyon in Speech 108, University of Georgia. Used with the permission of Miss Kenyon.

one-half to five and one-half billion years is a long time ago. Scientists tend to agree on several other points, too.

Our solar system was created when great whirls of cosmic dust and gas condensed rapidly, producing heat and pressure. Thermonuclear reactions began occurring, which produced our sun. The planets, including our earth, were formed after the sun, and began condensing and cooling. As the earth condensed, the various elements were stratified. Left near the surface of the earth were the primary elements of life: hydrogen, nitrogen, oxygen, and carbon. However, they were not present in the same proportion or in the same form they are present on the earth now.

As we all learned in our general science courses, our atmosphere right now is about 21 percent oxygen and 78 percent nitrogen. But when the earth first formed there was very little free oxygen; in fact, the word used to describe the early condition of the earth is anoxygenic, which means "not with oxygen." Also, there was very little free nitrogen. Most of the oxygen and nitrogen, as I have said, was not "free." This means they did not exist in a pure form in any large measure, but were parts of other compounds. Scientists think these compounds were ammonia, which is composed of nitrogen and hydrogen; water vapor, made up of hydrogen and oxygen; and methane which is hydrogen and carbon.

Now you may think this sounds awfully complicated up to now, and in reality I guess it is. In fact, I may be over-simplifying it a bit. But the main thing to remember is that here we have, in the very early stage of the earth's existence, the elements carbon, oxygen, nitrogen, and hydrogen. And it exists in the form of ammonia, water vapor, and methane. Now as the earth cooled, the water vapor condensed. And we all know what happens when water vapor condenses in the atmosphere, don't we? It rains, right? And that's what happened on our primordial earth—it rained. And all four of these elements essential to life—hydrogen, carbon, nitrogen, and oxygen—collected together in our primordial seas.

And here you have the conditions of the early earth. But how could life arise from ammonia, methane, water, and hydrogen? The molecules of these compounds are quite stable, and do not readily inter-react with one another to produce different combinations. What was needed was some catalyst to create the necessary reaction to form organic material from the inorganic primitive goo in the early ocean. These chemicals, like the head of a match, had the potential of reacting; to make a match strike, you add the heat of friction. Some such addition in the form of energy was needed to produce life in the dead ocean.

Now, what kinds of energy sources comparable to heat from friction were available then? There were two such sources. One was irradiation from the ultraviolet rays of the sun. The other was electricity: lightning.

Scientific experiments, using what we now believe was the composition of the primordial seas and either irradiation or lightning, have con-

Figure 8. *Diagram of Miller's apparatus. Adapted by Valerie Jo Gruner from the drawing in Encyclopedia Britannica, vol. 13, p. 1083H, 14th ed. (1971).*

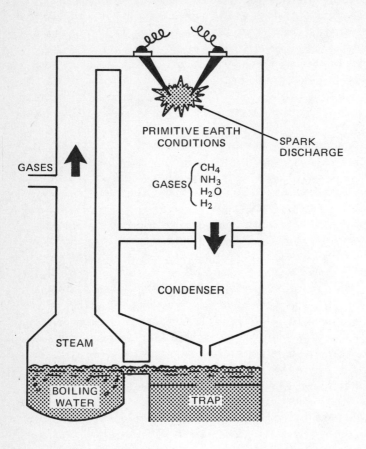

firmed that organic compounds can result. The first of these experiments was conducted by a man named Stanley Miller. For his doctoral project, directed by Dr. H. C. Urey, he constructed the apparatus you see illustrated here in my visual aid.

Miller mixed methane, ammonia, and hydrogen in a water solution and placed it in the bottom of this smaller side of the apparatus. To keep it circulating, as it would do in the sea, he kept the water boiling. At the top of the other side of the apparatus he kept a constant electrical spark operating; this was to simulate lightning on the early earth.

After a few days of this kind of activity, Miller's solution changed color. It became orange. The solution was analyzed chemically to determine what had happened to it. The analysis revealed that several amino *and hydroxy acids had been formed. These are "organic" compounds, and are very basic building blocks in our contemporary life.*

Miller's was a relatively simple experiment, beginning with what was thought to be the composition of the early earth and adding to it the energy known to exist at that time. In fact, the experiment is so simple that it has been duplicated many times, even by high school students.

Many other experiments with inorganic materials have produced primitive life in the form of amino acids and other materials. For instance, a Dr. Fox experimented with ordinary lava, like from a volcano, exposing it to intense heat. He found that these inorganic materials produced long protein chains, and these protein chains could reproduce themselves. Dr. Fox has also tested dust from our moon; and he has found that all conditions are present therein for life to form on the moon, with one exception: there is no water vapor.

I said earlier in this speech that the young earth had very little free oxygen. This is an important point in the theory I have here only sketched the beginning of. For if there had been as much free oxygen then as we have in our air today, these basic building blocks of life would die off quickly from oxidation. So the lack of oxygen in the early earth actually preserved these basic but primitive life forms. And, of course, without free oxygen, other micro-organisms which could feed on the building blocks of life could not exist.

Incidentally, you may wonder where all our present oxygen came from. Well, according to the theory I have been explaining here, life eventually evolved to the stage where plants could photosynthesize the sun's rays to produce oxygen. Our 21 percent oxygen in our present atmosphere, then, is largely from the photosynthesis of plants, like grass and trees.

Well, there you have it. Scientists believe that the early earth had all the necessary inorganic components of life. And they have demonstrated through experiments such as those of Dr. Miller and Dr. Fox that the organic basic building blocks of life could have been formed from them with a bit of help from lightning or irradiation. So now I hope you understand one of the most fascinating theories of all time, how life may have begun on our planet. And, maybe if you are clever enough you can go home now and "cook up a little life" for yourself!

REFERENCES

The Encyclopaedia Britannica, 1971 ed., vol. 13, pp. 1083G–1083J.

John Keosian, *The Origin of Life* (New York: Reinhold Publishing Corp., 1964).

M. G. Rutten, *The Origin of Life by Natural Causes* (Amsterdam, London, New York: Elsevier Publishing Co., 1971).

Lynn Margulis, ed., *Origins of Life: Proceedings of the First Conference* (New York: Godon and Breach, Science Publishers, 1970).

Miss Kenyon's speech, above, exemplifies several features which you as a speaker might do well to employ in your own speeches to inform.

First, the speech takes up only a small part—the very beginning—of a much larger theory of how life began and evolved. Limiting the topic, thus, permits detailed coverage in the short time allowed for the speech.

Second, the topic is one inherently interesting to educated people. The mystery of life's origin has always been a source of much specula- tion, and her introduction tells us this as well as employing the aura of mystery and suspense to add interest. The second paragraph clearly states the thesis of the speech and divides it into the two main ideas which the speaker intends to explain. Thus the audience has been told "what the speaker is going to tell them."

Note that the body of the speech is neatly divided into the two main ideas, one on the theory of the composition of the early earth and the second on the experimentation which has shown that *organic* mate- rials could be produced from the *inorganic* materials. In fact, the body of the speech might be outlined thus:

I. Scientists believe the earth contained all the inorganic elements necessary for contemporary life.
   A. Support, details, etc.
   B. Support, details, etc.
II. Scientists have demonstrated in the laboratory that the *inorganic* materials present in the early earth could have produced *organic* materials.
   A. Support, details, etc.
   B. Support, details, etc.

The speech uses a clear, simple visual aid, as well as specific and detailed supporting materials. Specific figures and names of experi- menters are supplied. Actual experiments are explained. How the apparatus works in one experiment is shown verbally and graphically. The need for a power source as a catalyst to the inorganic materials was compared to the need of a striking friction in order to light a match, a literal analogy since the two events are alike in principle. The names of the inorganic and organic materials are repeated several times throughout the speech, to reinforce the audience's memory of these details; frequent summaries and other repetitions are used. Clear-cut transitions between main and other points are employed. The language of the speech demonstrates many characteristics of a good oral style (Chapter 9) including much direct address to the audience and refer- ences to the speaker. Finally the conclusion of the speech, the last paragraph, aptly summarizes the thesis and the two main ideas of the speech. The last short sentence "rounds off" the speech conclusively.

In short, this is a speech to inform on a well-limited aspect of an important subject which is related to audience interests, and it lucidly explains the subject in clear oral style and with adequate supporting material. It is organized into two clearly distinguishable main ideas which are repeated several times and separated by clear transitions. And, most importantly, it depends for its effectiveness upon the learning of a single concept, a "proven" theory that the inorganic elements believed to be present in the early earth *could* have reacted together to produce organic materials. Even if the audience should forget the actual elements involved, the details of Miller's apparatus, and so on, they would be able to at least partially reconstruct some of these details from the *concept* of the theory they had learned.

The above speech, in other words, is a useful model for your own informative speeches—a model not merely to copy or imitate, but one you would do well to emulate.

THE ORAL REPORT

For four reasons the writers of this book feel that what we call the "oral report" is a distinct type of speech to inform.

1. The person who presents it is usually assigned the responsibility for making it.
2. The audience (either one person or a group) has generally assigned the responsibility for the making of the report.
3. The content of the oral report tends to be specialized and technical, usually based upon some specific investigation.
4. Because of its peculiar content, the oral report seems to fit best into its own unique pattern of arrangement.

What kind of person makes an oral report? One might be a chemist working in an industrial laboratory, who reports on an experiment designed to produce and test a better glue for furniture manufacturing. Another could be a member of a fraternal organization giving a committee report on the committee's investigation into and recommendations for the furnishings of a new club room. A junior vice president of a company reports on his investigation into reasons why an order takes an average of five days from the time it comes into the plant until the merchandise leaves Shipping and Receiving. There are hundreds of different types of oral reports, but the above three give some idea of the variety.

Who hears oral reports? Persons who "assigned" them in the first place, usually. The chemist reporting on his glue experiments was probably given the task of conducting experiments and then reporting on them by his superior. The "furnishings committee" was probably elected from the floor in a motion before a full membership meeting and given its task, with perhaps even a specified meeting date on which to report its findings. The vice president was probably assigned his job on the order-filling problem by his superior or a group of superiors.

What kind of content is unique to the oral report? As indicated above, it is usually concerned with a somewhat original investigation carried out by one or more members of a firm or organization for the purpose of solving a specific problem.

What kind of arrangement best suits the oral report's contents? As with any other speech, the report should consist of three parts—the introduction, body, and conclusion.

The introduction should establish interest and attention, and should clearly state the thesis or subject of the report. Reasons for the need for the investigation might be included. Since the audience is presumably already highly interested in the content of the report, there is usually less emphasis upon interest material in the introduction, and the "history" of how the investigation came to be conducted might suffice for interest material. The history would then lead up logically to the statement of the report's thesis or subject.

The data or findings of your report will be the meat of the report but this should come last in the body of the speech. Since the quality or usefulness of your data or findings is directly related to and a function of how carefully and thoroughly they were arrived at, the first part of the body of the report should be an explanation of how the data were gathered.

If you are reporting on a survey, for example, you will tell clearly and accurately how you picked your sample of the population to be surveyed, how the questions were chosen and worded, who asked the questions, and under what conditions they were asked. In the case of some laboratory-type experiment, you would tell how the experimental or "causational" variable was selected, measured, validated, and manipulated. For instance, you might report that, "To the experimental speech were added eight jokes chosen from a group of twenty by fifteen undergraduate students as funniest." You would tell your audience how you measured the dependent variable (or *effect* of the experiment). For instance: "The attitudes of the subjects hearing the funny and the non-funny speeches were measured by six semantic differential scales found by Osgood and colleagues to measure evaluation." Then you would state your standards or criteria for evaluating your results: "The five per cent level of statistical significance was set for evaluating whether the experimental speech produced different evaluations, or attitude, as compared with that produced by the control speech."

First, your conclusion might be your recommendation on what action should be taken: "Therefore I recommend that glue from Process 437 be substituted for the glue we now use." "So our committee recommends the package plan of furnishings offered to us by Hennings Department Store." "We therefore recommend that an additional employee be hired to help Miss Jones in the mailroom and that we automate Shipping and Receiving."

Perhaps your superior is the type of person who dislikes having underlings make recommendations to him. Your conclusion, then, might simply be a brief evaluation of the investigation and its findings: "I was only able to observe Miss Jones for two days, and that might not be a long enough period to ascertain a reliable estimate of her work load. Furthermore, ..."

Your conclusion might consist of a combination of an "evaluation" and the "recommendation": "The tests we conducted were rigidly and thoroughly controlled under various combinations of heat, humidity, and stress. Therefore, I recommend the glue from Process 437 . . . ."

A brief, skeletal outline of the oral report might look like this:

Introduction:
I. History of the problem and / or other interest material.
II. Thesis statement, or purpose of investigation.

Body:
I. How the investigation was carried out.
II. Standards for judging results.
III. Results.
   A. Data.
   B. Implications of data.

Conclusion
I. Evaluation of study, or
II. Recommendations, or
III. Both.

One final point about the oral report. Since it involves, either implicitly or explicitly, evaluation and/or recommendations for action, it inherently involves elements of *persuasion*. It is, after all, usually given as the result of investigating some problem that needs to be solved. However, it is included here as a form of speech to inform because of the high ratio of information to evaluation or recommendations.

EXERCISES/ASSIGNMENTS

1. Prepare a four to six minute informative speech in which you clearly explain the basic steps in a process. Use visual aids when appropriate.

2. Prepare a four to six minute informative speech in which you will present instructions to an audience on some activity. For example, you might discuss a camping trip all of you are about to take, reminding them of equipment they will need, the schedule they will follow, and so forth.

3. Prepare a three to four minute oral report in which you will explain the organizational structure and chain of command in an organization (business, education, church, government).

4. Prepare a three to five minute statement in which you define a concept such as liberty, love, brotherhood, democracy, prejudice, or freedom.

5. Prepare an introduction of several sentences for a speech on each of the following topics. Stress in these introductions the reasons the audience (your classmates) should want to learn the information in the speech.
   - How to navigate an airplane by dead reckoning.
   - The aerodynamics of hot-air balloons.
   - Understanding the concept of "Double Jeopardy."
   - How to use the library's special collections holdings.
   - Features to be found in a topographical map.

6. Read a newspaper or magazine article on a complicated national or international news story. Reorganize it into main and supporting points as if for a speech to inform. How would this new organization differ from the journalistic organization? In a speech would you retain all the information in the article? Would you wish to add more? Would you provide for more repetition of some points in the speech?

7. Assume you have been appointed by your club, fraternity, service organization to be a committee of one to investigate the feasibility of making a purchase for the organization (new T.V. set, record player, pool table, etc.). Develop a plan for visiting the stores in your area which sell the item. Develop a set of questions you would ask at each store to determine the best buy for your organization. Then make a brief outline of how you would make your oral report at a meeting of your organization once you had completed your investigation.

CHAPTER 11

THE PROBLEM-SOLVING PROCESS

$\mathcal{A}$lthough people have achieved impressive accomplishments in areas of society such as transportation, medicine, education, and space exploration, we continue to confront very serious social problems. In this chapter we discuss in detail the importance and role of the Problem-Solving Process to the speaking situation.

There is a critical need to know more about how problems can be solved. Today we are confronted with our desire for material progress while, at the same time, preserving the quality of the air and water in our environment. We wonder how countries with conflicting political philosophies can get along peacefully in the world. Concerned citizens ask what can be done about corruption in government, human poverty, unequal opportunity, and discrimination because of race, sex, creed, or color. Our present and future lives will, to a large degree, depend upon the choices we make. Making enlightened cooperative decisions is a basic concern of this book. Wise choices require both self-enlightenment and meaningful communication with others. In our study of the Problem-Solving Process we will first consider the wide variety of communication which we might encounter.

COMMUNICATION COMBINATIONS

The Problem-Solving Process is the procedure by which one or more persons go from the recognition of a problem, such as decline in reading skills among elementary pupils, to actually doing something about increasing the reading skills—from communicative analysis of the problem to action. If you were to study only on your own the problem of poor motivation for learning among college students, the process would stop with self-enlightenment. If you go beyond learning and try to solve the problem, this means communicating with others in order to improve student motivation.

Before looking at each step in the Problem-Solving Process, you should have a clear picture of the part speaking can play in that procedure. A few examples will demonstrate the kinds of communication combinations which might occur. One person could face a personal problem and decide to think through the problem mostly on his own and might well reach a decision without involving others. But here too, when struggling with a personal concern, one would do well to consider the Problem-Solving Procedure discussed below. Such a consideration might not be as formal or as organized as if one were working with other people, but the method of analysis explained below would be helpful.

A second example of how speaking contributes to the solution of problems is when one works with a group. Members of a Chamber of Commerce meet to discuss the increase in shoplifting in their community. In this situation one is involved with other people from the beginning. A third example is a woman who decides on her own to improve the playground equipment at a local public school. After studying the situation carefully she must now come into communication with persons who have the authority to do something about the equipment. So we have seen three examples, one when a person communicated with himself, a second when a group worked together, and a third when a woman worked alone until she found it necessary to communicate with others.

Regardless of the nature of the situation or the problem, the activity which is common to all is speaking. Now that we have explained several kinds of speaking situations, we will present three broad areas of the Problem-Solving Process: the problem, the solution, and the implementation of the solution. While our discussion at times may sound quite prescriptive, most social problems are such that one cannot prescribe an easy cure. These three areas should be thought of as the fundamentals of problem solving, not a sure plan one always follows. Each personal and social problem is different and complex. We believe the insight you gain from understanding this process will help. But you must contribute much to the situation as you make wise choices. Communication with other people becomes critical, for only by sharing concerns and suggestions can you make the best decisions.

THE PROBLEM

Whether you are concerned about the sales of hard drugs in your community or the decline of membership in your favorite organization, the first step is to study the problem.

Recognition of the Problem

Too often in society and in courses in speaking, persons rush to offer advice or persuade an audience to believe a certain way or take a specific action before they understand if there is a problem or what the problem is. On occasions the problem is obvious. A school building roof may be leaking and impossible to ignore. A private school which yearly goes further in debt has an obvious problem. With such conspicuous situations the speaking assignment is to communicate clearly to the appropriate persons the presence of the difficulty.

On occasions it is difficult to communicate to others that a need exists. A soldier may observe misconduct on the part of some fellow soldiers in a war zone, but communicating that activity not only takes great courage but also considerable strategy. Organizations and individuals resist public communication about their own failures. A worker in a political campaign who witnesses illegal campaign tactics or an executive who learns of illegal transactions may confront powerful obstacles when simply attempting to speak about his observations. The task of reporting the recognition of a problem can be complex.

Defining the problem, then, is important. Life is too complex to study as a whole, but we can take one segment at a time and accumulatively improve society. Define the need carefully and you will help communicate a better awareness of the situation.

Analysis of the Problem

To understand a problem one must analyze it. To analyze a problem is to partition it into its inherent parts and to discover its causes. Can you imagine a physician taking a quick look at a rash on your left arm and, without further inquiry into what caused the rash, prescribing surgery to remove your limb? Such an example sounds absurd, but we often approach social problems in this manner. On the basis of little study and consideration of causes people conclude that: "All welfare programs should be abolished," or "The government should guarantee each family an income of $6,000." Too often we are willing to prescribe instant remedies to complex social situations without prior analysis. Communication which ignores causes is not likely to be as successful as it should be.

Causal analysis is critical to your understanding of human events and to the successful analysis of social problems. How you perceive an event to have been caused will determine to some degree what you would recommend to imporve the situation. What, for example, would you believe if you saw a youth throw a brick through a window? If you immediately said, "That mean bum should be locked up," your understanding of the event probably is that meanness caused the youth to throw the brick. This causal reasoning would then help determine how you would solve the problem. Either you would look for some way to rid the youth of his "meanness" or you would throw up your hands and advocate getting him off the streets and into a jail. What, however, if you perceived the event differently—that the brick-throwing was caused by deep personal frustrations? This causal conclusion would lead you to ask, "What caused the frustration?" His frustration might be caused by lack of parental interests, inadequate schools, forced unemployment, no opportunity for meaningful recreation, and so on. This second perception of the event would influence one to advocate quite different solutions from the first. Here the person would probably recommend specific programs to provide the youth an opportunity to develop his or her potential as a human being.

To find the causes of a problem often involves study of the history as well as the present conditions of a situation. For example, if you wanted to do something about traffic congestion in a large city, whether as an individual or with other people, you would do well to research the background of that subject before recommending that "all cars be abolished" or that "we allow the problem to work itself out." One must ask: When did the problem begin? What was done (or not done) earlier to better control traffic? Why didn't these plans work? Why weren't certain actions which were advocated earlier implemented? Did public opinion prevent meaningful actions? Were funds not available? Do the same obstacles still exist? If so can something be done now which will overcome the obstacles?

Finally one works his way up to the present situation: Does a serious problem now exist? What is the problem? What are the causes of the problem? With the traffic problem, is it caused by the number of vehicles? Is it the kinds of vehicles? Is it the roads? Is it the fuel? Or is the source of the difficulty the attitude of the public? What available solutions are being tried, which ignored? Why?

In determining whether a possible cause is the only cause of the problem there are certain tests one can apply. With an earlier example used, that of the person with a rash on the arm, the physician might have allergy tests made and discover that a certain food caused the rash. Thus, the doctor knows how to cure the rash. With sociopolitical problems, however, isolating causes seldom is so easy. What are the actual causes of pollution, poverty, human frustration, and political corruption? Because the causes are difficult does not change our aim; we should search diligently for the causes so our recommended solution will be sound. When testing possible causes of a problem, ask the following questions: Can a causal relationship be demonstrated (for example, between "meanness" and "brick throwing" or between "personal frustration" and "brick throwing")? Is the alleged cause adequate to produce the alleged effect? Are there possibly several causes of the problem? Are there forces at work which prevent a probable cause from being the correct one? Such tests are vital to the success of the Problem-Solving Process. A mistake in the analysis of the causes of the problem will be reflected accumulatively in the results of the Problem-Solving Process. An awareness of the perils of faulty causal analysis warns us not to rush to advocate a position which we really don't fully understand, but to approach complex social problems with some sense of humility. There will be times when our goal is to persuade the listeners, not that we have found the best solution, but of the fact that a problem does exist and they should join the search for a better understanding of the problem and for the most appropriate solution.

The first step of the Problem-Solving Process, then, is a careful study of the problem. Two examples of this stage are outlined below. Notice how different factors, such as "lack of work," could be either a "cause," a "sympton," or an "effect." How one analyzes the problem reflects his perception of it. Two different perceptions of a human situation are provided in the two examples.

THE PROBLEM

Symptoms	Causes	Effect
Example 1: Shabby clothes, poor health, loitering.	Lack of work, poor education, small income.	Depressive condition of personal poverty.
Example 2: Shabby clothes, poor health, loitering.	Laziness, meanness, "no good."	A person who won't take advantage of his or her opportunities.

THE SOLUTION

The second step of the Problem-Solving Process is the solution stage. Now that the individual or group has a thorough knowledge of the problem and its probable causes, they are in a position to consider alternative actions.

As noted above, your perception of the problem and its causes will influence the line of reasoning and solution you will suggest. For example, after one of the large urban riots in the 1960's, some persons advocated "more policemen." Later it was discovered that one basic cause of the unrest was the inability of the people in the area to find transportation from their neighborhood to their places of work. While "more policemen" may have been necessary to keep order during the event, if one hoped to offer a long-range plan he would have to also consider the causes, one being the matter of transportation from home to work.

Consideration of Criteria

In addition to causes one must also ask what criteria or standards his or her solution should meet. For example, if one were considering a way to repair a leaking roof he would have to weigh the criteria of cost, time, looks, labor, extent of damage, age of the roof, insurance, and others. Some solution criteria, such as cost and time, are so commonly appropriate to so many different possible problems that they might be called "stock criteria." Other factors grow more out of the peculiar nature of the problem. For example, the list of criteria one would consider when raising taxes not only includes economic matters but also public opinion.

If you do not consider causes and criteria during the solution stage, you will confront them when you later attempt to implement a solution. Then, however, they will be obstacles to implementation. For example if, during the solution stage, you decide to use a rare material for a new roof without any concern for the criteria of cost and availability of materials, when you go to purchase the material it may be too costly if available at all. Time invested in careful deliberation of the nature of a problem, criteria, and causes is time well spent.

Weighing Alternative Solutions

After defining the problem and studying criteria by which you will judge solutions, you are now ready to consider all possible solutions. The purpose here is to gather as many ideas and alternatives as possible; welcome all suggestions. Most persons will attend a meeting with personal preferences as to what should be done. It takes self-control to be willing to listen fairly to the preferences of others. Yet this is an important aspect of problem solving. If we develop an attitude of inquiry and cooperation and are open to all suggestions, we are less apt to be ruled by prejudice and poor information. After the possibilities are exhausted, you are ready to weigh each suggestion and combinations of alternatives to determine whether they treat the causes of the problem and fit within the selected criteria.

Choosing a Solution

Finally, in the solution stage of the Problem-Solving Process, one person or a group decides upon the best solution. This may mean a compromise with one's own thinking or among several persons in an organization. What you or the majority in a group may believe to be the best decision may cost too much or take too long to implement. The solution which best removes the causes of the problem and meets the criteria you established (such as cost, feasibility, public opinion, time, and honesty) is one you can defend with considerable confidence. The first two stages of the Problem-Solving Process can be summarized as follows:

THE PROBLEM

THE SOLUTION

	Symptoms	Causes	Effect	Possible Solutions	Criteria	Best Solution
Example 1:	Shabby clothes, poor health, loitering.	Lack of work, poor education, small income.	Depressive condition of personal poverty.	Federal work program, state work program, program sponsored by private industry, vocational schools, adaptation of college education, adaptation of public schools.	Cost, time, public opinion.	Program jointly sponsored by business community and state government, integrating education and employment opportunities.
Example 2:	Shabby clothes, poor health, loitering.	Laziness, meaness, "no good."	A person who won't take advantage of his or her opportunities.	Put loiterers in jail, pass a clothing code, if a person wants to be lazy let him, be certain he does not break the law.	Rights of poor, needs of society, available funds, economic conditions, attitudes of businessmen, educators, and government officials, job market.	Build more jails and put lazy loiterers in them.

IMPLEMENTATION OF THE SOLUTION

The third step in the Problem-Solving Process is the implementation of the selected solution. It is one thing to reach a decision in theory, whether by one person or a group, and something entirely different to have that decision accepted. What, for example, if you personally decided you wanted to stop a particular factory from pouring pollutants into a river near your home? Or what if you had been meeting with other people periodically for six months and had decided on a specific plan to reduce crime in your community? In the first example, you now are faced with the difficult task of convincing persons with decision-making power in the local factory to make changes in order to stop the pollution of the river, changes which will add to their expenses. Not an easy job! In the second case the work of simply identifying all the necessary people and agencies concerned with crime would be a challenge. Would you work through the town council or the county commissioners? At what point would state and federal laws and officials have to be considered? Unless your solution is only something like, "Everybody write your congressman," the task of implementation will involve as much planning, organization, and communication as the discovery of the solution.

One is faced with the challenge of communicating his recommendations to the appropriate decision-making person or body. If the person or group which reached the solution has the authority to implement the solution the task is easier, but they still must convince others involved that it is an improvement over the present procedure and deserves support. Usually, however, solutions have to be sold to a board of directors, the person next up the chain of command, or to the public.

After the solution has been explained and advocated, three factors are critical to the implementation of the solution: the persons who want a change, persons who must be influenced if the suggested change is to take place, and situational factors which should be considered.

Role of Speaker

After going through the first two stages of the problem-solving analysis—consideration of the nature of the problem and the best solution—the persons who want a change are in a confident position. Unlike the speaker who has a beautifully polished speech but little understanding of his subject, this person (or persons) is well informed. He is not disturbed by difficult questions. Usually such questions have already been confronted in earlier steps in the Problem-Solving Process. Those who are advocating the solution welcome the opportunity to share their insights and findings with those who may not have their background or knowledge. When one works long and hard on a project, he is delighted with the chance to show what has been accomplished. One can be open and candid and quite willing to listen to suggestions by others, suggestions not thought of before. After all, the purpose is not to win points but to improve a situation. The best strategy and most convincing argument may be simply to explain as carefully and as candidly as one possibly can the definition and nature of the problem, its causes, some of the better solutions considered, and why a particular solution was chosen. In other words, those persons advocating a new program take the audience on a verbal tour of the analysis they went through in getting to their present thinking on the subject. There may be, however, a more appropriate method of organizing one's presentation of the solution. Other methods are discussed in Chapter 5.

Role of Audience

This brings us to the second aspect of the implementation-speaking situation—the persons who must be influenced if the suggested change is to take place. The person or persons with final decision-making authority may vary greatly. If you are the only one involved in the entire Problem-Solving Process, you have to convince yourself: to go back to school; to take a job, to take a trip. When others are involved you first must discover who has the responsibility or authority to make the final decision. This may be the president of a company, the faculty, students, a Chamber of Commerce, or a body of government. Public opinion, possibly involving a vote, may be the final arbiter.

After deciding who has the decision-making power, you or your group will attempt to convince that person or persons that your suggested solution will remedy a recognized problem and thus merits adoption. Your strategy will depend upon how your "audience" perceives the situation. If those who have power to make a change do not view the situation as a problem, you must first demonstrate that there is indeed a problem. If you have followed the Problem-Solving Process carefully and candidly you will know the nature, extent, and probable causes. You now have to share those findings with the decision-making body. If, however, you are unable under rigorous questioning and deliberation to demonstrate a justification for a new way of looking at what you perceive as a problem, you will likely fail in your attempt to have your recommendation adopted. Remember, the decision makers may perceive the entire subject differently from you because of self-interests, tradition, ignorance, cost, public pressure, lobbyists, sincere concern for people, different personal experiences relating to the topic at hand, and other factors. Communicating with persons with perceptions different from your own about complex social problems is extremely difficult under the best of conditions. Even after having convinced yourself of the worth of a particular solution on the basis of long hours of research, study, and reflection, you will have to explain your thinking in such a way as to ensure your plan a fair hearing. Unless the situation is of crisis proportions and easily recognized, there is a tendency for people to avoid or ignore it. Review Chapter 3 on audience analysis for more help in adapting to such attitudes.

Situational Factors

The third aspect of the implementation stage includes the situational factors involved. Of course audience reactions could be considered a factor of the speaking situation. Other factors are sociopolitical forces at work at the time, economic conditions, interests of different parties, personal prejudices, knowledge of the subject, quality of the solution, the occasion, personalities involved, profit, concern for quality of life, intensity of the problem, immediacy of the problem, ability to communicate, and others. These examples are listed to illustrate the wide variety of determinants which can influence whether even a defensible solution can be implemented. Some of the factors may seem more "reasonable" than others, but any or all could delay implementation of the solution or prevent its adoption. There is no prescription one can write which will guarantee the desired results. Each speaking situation is one of a kind. Look for factors, inherent to the situation and subject with which you are concerned, that will influence how your solution will be received. At every step in the Problem-Solving Process important judgments have to be made concerning these situational factors. If you have analyzed the nature and causes of the problem, have carefully weighed all possible solutions, and have, on the basis of the causes of the problem and the criteria established, selected what seems to be the best solution, you can have considerable confidence in your understanding of the situation and in your recommended remedy. Your entire problem-solving procedure can be charted as follows:

THE PROBLEM

Symptons	Causes	Effect
Example 1: Shabby clothes, poor health, lazy, loitering. *Example 2:* Shabby clothes, poor health, loitering.	Lack of work, poor education, small income. Laziness, meanness, "no good."	Depressive condition of personal poverty. A person who won't take advantage of his or her opportunities.

THE SOLUTION

Possible Solutions	Criteria	Best Solution
Federal work program, state work program, program sponsored by private industry, vocational schools, adaptation of college education, adaptation of public schools.	Cost, time, public opinion.	Program jointly sponsored by business community and state government, integrating education and employment opportunities.
Put loiterers in jail, pass a clothing code, if a person wants to be lazy let him, be certain he does not break the law.	Rights of poor, needs of society, available funds, economic conditions, attitudes of businessmen, educators, and government officials, job market.	Build more jails and put lazy loiterers in them.

IMPLEMENTATION

Strategy of Persons Advocating Change	Persons Who Must Be Convinced	Situational Factors To Be Considered
To enlighten and persuade officials through problem-solving method of analysis and organization.	State government officials, leaders in business community, leaders in education, the public generally.	Cost, workability, availability of personnel, attitude of persons in government, business, education, and the home, time involved, probable results.
Show common sense of a solution which rewards those who do their part in society, while not rewarding those who do not do their part.	Government officials, the public generally.	Attitude of persons in government and in society generally, reaction of the poor, cost to society of effects of poverty, morality of the decision.

THE PROBLEM-SOLVING PROCESS: A CONTINUING PHENOMENON

In the discussion above concerning how the Problem-Solving Process operates, there appears to be the implication that most problems can be solved by this formula. This is not always true. Most problems of society (economic, religious, educational, political, social) are complex and not easily analyzed or solved. Even experts may disagree as to the causes and cures of problems relating to alcohol, drugs, poverty, education, business, government, and human relations. Often we have been deceived, and we have deceived ourselves, into believing that some candidate, party, or group has *the* platform for progress. In fact the progress of individuals and society undergoes constant change.

With many perplexing situations there are times when we have to act before we fully understand their nature and their causes. If society is threatened by crime, we may have to attempt to do something to help prior to discovering the causes and the best long-range course to follow. One cannot always wait before taking initial action. Also, such situations are continuously changing and so demand preventative measures and long-range planning.

Although we should study a problem carefully, search for the causes of that problem, and conceive a workable solution, many social matters will demand constant attention. With the many problems where no final solution has been discovered, communication becomes even more critical. Channels of communication should be open and active. Accurate and continuous communication is vital because so many social and human matters are unpredictable; you have to feel your way as you go from decision to decision. The success of your choices will depend to a large degree upon how well individuals and groups communicate about the problem. To achieve understanding of matters in society one would do well to first study the Problem-Solving Process.

EXERCISES/ASSIGNMENTS

1. Study a situation in your community where people are attempting to solve a specific problem. Keep a record of the people involved and the kinds of speaking which take place.
2. Select a problem you believe needs attention and, using the Problem-Solving Process, analyze the problem and decide what should be done and how you should go about it.

3. Interview a person in a business, school, church, or government office and ask the person what method he uses to solve problems.

4. Study a problem situation that existed in the past. Using the Problem-Solving Process, show why the solutions attempted did or did not work.

CHAPTER 12

PERSUASIVE SPEAKING

$\mathbb{T}$ his chapter is concerned with how one constructs persuasive speeches to accomplish particular goals. As a starting point, let us offer a working definition: *Persuasive speaking is the use of verbal and nonverbal communication to affect attitudes and/or behavior.* In Chapter 10 the topic of informative speaking was covered. Informative speaking is primarily intended to raise the audience's informational level only. In persuasive speaking there is always some "informing," but the purpose of using the information in the speech is to create, shape, modify, strengthen, or weaken audience *attitude* and/or to cause them to do or not do some particular act. Much of what has already been said in regard to speech making in general applies to persuasive speaking. However, there are three major topics which have been dealt with earlier that deserve special notation at this juncture: *supporting materials, methods of organization,* and *types of reasoning.*

The topic of supporting materials was discussed in detail in Chapter 6. The major supporting materials discussed were the following: facts, statistics, examples, comparison and contrast, testimony, restatement, repetition, definition, and description. These same major categories of supporting materials are important to the persuasive speaker.

Methods of organization were considered in Chapter 5. The major organizational approaches discussed there, namely, chronological, spatial, topical, cause-effect, and problem solution are likewise useful in persuasive speaking. In this chapter we have added a consideration of the motivated sequence as an additional organizational strategy that is available to the persuasive speaker.

The third and final area that deserves mention is the types of reasoning that were elaborated in Chapter 6. At that time we considered the following types of reasoning: use of authority, cause and effect, analogy, induction, deduction. These types of reasoning are of major importance to persuasion. At this point we would suggest that the reader reread these three critical areas of supporting materials, methods of organization, and types of reasoning, as they will be most helpful to him as he prepares to study and practice persuasive speaking.

We will approach persuasive speaking from the following perspectives: (1) the nature of persuasion, (2) the relationship between motivation and persuasion and (3) the contributions of empirical research to persuasive speaking.

THE NATURE OF PERSUASION

To develop an understanding of persuasive speaking you should know something of the history of the subject. Persuasive speaking and attempts to teach persuasive speaking flourished during Greek civilization. During the fifth century B.C. speech teachers, called Sophists, provided their students with intensive training in persuasive speaking as an important part of their liberal education. Some of the early Sophists included Gorgias, Hippias, and Corax. Corax is usually credited for developing one of the first systematic approaches to persuasive speaking. Central to his system of persuasion was the concept of probability. That concept simply meant that a speaker attempting to persuade should use arguments which are plausible. That may seem like common sense today, but in mid-fifth century B.C. it represented one of the first principles in what was to become a substantial body of literature dealing with the topic of persuasive speaking. Aristotle (384–322 B.C.) wrote the most important and influential treatment of persuasive speaking during the classical period.

Aristotle and the Modes of Persuasion

Aristotle defined rhetoric as "the faculty of observing in any given case the available means of persuasion." Aristotle maintained that there were three major means of persuasion, and he described them in the following manner in his book, the *Rhetoric:*

> Of the modes of persuasion furnished by the spoken word there are three kinds. The first kind depends on the personal character of the speaker; the second on putting the audience into a certain frame of mind; the third on the proof, or apparent proof, provided by the words of the speech itself. Persuasion is achieved by the speaker's personal character when the speech is so spoken as to make us think him credible. We believe good men more fully and more readily than others: this is true generally whatever the question is, and absolutely true where exact certainty is impossible and opinions are divided. This kind of persuasion, like the others, should be achieved by what the speaker says, not by what people think of his character before he begins to speak. It is not true, as some writers assume in their treatises on rhetoric, that the personal goodness

revealed by the speaker contributes nothing to his power of persuasion; on the contrary, his character may almost be called the most effective means of persuasion he possesses. Secondly, persuasion may come through the hearers, when the speech stirs their emotions. Our judgements when we are pleased and friendly are not the same as when we are pained and hostile. It is towards producing these effects, as we maintain, that present-day writers on rhetoric direct the whole of their efforts. This subject shall be treated in detail when we come to speak of the emotions. Thirdly, persuasion is affected through the speech itself when we have proved a truth or an apparent truth by means of the persuasive arguments suitable to the case in question.[1]

Those three major modes of persuasion—ethos, pathos, and logos—are still referred to today by many writers in the area of persuasion. Let us examine what recent scholars of persuasion say about these three kinds of proof.

Ethos.   Ethos or ethical proof refers to the quality of proof that is found in the speaker himself. In other words, if you tend to believe (or disbelieve) what a speaker says mostly because of *who the speaker is,* you have been persuaded primarily by that speaker's ethos. Most students of persuasion, including Aristotle, distinguish between two kinds of ethos, what we might call "acquired ethos" (or reputation) and "developed ethos."

Acquired ethos—reputation—is that ethos which the speaker brings to the speaking situation based upon past actions and performance. If you are impressed (or disenchanted) with the speaker because of his present or past public offices, his wealth, his associates, his education, his past speeches and/or writings, and other factors, this reputation will affect how you respond to his persuasive messages. If he has a good reputation with you, you will tend to believe him; if you have grown to dislike and distrust the man because of his past and present activities, you will tend to reject his proposals.

Few beginning speakers have much of a reputation as experts or as speakers worthy of instant credibility. They must depend upon "developing" ethos *while* they are speaking.

How is this done? How does a speaker gain credibility as he speaks? Research studies in the field of speech communication reveal that a number of speaking attributes will help the speaker develop ethos. These are: (1) specific, clear, and fresh supporting materials; (2) poise and forcefulness in delivery; (3) manifestation of an appearance of earnestness and sincerity; and (4) even a sense of humor.

1. Aristotle, *Rhetorica,* trans. W. Rhys Roberts, in *The Basic Works of Aristotle,* ed. Richard McKeon, Random House, 1941), pp. 1329–30.

Audiences tend to believe the speaker who seems to know what he is talking about, who has at his disposal facts, statistics, examples, analogies, testimony, and other materials to support his contentions; who speaks as if he is so "wrapped up" in his speech that he has lost all self-consciousness and is speaking to his audience "from the heart"; and who does not take himself so seriously that he cannot smile at his own foibles.

Pathos.   Pathos, or what is often referred to as "emotional proof," is that form of proof which resides within the audience itself. Why do we say that *proof* resides within the *audience?* It is because people share in common many types of emotion. When these emotions are properly appealed to by a speaker, and the audience responds favorably, the speaker has utilized qualities already possessed by the audience. For instance, people universally fear injury and death. If a speaker can convince you that there is a good likelihood that you will become injured or killed unless his proposal is adopted, you will probably adopt his proposal.

Modern writers tend to place the consideration of emotions under the topic of "motives" because emotions are usually aroused by appeals to motives, and these appeals to motives will in turn arouse the emotions. Brigance, for example, argues that speakers should speak to motives rather than emotions:

> People have emotions to be sure. But effective speakers usually don't deal with them as such. Rather, they deal with wants, motives, hopes, ideals, ambitions and those habits of society known as culture patterns. Therefore, it is more effective for speakers to think in terms of these human drives with which they must deal: wants, motives, hopes, ideals, ambition, and culture patterns.[2]

Some people in the speech communication field contend that the use of pathos should be given little priority; many consider it "unfair" to play upon the emotions of a "helpless" audience. We believe that all kinds of proof should be used responsibly and with the highest integrity. There is no doubt that emotional appeals are more persuasive than nonemotional appeals; this contention is supported by a number of research studies, such as an early study by Hartman quoted by Minnick:

> Hartman prepared two leaflets urging people to vote for the Socialist Party. One of these leaflets was emotionalized by pointing out the threat of war, economic depression, and the like, and emphasizing the satisfactions to be gained from a

2. William Brigance, *Speech: Its Techniques and Disciplines in a Free Society* (New York: Appleton-Century-Crofts, 1961), p. 153.

Socialist program. The other leaflet, a so-called "rational" leaflet, merely set forth a series of statements encompassing major aspects of the Socialist program and urged those who agreed with the statements to vote Socialist. One groups of wards received the emotional leaflet; another group received the "rational" leaflet; a third, serving as a control group, received no communication at all. These were the results:

In the wards receiving the emotional communication, the Socialist vote increased 50 percent.

In the wards receiving the "rational" communication, the Socialist vote increased 35 percent.

In the wards that received no communication, the Socialist vote increased 25 percent.

In this and subsequent experiments of the same type, two factors appeared to account for the greater effectiveness of the emotion-arousing communication. First, emotion tends to focus attention on the communication and to prevent mind-wandering. Second, since the emotional communication stresses the relationship of the communication to the listener's needs and wants (and improves attention), it probably increases the listener's comprehension of the material.[3]

Logos. We say that logos, or logical proof, resides in the speech since it refers to the logical materials used by the speaker to develop his ideas. This type proof consists of evidence, arguments, and other supporting materials covered in detail in Chapter 6.[4]

In summary, ethical proof is that type of proof which is found in the character or reputation of the speaker. Emotional proof is directed toward the motives and emotions of the audience, and logical proof comes from the type of supporting materials and the way the speaker uses them. While we have described the three major forms of persuasion independently, we have done so only for purpose of clarification and explanation. In reality the three forms of proof—ethos, pathos, and logos—are interrelated. Frequently, audiences cannot distinguish between the three types and even communication experts cannot always agree as to how persuasive appeals should be classified.

Persuasion and Attitude Change

At the start of this chapter we noted that persuasive speaking was concerned with influencing attitudes. Current ideas about persuasion necessitate some basic understanding of what attitudes are and how they change. An attitude may be defined as a psychological set to act in

3. Wayne Minnick. *The Art of Persuasion.* 2nd ed. Boston: Houghton Mifflin Company, 1968), p. 239.

4. See Samuel L. Becker, "Research on Emotional and Logical Proofs," *Southern Speech Journal* 27 (Spring 1963), pp. 198–207.

a particular way under certain circumstances. For instance, if you hold a generally favorable attitude toward your town's public schools, you are likely to vote for a school bond issue should such a vote take place. Attitudes of people can be discovered, in general, in two ways: you can observe their overt, observable behavior, or you can *ask* them what their attitudes are.

A logical question to arise at this point is how do people develop and change attitudes. One answer to that question is provided by Sarnoff, Katz, and McClintock when they suggest that people are likely to develop and alter their attitudes in the following three motivational contexts:

> (1) Attitudes may be acquired in the interest of rationally structuring the individual's world and of testing what the world is like; (2) they may be formed as an adaptation to rewards and punishments imposed by the social situation; and (3) they may be a function of the ego-defensive needs of the individual.[5]

Sarnoff and colleagues go on to point out that any one person is likely to have different attitudes anchored in different motivational contexts. For instance, a school teacher may have developed an attitude which has led him to become a "defensive driver" because his experience indicates to him that some careless driver may smash into him if he does not drive defensively. He may have grown up to be a Republican (or a Democrat) because his family reared him to be so through praising him for making pro-Republican (or Democratic) statements as a child. So it is apparent that a persuasive speaker will need to take into accounts not only his audience's general attitude toward his topic, but how the audience was motivated to adopt that attitude. For example, if you have reason to suspect that your audience, whom you wish to persuade to use automobile seat belts regularly, is basically opposed to the use of such belts because they do not want to be considered "scaredy-cats" (ego-defensive need), your course is clear. You must convince them that others will consider them quite sensible and logical and not lacking in courage for wearing seat belts.

In recent years some writers concerned with studying persuasion and attitude change have suggested a theory called "balance" or "congruity" theory. In essence, balance theory contends that people strive to maintain an internal belief structure that is consistent. The basic components of balance theory are set forth by Minnick:

> 1. Each person develops cognitive units or attitudes toward a variety of objects and issues in his life space. The elements of such units are either all plus or all minus.

5. I. Sarnoff, D. Katz, and C. McClintock, "Attitude Change Procedures and Motivating Patterns," *Public Opinion and Propaganda*, ed. D. Katz, et al. (New York: Dryden Press, 1956), p. 307.

2. When an incongruous piece of information is communicated in relation to a particular unit, the balance is upset, and uncomfortable tension or dissonance develops which motivates the organism to restore balance.
3. Balance can be restored by restructuring the cognitive unit / attitude or by reaffirming one's own position.
4. Whether one changes his cognitive structure or reaffirms his own stand seems to depend on factors not fully understood. One of these may be where the individual places the communication on his own acceptance / rejection latitude scale.[6]

Following the directives of balance theory a persuasive speaker would essentially prepare his message to affect the audience in two ways. First, he would attempt to create imbalance or incongruity in some manner so that the listener would develop tension or dissonance in his attitude structure. Second, the speaker would show that the tension or dissonance can be alleviated if the listener restructures his attitude to closely coincide with what the speaker advocates. While the persuasive speaker is basically concerned with changing attitudes in his listeners, there are some major purposes to persuasive speaking and a consideration of those is appropriate at this point.

Purposes of Persuasive Speaking

Traditionally, persuasive speeches have been classified as speeches to convince, to actuate, and to stimulate. The speech to *convince* supposes the audience to be *opposed* to the speaker's thesis and seeks to change that opposition. An audience may be opposed, say, to amnesty for draft evaders and deserters from the armed forces, and a speaker may seek to convert their minds to an attitude favorable toward conditional amnesty. The speech to *actuate* assumes that an audience needs motivation enough to cause them to perform some overt act. A speaker might realize that his audience thinks that giving blood to the Red Cross is a nice idea, but they want nothing to do with needles. He must, therefore, motivate the audience to act upon their originally favorable view toward donating blood. The speech to *stimulate* is mostly motivational also, for it seeks to heighten belief or energize action already ongoing. For instance, the typical sermon does not seek to convince people opposed to its message; its purpose is to heighten belief in the creed and beliefs the congregation already agrees to. And the "pep talk" by the football coach at half-time or that by the sales manager at his weekly meeting with his corps of salesmen is designed to motivate their charges to work harder.

6. Minnick, *The Art of Persuasion*, p. 116.

Although the system of classifying speeches to convince, actuate, or stimulate has been a useful system throughout the years, we are of the opinion that a very useful way of incorporating speech types is the framework provided by Wallace Fotheringham.[7] His view of the persuasive purpose has two thrusts—instrumental effect and goals. Fotheringham's rationale for this type of a decision is based on the belief that a persuasive message is *part* of a total persuasive campaign. In the total persuasive campaign an individual message attempts to achieve with its audience a particular "instrumental effect," but the overall *goal* of the persuader is to achieve some particular action from his target audience.

Fotheringham's concept can be illustrated in the following example. Suppose Max Brown is running for State Superintendent of Education. Using Fotheringham's campaign diagram his persuasive campaign could be diagrammed in five stages as follows:

1. *Source:* Max Brown—Candidate for State Superintendent of Education
   Receivers: Eligible voters
   Instrumental Effect: To become known to voters
   Goal: To be elected to office
2. *Source:* Max Brown—Candidate for State Superintendent of Education
   Receivers: Eligible voters
   Instrumental Effect: To have voters believe state is falling behind educationally
   Goal: To be elected to office
3. *Source:* Max Brown—Candidate for State Superintendent of Education
   Receivers: Eligible voters
   Instrumental Effect: To have voters believe the current superintendent is incompetent as an administrator
   Goal: To be elected to office
4. *Source:* Max Brown—Candidate for State Superintendent of Education
   Receivers: Eligible voters
   Instrumental Effect: To have voters believe that currently their state is not getting its fair share of federal funds because of a lack of effort on the part of their current superintendent
   Goal: To be elected to office

7. Wallace Fotheringham, *Perspectives on Persuasion* (Boston: Allyn and Bacon, 1966).

5. *Source:* Max Brown—Candidate for State Superintendent of
   Education
   Receivers: Eligible voters
   Instrumental Effect: To convince voters that he has the ability to be an
   effective State Superintendent of Education
   Goal: To be elected to office

In all of these messages the goal of the message remained the
same, but the instrumental effect changed. In any persuasive speaking
situation the speaker must keep not only his goal in mind but also what
instrumental effect he strives for with a particular message. It would
appear that the concept of *instrumental effect* is helpful in determining
the role of persuasion in society.

Now that we have briefly considered the nature of persuasion we
are ready to examine how one actually goes about giving a persuasive
speech. Much of what we have said earlier in regard to giving informative speeches applies to persuasive speeches; however, in the case of
the persuasive speech there are some motivational considerations that
are of major importance to the persuasive speaker.

MOTIVATION AND PERSUASION

We must understand what is motivation and how it relates to persuasion. Motivation may be defined as a need and goal state. To the
extent that a person feels a need for something (e.g., food, house), we
say that the person is motivated. Motivation may vary quantitatively; we
may be more or less hungry. Some amount of motivation must, however, be present in order for any behavior to occur. If you have just
eaten a large T-bone dinner, it is unlikely that you will eat a hamburger
placed before you. Having fulfilled a need of hunger with the steak, you
are no longer motivated by the presentation of additional food.

To persuade an audience, to actuate, to alter behavior, it is necessary that the audience be motivated. Alan Monroe has developed an
organization sequence which arouses a need for something in the listener and offers a goal which will reduce the need.[8] This "motivated
sequence" proposes to carry the listener to the point of agreement with
the speaker. Below we elaborate upon Monroe's motivated sequence
by drawing appropriate examples for each of the steps from recent
speeches.

8. Alan H. Monroe and Douglas Ehninger, *Principles and Types of Speech Communication,* 7th
   ed. (Glenview, Ill.: Scott, Foresman and Co., 1974), chapter 13.

Attention

Step one in the motivated sequence is little different in its requirements from any other introduction; you arrest the attention of the audience. As such, it should arouse some interest in the speech through any of the normal procedures outlined in Chapter 5. A little humor, an unusual, or possibly a frightening statement will encourage the audience to listen. Whatever its form, it is necessary that the audience recognize some reason for paying attention to the speaker.

Howard Hardesty, the executive vice president of Continental Oil Company, caught the attention of his audience with a somewhat frightening representation of the dilemma we face in balancing the forces of sound ecological use of our resources with the necessity for the continued exploitation of those resources.

> Ladies and Gentlemen, I have been asked to make two announcements: "Because of fuel shortages, the local utility is unable to continue generating electricity at fully capacity. At noon the lights will go out, elevator service and telephone service will be discontinued. To avoid any hazard, the management requests that we vacate the hotel by 11:30 A.M."
>
> Regrettably we have also just received the following news bulletin: "An oil well platform off the Delaware Coast has blown out and is on fire. Unless containment efforts are successful, oil will wash ashore along the Delaware and New Jersey Coasts."[9]

With a familiar bit of American history, Louise Bushnell was able to interest her audience and introduce the subject of her speech—her conceptualization of America.

> There is something personal and unique in remembering that Thomas Jefferson hitched his own horse outside the White House, to show that a President is no better than the people.
>
> That Ben Franklin came to Philadelphia, his pockets stuffed with buns. He worked hard. He saved. He soon became a leading citizen.
>
> That Abraham Lincoln, born humbly, studied by firelight. With nothing to help him but his brain and his hands. He left us a heritage of words and deeds unsurpassed in American history.[10]

Need

With the attention of the audience in hand, the speaker must show the audience that some need exists. These needs may be physical, psychological or social. The purpose of this portion of the speech is to bring to

9. C. Howard Hardesty, Jr., "Energy vs. Ecology," *Vital Speeches of the Day* 39 (March 1, 1973), pp. 314–15.
10. Louise Bushnell, "What Is America?" *Vital Speeches of the Day* 39 (April 1, 1973), p. 371.

consciousness a problem which already exists. The need for maintenance of life is pervasive and basic. Under its mantle lie needs such as those of food, shelter, and sex. Robert Browne emphasizes the need to bring blacks into a productive role in the American economy:

> The ghettos are fuller than they have ever been, with 500,000 people moving into them each year and only some 40,000 moving out. They are the same old Bedford-Stuyvesant, Harlem, Detroit and Watts, only they are much bigger, with more rats, more roaches, and more despair. There are more Negro youngsters in segregated schoolrooms than there were in 1954—not all due to segregation or discrimination, perhaps, but a fact. The number of youngsters who have fallen back in their reading, writing, and arithmetic since 1954 has increased, not decreased, and unemployment for Negro young women is up to 35, 40, and 50 percent in the ghettos. For young men in the ghettos, it is up to 20 percent, and this is a conservative figure.[11]

It is not, however, necessary to resort to a physical need in motivating an audience. The availability of more abstract, social needs provides ample area for establishing a motivational appeal. The Chief Justice of the United States, Warren E. Burger, uses an anthropological metaphor to arouse a need for legal restraints as viable authors of general freedom.

> As people gradually began to gather to live in larger and larger groups, in tribal villages, and later in towns, tribal customs developed with crude rules to curb the same aggressiveness that had enabled people to survive. Thus the idea of the rule of law was born even before Man's comprehension was able to grasp this as a concept. From hard experience our primitive ancestors learned that communal life and unrestrained aggressiveness could not co-exist. In their own way they discovered that total freedom was not freedom.[12]

The variety of needs provides the speaker with innumerable alternatives; however, he may be dealing with an issue which appears to be more problem-oriented than need-oriented. Ross Smyth provides an example of such a problem-oriented issue. He proposes that we adopt some form of world government. The rationale or the need for this government is derived from a problem which he presents near the beginning of his speech.

> Sovereign national governments cannot adequately defend themselves in the nuclear age, nor can the traditional nation-state system designed in the horse-and-buggy era resolve today's difficulties. Global problems definitely require global solutions.

11. Robert Browne, "A Case for Separation," in Lester Thonssen, ed., *Representative American Speeches 1968–69* 41 (New York: H. W. Wilson Company, 1969), p. 158.
12. Warren E. Burger, "The Fragility of Freedom," *Vital Speeches of the Day* 39 (June 15, 1973), p. 514.

> If we have learned the lessons of history, it is that the operation of the traditional nation-state system with its great emphasis on sovereignty has always led to warfare and violence.[13]

Actually Smyth's "problem" is a need. It is a need for a social harmony, a more abstract need than Piccard's survival (see below) but similar to Burger's need for legal restraints. In Burger's speech the issue is expressed as a need; in Smyth's speech the issue is couched in terminology which reveals a problem—international harmony. Although problems may be reduced to a lower common denominator—needs— the procedure is unnecessary when a problem formulation better serves the speaker's uses.

Satisfaction

Once a need has been established, the speaker should offer some solution which satisfies the need. In essence, the speaker offers a plan which solves the need-problem much as a debater would. After Jacques Piccard developed his thesis—that control of ocean pollution is necessary—he offered the following solution or satisfaction of the need.

> I am convinced that in the future only an international agency with global authority could oblige the world industries to really and radically decrease the pollution level. I know, of course, that for the time being, this worldwide authority is pure utopia. But one door is still open on the international level; it is the one of the multinational agreements and treaties.[14]

In fact, Piccard merely suggests a plan or method of problem resolution.

Bruce Johnson proposed that there is a need to understand and control inflation. Most people connect inflation with a reduced income and thus with reduced satisfaction of needs such as shelter, food, or recreation. The causal chain from inflation to food is rather simple. With this need established, Johnson proposed that we alter our concept of money as a storehouse of value and think of dollars in relative terms. His solution:

> I would recommend that we take away from the dollar its store of value or measure of deferred payments function and transfer this function to legal instruments, contracts.
> Reference is now made to a method that Congress could choose to "regulate the value thereof," i.e., the value of money. One can regulate

13. Ross Smyth, "Humanity's Choice," *Vital Speeches of the Day* 39 (March 15, 1973), p. 347.
14. Jacques Ernest Jean Piccard, "How Modern Technology Is Endangering Our Lives," *Vital Speeches of the Day* 39 (January 1, 1973), p. 179.

value if he explicitly recognizes any changes in the yardstick by which said value is measured. The choice of the method herein proposed raises the two main questions of (a) the legal necessity and (b) the economic wisdom of relieving the dollar of its function as a standard of deferred payments and the transfer of this function to obligational instruments.[15]

Of course Johnson and Piccard elaborate beyond the statements quoted herein. While a debater's plan is characterized by brevity, this third step of the motivated sequence may represent a large portion of a speech. In this portion of your speech you can define your solution clearly and demonstrate why and how it will satisfy the existing need.

Visualization

This step involves picturing what will happen in the future and may take one of three forms. The speaker can vividly describe dire consequences that will occur if his proposal is not adopted (the negative method). He can give a glowing description of how beneficial things will turn out if his proposal is accepted (the positive method). Or he can present *both* the negative and the positive side of accepting his proposal (the combination method). Jean Way Schoonover used the combination method in her exhortation to businessmen to stop fearing women in business. After detailing the ten fears that businessmen have of businesswomen and how to overcome them, she said:

> My friends, there you have them: ten keys to understanding, ten real, ten common fears in executive America, in corporate America, of the new woman, fears held by the "old man."
> The old culture.
> The old work ethic.
> The old wisdom.
> The old fears.
> The old *waste.*
> Yes, I said waste.
> We see it so often. I'm sure you do, too. In your board rooms, in your executive offices, in your clubs and bars, wherever good men gather: the pain, the real anguish, the joylessness of executive America, of corporate America, thinking about, grappling with, *The Problem of the New Woman—of Business and the New Woman.*
> What waste, what a colossal waste!
> What a stunning example of the negative effect of this culture's conditioning! [Note: end of negative, beginning of positive method.]
> America's businessmen are the best in the world, the most creative, the

15. Bruce Johnson, "Inflation and Money Markets," *Vital Speeches of the Day* 39 (June 1, 1973), p. 509.

boldest, the most enterprising, and yet they do not see an opportunity of historic proportions, a monumental opportunity to use—to harness, virtually untapped energy; to put into the service of this culture, of this business society, limitless new brainpower, a totally fresh perspective—the energy, the brainpower, the perspective of Woman, modern woman, the liberated woman . . . the woman who is free to hunt with the man, free to run with him, build with him, free to build a new way of business, and entirely new way of business life. Better. Different. Richer. Variegated. Male and female.

A society not of free men only, nor of liberated women only, but a society that is totally liberated—a society that liberates humankind from the cave and the loneliness of the hunt.[16]

Action

The final step is the speaker's call for action. He asks that the audience adopt his solution and solve the problem or reduce the need by taking some action or by altering some belief. Ross Smyth provides a clear example of this final element—a call to action, when he exhorts his listeners to take up the cause of world government.

> If you agree with much of what I have said, you may ask: "What can I as an individual do about it?" Take an active interest in foreign policy and world affairs. Become a well-informed layman, and then inform others. Support the world federalist organization and those working in related areas such as the United National Association, the Canadian Institute of International Affairs, the Futurist Society, etc. And it is of key importance that you write and discuss these affairs with your elected representatives.[17]

A similar, although more general call to action, comes from Professor Ralph Eubanks in a speech to the Florida Scholastic Press Association.

> Writing the truth is a sober business, an awesome undertaking. It's an undertaking that calls for wisdom no less than courage, for idealism as well as pragmatism. It begins with the affirmation that life and the world are to be held dear. Yet at the same time it requires us to face a hard historical reality—the reality that unrestrained utterance is the certain route to the loss of freedom.[18]

The sequence just described is an outline; it is not intended to be rigid, nor is it designed as a dogmatic prescription. It is merely a plan for employing motivation in obtaining behavioral change through the medium of persuasion. The plan recognizes that man behaves because he is motivated to behave. He has numerous needs and acts to satisfy

16. Jean Way Schoonover, "Why Corporate America Fears Women," *Vital Speeches of the Day* 40 (April 15, 1974), p. 416. Quoted by permission of *Vital Speeches of the Day*.

17. Smyth, "Humanity's Choice," p. 348.

18. Ralph T. Eubanks, "Writing the Truth," *Vital Speeches of the Day* 38 (December 15, 1972), p. 160.

those needs. Monroe's motivated sequence graphically prescribes a method for capitalizing on this characteristic of man.

Having considered the nature of persuasive speaking and the relationship between motivation and persuasion, we will complete the treatment of persuasive speaking with an examination of some of the empirical research relating to this area.

CONTRIBUTIONS OF EMPIRICAL RESEARCH

Persuasive speakers have frequently been concerned with such practical questions as should one or both sides of the issue be presented, should the strongest arguments be presented at the beginning or at the end of a speech, and are fear appeals persuasive. Our purpose here is to look at some of the most frequently asked questions in regard to persuasive speaking. While specific research studies in the area of persuasion abound, the suggestions that can be drawn from these studies are many times contradictory and frequently inconclusive.

The following questions about persuasive strategies should be of some interest to those of us engaged in persuasive speaking.

Will Information Itself Change Attitudes?

Frequently, we hear the idea expressed that if you give people enough information on a topic they will see the subject the same way that you do, and indeed it would appear at first glance that simply providing information to people on a particular topic might change their attitude in regard to that topic. However, it is only in limited cases that the mere presentation of information will be persuasive. The major instance where information may be persuasive is when a person has no knowledge whatsoever of a particular topic, and in this day and age that condition will not be found that often.

Haskins has reviewed many advertising and psychological studies to see if any relationship exists between factual learning and opinion change. From the twenty-nine studies he reviews, Professor Haskins concludes: "Learning and recall of factual information from mass communications does occur. However, recall and retention measures seem, at best, irrelevant to the ultimate effects desired—the changing of attitudes and behavior." Haskins' review of the literature would indicate that telling the facts does not necessarily influence attitude change.[19]

19. J. B Haskins, "Factual Recall as a Measure of Advertising Effectiveness," *Journal of Advertising Research* 6 (1966), pp. 2–8.

While information by itself then is not necessarily persuasive, we cannot conclude that the use of information is useless in persuasive speeches. There is some evidence that tends to indicate that new information can strengthen desirable attitudes that people have, and in some cases, if the new information is articulated in a clear fashion, it will provide people a way to verbalize their attitudes.

Should One or Both Sides of a Given Issue Be Presented?

In this area there have been several studies conducted, but results are somewhat inconclusive. One of the more interesting studies has been conducted by McGinnies. In a study he conducted with Japanese university students, the university students were first asked to fill out attitude scales assessing their position toward two relevant international issues: (1) American handling of the Cuban missile crisis, and (2) visits by American submarines to Japanese ports. A week later each subject was exposed to one of four pro-American speeches, all presented in a similar manner by a Japanese dramatic arts student. The four messages were:

1. One-sided argument—Cuban missile crisis: This presentation was based on the commentary of Ambassador Adlai Stevenson defending United States action on Cuba to the United Nations.
2. Two-sided argument—Cuban missile crisis: In this communication "cognizance was taken of certain points raised by Premier Nikita Khrushchev on the matter of missile bases in Cuba."
3. One-sided argument—American submarine visits: This statement was composed from Japanese editorial comments favoring such visits.
4. Two-sided argument—American submarine visits: This speech included arguments against such visits by a "left-wing" Japanese newspaper.

After hearing one of the four speeches, each subject was given the same attitude survey he had been given a week earlier. The two-sided communcication was superior to the one-sided appeal for individuals initially opposed to the position advocated. For the subjects who initially agreed with the opinions of the speaker, the one-sided communication tended to be more effective.[20]

While more work is needed in the area, the findings of McGinnies would appear logical. In other words, when the audience initially disagrees with you or may hear the other side presented by someone else,

20. E. McGinnies, "Studies in Persuasion: III, Reactions of Japanese Students to One-sided and Two-sided Communication." *Journal of Social Psychology* 70 (1966), pp. 87–93.

you should probably present both sides of the argument. However, when the audience is already in general support of your position and you desire a quick, even though it may be a temporary attitude change, your best strategy may be to present only one side.

Should Your Strongest Arguments Be Presented at the Beginning, the Middle or the End of Your Speech?

One of the earliest studies in this area was conducted by Tannenbaum when he tested the ability of individuals to recall information. He found that recall was better at the beginning and at the end than in the middle of presentations. More recently, Shaw conducted an investigation to see if there were any relationship between the time an idea was presented to a group and whether or not they accepted it. Shaw concluded that opinions stated first and last had a significantly better chance of being adopted.[21]

Will Active Participation by the Listener Enhance Persuasion?

The fundamental issue in this question is simply will a person be more likely to be persuaded if the information is "given" to him by a speaker or when he "exerts" himself to obtain information. Several fairly recent studies would indicate that the latter is true. For example, a study by Elms concludes that subjects engaged in role playing had more attitude change than those who simply listened to a tape recording of the role players' persuasive arguments.[22]

Finally, an interesting study by Wicklund, Cooper, and Linder suggests that when persons exert more effort to hear a persuasive communication they change their attitude in the desired direction.[23]

Is the Use of Fear Appeals Persuasive?

Many studies in this area indicate that fear appeals are persuasive. In recent years this question has been refined to the point of asking

21. M. E. Shaw, "A Serial Position Effect in Social Influence on Group Decisions," *Journal of Social Psychology* 54 (1961), pp. 83–91.

22. A. Elms, "Influence of Fantasy Ability on Attitude Change through Role Playing," *Journal of Personality and Social Psychology* 4 (1965), pp. 2–8.

23. R. Wicklund, J. Cooper, and D. Linder, "Effects of Expected Effort on Attitude Change Prior to Exposure," *Journal of Experimental Social Psychology* 3 (1967), pp. 416–28.

whether strong fear appeals or mild fear appeals are more persuasive. One of the most interesting studies in this area has been conducted by Sidney Kraus. He and his research team selected eighty-seven individuals from a cross-section of an adult community and studied their reaction to mass media recommendations for avoiding eye damage while viewing a solar eclipse. The fear appeal they used was simply "heed these suggestions or you'll burn your eyes out." This fear appeal was followed by suggestions as to how one should properly watch the eclipse by using "pinhole boxes" or by looking through exposed film. Forty-one percent of the sample population adopted one of the suggested procedures for viewing the eclipse. Kraus and his colleagues concluded that in some cases appeals containing elements of strong fear may be used quite successfully to promote the behavior desired by the communicator.[24]

Should You Explicitly State Your Conclusion?

Sometimes persuasive speakers feel that if they present the evidence supporting their position the audience will draw the desired conclusion for themselves. A study by Weiss and Steenbock in 1965 provided support that the speaker should present his conclusion for the greatest persuasive effect. The study asks the question: Would subjects be more persuaded by a communication that contained explicit conclusions, even when those conclusions recommended actions objectionable to the listener? Two groups of college undergraduates were asked to read a communication supporting the need for a history of science course— a viewpoint strongly opposed by the students. One group read a form of the communication without a concluding section; a second group received the material given the first group *and* the concluding segment as well. A third group (control) did not read any communication. Subjects' opinions of the value of a history of science course were assessed before and after the communications were read. The researchers concluded that communication in which the conclusions were presented was more effective in changing attitudes than when conclusions were not specifically stated.[25]

The previous studies should provide some additional insight into the qualities that make for effective persuasive speaking.

24. S. Kraus, E. El-Assal, and M. DeFleur, "Fear-threat Appeals in Mass Communication: An Apparent Contradiction," *Speech Monographs* 33 (1966), pp. 23–29.
25. W. Weiss and S. Steenbock, "The Influence on Communication Effectiveness of Explicitly Urging Action and Policy Consequences," *Journal of Experimental Social Psychology* 1 (1965), pp. 396–406.

SUMMARY

In this chapter we have pointed out that much of what we have said earlier in the text applies to persuasive speaking. We have focused upon the nature of persuasion, the relationship between motivation and persuasion, and finally we have examined some basic principles of persuasion. Persuasive speaking requires the same type of rigor and preparation as other kinds of speaking and in addition the persuasive speaker has the burden of bringing about some change in the behavior or attitude of his audience.

EXERCISES/ASSIGNMENTS

1. Observe a speaker and analyze his or her use of ethical and emotional appeals.
2. What personal factors would a speaker need in order to have favorable "ethical" appeal to you?
3. Prepare a four- to six-minute (written/oral) presentation in which you use the "motivated sequence." Label each step carefully and, using a wide margin, note how each step is used.
4. Select an ad on TV and write an analysis of the persuasive appeals employed in that ad.
5. Select a political or advertising campaign and attempt to show how it does or does not employ the "motivated sequence."

CHAPTER 13

SPEECHES FOR SPECIAL OCCASIONS

$\mathbb{T}$his chapter deals with those types of speaking that do not fall under the general headings of informative or persuasive speaking. Speeches for special occasions are usually very short and in keeping with the circumstances in which they are used. Much of what we have said about public speaking in general in the rest of this book applies to speeches for special occasions. However, said speeches do merit some specific considerations and observations which we will take up at this time.

THE SPEECH TO ENTERTAIN

The speech to entertain is the third in a classification which includes informative speaking and persuasive speaking, respectively described in chapters 10 and 12. The principal purpose of a speech to entertain is, of course, to amuse the audience; the speech is arranged and presented with the pleasure of the audience as its principal concern. Although this type of speaking may be informative or, on occasion, persuasive as well as entertaining, the audience's enjoyment is the primary interest of the speaker.

One may immediately assume that the speech to entertain is humorous. This is not necessarily the case; however, an entertaining speech is usually characterized by humor. Many people attend public and academic lectures as a form of entertainment, and, while those speeches may contain humor, their primary focus is informative speaking. Many social and semisocial situations require speeches which the audience finds entertaining, yet these speeches are informative or persuasive in design. That one finds speeches to entertain which are not humorous and informative, or persuasive speeches which contain sizable amounts of humor, produces a definitional problem. One may resolve this problem only partially by focusing his attention on the *speaker's perspective* in a definition of a speech to entertain, the central aim of which is to amuse the audience. The material presented in the

211

remainder of this chapter may be used by the speaker who wishes only to amuse the audience or to inform or persuade in an amusing way.

Why Use Humor?

Of major importance to the speaker who wishes to present a speech to entertain is humor. The subject of humor has occupied the attention of many writers in the past. Analyzing the determinants of humor led Cicero in his *De Oratore* to write the following response from Caesar to Antonius and Crassus.

> For it is by deceiving expectation, by satirising the tempers of others, by playing humorously on our own, by comparing a thing with something coarse, by dissembling, by uttering apparent absurdities, and by reproving folly, that laughter is excited.[1]

Most textbooks today give little attention to the use of humor in speeches. Studies indicate that the use of humor does not help people remember information from the speeches nor has the use of humor been proven as a persuasive device.[2] The question arises then as to what roles does humor play in speech making. It appears that there are two reasons for the use of humor. First, humor adds *interest* to speeches.[3] By adding interest, one is able to maintain the attention of the audience. The second is that humor enhances the credibility or character of the speaker. Audiences seem to *like* the speaker who uses humor more than the speaker who does not use humor.

Appropriate Use of Humor

Few events or behaviors are inherently humorous. The devices of the speaker, the environment, and the composition and attitudes of the audience determine what is humorous. What excites laughter from one audience may seem dull to another group. Academicians may find a speech which lampoons the trade-off between teaching and publishing extremely laughable. The local Optimist Club, listening to the same speech, might react with concern for their children who attend the university or their tax dollars which support it. This same audience may

1. J. S. Watson, trans. or ed., *Cicero on Oratory and Orators: With His Letters to Quintus and Brutus* (London: George Bell and Sons, 1896), p. 308.
2. Charles R. Gruner, "Effects of Humor on Speaker Ethos and Audience Information Gain," *Journal of Communication* 17 (September 1967), pp. 228–33. Also Donald Kilpela, "An Experimental Study of Effects of Humor on Persuasion" (M.A. thesis. Wayne State University, 1962).
3. Charles R. Gruner, "The Effect of Humor in Dull and Interesting Informative Speeches," *Central States Speech Journal* 21 (Fall 1970), pp. 160–66.

also react to the context in which the speech is given. A speech which satirizes newsmen may achieve some amount of success at the Press Club luncheon; the same speech might be ill received at an awards banquet. Both the audience and the environment deserve careful attention and analysis in preparing a speech to entertain. The student should find some helpful suggestions on audience analysis in Chapter 4.

With the constraints of audience and environment under consideration, the speaker must find an appropriate topic. Unlike an informative speech, topics are not readily identifiable for an entertaining speech. Many topics become entertaining with the addition of several devices which create humor. One should examine everyday instances with which he is familiar. His work, a recent vacation, pets, his lifestyle, recreation, and others may become topics for an entertainment speech or entertaining incidents within one of the other two types of speeches. Anyone participates in events which have the potential for humor, but the manner in which these events are presented is crucial in determining whether they will be mirth provoking.

Supporting Materials for Entertainment Speeches

Several mechanisms are available for enhancing interest and increasing the likelihood that an event or incident is perceived as humorous. The mechanisms here described are usually employed in the context of a narrative or descriptive form. The key element in entertaining is the use of a story form rather than argument or exposition.

Sequence.   In any story the sequence of events must be carefully planned. In relating some incident, forgetting a fact along the way may result in a reduction of suspense and a consequent minimization of humor.

Vividness.   This element lends much aid to the development of humor. The speech may be enhanced with exciting and descriptive language. The narrative form of humor requires that the vocabulary be carefully chosen in order to adequately convey the mood as well as facts of an event.

Dramatization.   Closely related to vividness is dramatization. The use of dialogue can enhance the realism of narration. If dialogue is used, the characters should be named. A continuous sequence of "he said" and "she said" is boring rather than humorous. A dialect or an accent, used with discretion, can add to the value of the dialogue.

Timing.   First, an entertaining speech should move rather swiftly. The incident which requires lenghty elaboration will prove to be more laborious than entertaing. Numerous brief stories are more desirable than lengthy ones. The second aspect of timing is its use as a device to create suspense or provide emphasis. Samuel Clemens's use of timing in his lectures was particularly admirable. Hal Holbrook's re-creation of Mark Twain possesses this same quality, as does James Whitmore's re-creation of Will Rogers.

Satire.   In addition to the above aspects of a speech to use to encourage a humorous response, several forms of humor may be employed. Satire is one of the most common devices, and one of its most effective uses occurs when the speaker directs the satire on himself. The satirist lampoons eccentricities, foibles, follies, abuses, and vices. Holding a person, institution or idea up for ridicule is the essence of satire. One warning is necessary. A satire directed at someone besides the speaker himself can, on occasion, antagonize the audience. As already observed, audience analysis is crucial in entertaining.

Exaggeration and Understatement.   These devices are easily used by the speechmaker. Mark Twain, adept at exaggeration as well as understatement, provides an example of exaggeration about the French in his often-quoted passage which places the nature of man somewhere between that of the angels and the French.

Irony and Sarcasm.   Irony consists of a contradiction between the literal and the intended. It is more playful than *sarcasm,* a device which should be used prudently, as its caustic or hostile undercurrent necessitates a mood of good-humored jesting for its use.

Unexpected Turns.   This is usually employed in conjunction with suspense. The unexpected turn occurs at the climax of a story.

Burlesque.   The final form of humor is the burlesque, the ludicrous characterization of the sensible and the sensible characterization of the ludicrous.

Organization

Although the story form is basic to the speech to entertain, a further comment about organizing the speech should be made. Relevant information about organizing a speech is available in Chapter 6. Although the entertainment speech is designed to amuse, a central thesis or issue around which anecdotes and stories are organized is essential. Without this focus, the speaker will appear to be more a jokester than speaker. A basic issue helps to create a natural sequence into which anecdotes may be organized. The basic form of the entertainment speech is quite similar to the informative speech in that the speaker uses an introduction, states the essential thesis of his speech, develops this thesis with satires, anecdotes, stories, and other materials and closes with a restatement of the speech's thesis.

THE SPEECH OF INTRODUCTION

After the speech to entertain, the speech of introduction is probably the most common of the occasional speeches. It may vary in formality as well as length, depending upon the status of the speaker being introduced and the nature of the occasion. An introduction of a local celebrity at the Kiwanis meeting may seem rather remote from the introduction of the keynote address at a political convention; however, both introduction speeches, if adequately designed and delivered, are presented for the same reasons and should achieve similar goals. Admittedly, one situation may require greater elaboration and more details, but the essential requisites remain fairly constant.

A speech as well as a speaker is introduced with the following purposes or goals. The speech of introduction should prepare the audience for the speaker and his speech. It should create a friendly and receptive attitude in the audience, stimulating a desire to listen— should motivate the audience, in effect. A well-designed introduction can also motivate the speaker to perform at a superior level. The person who presents a speech of introduction has the opportunity to increase the audience's receptivity and the speaker's potential.

The speech includes four major elements: biographical data, the nature of the occasion, information about the speech, and the name of the speaker and the title of his speech. In order to make the speaker as interesting as possible, accurate biographical information is essential. This information may include the speaker's education, his professional achievements, and facts of particular concern for the audience. When appropriate, a humorous anecdote about the speaker can act as a bridge from introduction to speech, providing the speaker an opportunity to respond in a manner which gets things off to a good start.

Any other biographical information particularly relevant to the situation may also be included. For example, if one were introducing a speaker at a fraternity meeting, he would certainly want to mention the speaker's membership in a fraternity. The subject of the speech should also be briefly related to the audience. These two elements of the introduction are motivational and their accuracy is essential. Checking the information with the speaker is desirable just prior to the time of presentation. Errors can embarrass the speaker and reduce any motivational aspects of the introduction.

Two more elements complete the requisites of the speech of introduction. The nature of the occasion should be related to both the presence of the major speaker and the particular topic on which he is speaking. Finally, the speaker's name and the title of his speech should be told to the audience. Usually it is recommended that these last elements (name and title) be used as a climax to the introduction speech. The title of the speech certainly belongs in the conclusion of the introduction. If the speaker is well known, there is little reason to give his name until the conclusion of the introduction. Providing the name of an unfamiliar speaker at the beginning of the speech, however, gives the audience a reference point to which biographical information may be related. This does not, though, obviate the need for including the name and title in the conclusion.

Two final suggestions will help to make the speech of introduction successful. The speech of introduction is not the main event; it should be designed with cognizance of its subordinate nature. Likewise, brevity is essential.

THE SPEECH OF WELCOME

A formal welcome may be extended to an individual or group of individuals in the form of a welcoming speech. The speech should begin with a simple statement of welcome and should mention the group which is extending the welcome. The purpose of the meeting requires mention, and this statement may be accompanied by an explanation of the reasons for the extension of the welcome. Finally, the speaker would want to conclude by wishing the visitor(s) an enjoyable and profitable visit.

The above elements are the essentials of a public and formal speech of welcome. Several additional components may be included with the situation determining which, if any, are necessary.

1 Compliment the visitor for his choice of this place or time or for some attribute.
2. Explain common bonds between visitor(s) and host.

3. Note any contributions to the community which may be expected from the visitor.
4. Predict pleasant experiences for the visitor and/or the host as a consequence of the visit.
5. The speaker may wish to describe the accomplishments of the visitor(s).

RESPONSE TO A SPEECH OF WELCOME

The contents of a response to a welcome are particularly difficult to prescribe since the contents of the welcome may warrant a variety of elements being included in the response. If the speaker who welcomes chooses to mention common bonds between visitor and host, the response should probably include a reinforcement of those bonds. The necessity for adaptation is particularly relevant for the response to a welcome.

Certainly the speaker who delivers the response to a welcome would want to indicate for whom he is speaking and express appreciation for the welcome. Anticipating a pleasant or fruitful stay may be common to many situations, as well. Other elements cannot be dictated; nevertheless, the reader may prepare himself by familiarizing himself with the potential elements of the welcome speech.

THE SPEECH OF PRESENTATION

At an anniversary, on the occasion of a retirement, or in numerous other situations, the need for a brief speech accompanying the giving of some gift arises. The speech of presentation can enhance the value of the gift and the occasion for those who are giving and for the recipient. Its primary purpose is the formal and public exhibition of the recipient's worth. Secondarily, the speech of presentation may heighten the sense of appreciation felt by the donor.

Five elements are needed in the speech of presentation. First, the recipient should be named and the donor given recognition. Second, some rationale for the presentation should be included. If the recipient of the gift is retiring, this fact requires notation. Third, the award, gift, or trophy should be named. Fourth, any particularly appropriate or symbolic qualities of the gift will, when explained, heighten the value of the gift. Finally, the sentiments of the group should be summarized.

THE SPEECH OF TRIBUTE

A speech of tribute is rather similar to one of presentation. However, the speech of tribute is more formal and may be longer than the speech of presentation. Certainly more time should be spent in explaining specific qualities of the person being honored. A gift may be presented, but the presentation is subordinate to the speech and the gift is more likely to be symbolic.

The speaker should note the occasion which provides the opportunity for paying tribute to the individual. If this occasion is a visit or a farewell dinner, mention of the fact will introduce the speech and orient the audience to the purpose of the speech. The major portion of the speech is spent in honoring the individual to whom tribute is being paid. Describing the person's exploits, his achievements, or praising special qualities of his character are examples of components of this portion of the speech. The third and final division of this speech is the presentation of an award or gift. At this time, elements of the speech of presentation may be included. These ingredients may be a description of the qualities of the gift, a summarization of the sentiments of the group, and naming of the donors. Since the purpose of this speech is the paying of tribute rather than a presentation, this last section of the speech should receive less emphasis than the poriton of the speech in which the individual is verbally honored.

THE SPEECH OF ACCEPTANCE

The speech of acceptance is familiar to anyone who has ever watched the televised Academy Awards Presentation. Although five elements are listed below, past audience experience with the acceptance speech may argue for a simpler and more honest expression of appreciation than is typically observed.

Where appropriate, this type of speech may include:

1. Thanks for the gift or honor.
2. Expression of goodwill toward the donors or those who honor.
3. An expression of modesty by sharing credit with others. (Unfortunately the honesty of such a statement may be questioned by the audience; consequently the speaker should consider his motives as well as the perception of the audience carefully before choosing to share the honor or credit with others.)

4. If the gift is a symbol, the speaker should devote some time to the appropriateness of the symbolization.
5. An explanation of the importance of the occasion will help to establish the sincerity of the speaker.

The difficulty of this speech is conveying the speaker's sincerity. Many people believe that sincerity is characterized by spontaneity and emotion. A lengthy speech may therefore cause the audience to question the sincerity of the speaker. Although most occasions on which an award is presented or tribute is paid are expected ahead of the occasion, the audience's perception of preparation may be viewed as somehow a violation of the spirit in which the donors give or the group honors. This may be unfortunate, but the speaker can handle an audience's expectation with brevity and simplicity, two qualities which seem to epitomize sincerity.

THE SPEECH OF FAREWELL

The speech of farewell is delivered by an individual who wishes to express regrets over his departure. It may be given upon receipt of a gift and may, therefore, be given in response to a speech of presentation, or it may be given at a dinner at which the speaker is honored.

The speaker usually begins by expressing his regrets about leaving. Admittedly, not every departure is regretful, but it is assumed that if someone is offered and accepts the opportunity to deliver a speech of farewell, he implicitly regrets his departure. Appreciation for the group may be expressed in a straightforward statement, or it may be combined with reminiscences about happy times and memories. If the speech is given as a response to the presentation of a gift, gratitude for the gift can be expressed in conjunction with appreciation for the group itself. Any symbolic qualities of the gift may be utilized, if appropriate, in recalling happy times. Praise for the group may be appropriate, if some or all of the group have worked as subordinates of the speaker. Before completing the speech, the speaker can look to the future with comments concerning potential of the group or plans in the making. Finally as with all speeches, a closing, which, in this case, is a statement of farewell, is necessary.

These elements may be summarized in the following list:

1. Regret over departure.
2. Appreciation for the group.

3. Reminiscence.
4. Praise for the group.
5. Look to the future.
6. Closing words of farewell.

THE EULOGY

The eulogy is designed to pay tribute to a deceased person; this speech commemorates the character of a person in the form of a funeral oration, on the occasion of the person's birthday or the anniversary of his death, or on some occasion which makes the individual's personal characteristics particularly appropriate for the audience's consideration. Incidents from the person's life provide supporting illustrations for the development of a eulogy. Evidence for this speech may be drawn from traits of character, aspirations or goals, outstanding accomplishments, and influences of the individual on his peers and period. Sources for such evidence are direct contacts, biographies, biographical dictionaries, and actual legacies of the person such as his writing, paintings, society he founded, or others.

In developing the eulogy, one should avoid a simple chronology of the person's life. An organization which focuses upon one particular aspect of the person's life has the advantage of creating greater interest among listeners and the potential advantage of providing some insight into the person's contributions.

THE SPEECH OF NOMINATION

A speech of nomination, like the introduction speech, will vary in length and formality according to situational variables. Five elements are essential. First, the speaker should explain that he is nominating someone for a particular office and name the office. Second, he should remind the audience of the qualifications required by the office. If the organization is a small one, this element may not seem necessary, but even in an informal environment, elucidating qualifications provides an introduction and transition for the presentation of evidence of your candidate's qualifications, the third element in the speech of nomination. Fourth, the speaker should suggest how the organization will benefit from this person's experience and ability. Experience could include holding a similar office in this or some other organization. Finally, the candidate's name should be presented and the group should be urged to vote for your candidate.

EXERCISES/ASSIGNMENTS

1. Prepare a brief speech of introduction, welcome, or tribute.
2. Write a eulogy for a person you admire. In addition to advice in this chapter, review Chapter 8 on language choice.
3. Find a nominating speech given at one of the national political conventions and study its content, strategy, and effect.
4. Take a speech of farewell and analyze it according to the principles set forth in this chapter.

NAME INDEX

SUBJECT INDEX